Finally found th
Terminal market in Philadelphia
after 3 year search.

The Frog Commissary Cookbook

by Steven Poses, Anne Clark, and Becky Roller
illustrated by Becky Roller

CAMINO BOOKS, INC. • Philadelphia

Published by arrangement with Doubleday, a division of The
Doubleday Broadway Publishing Group, a division of Random
House, Inc.

Manufactured in the United States of America

 2 3 4 5 6 7   07 06 05 04 03 02

Library of Congress Cataloging-in-Publication Data

Poses, Steven.
   The Frog Commissary cookbook / by Steven Poses,
   Anne Clark, and Becky Roller; illustrated by Becky Roller.
        p. cm.
   Originally published: Garden City, N.Y.: Doubleday, 1985.
   Includes index.
   ISBN 0-940159-73-2 (trade paper: alk. paper)
   1. Cookery, American. 2. Frog Commissary Restaurant.
   I. Clark, Anne. II. Roller, Becky. III. Title.

   TX715.P863 2002
   641.5′09748′1 I—dc21   2001043691

This book is available at a special discount on bulk purchases for
promotional, business, and educational use. For information
write to:

Camino Books, Inc.
P. O. Box 59026
Philadelphia, PA 19102

www.caminobooks.com

Contents

Introduction

The Frog/Commissary Cookbook is a useful compilation of flavorful and often unusual recipes. The recipes are at once sophisticated, highly accessible, and generally easy to follow. The cookbook is a result of the efforts of scores of exciting cooks who have worked in a family of unique restaurants in what has become one of America's most interesting restaurant cities—Philadelphia. In addition to the recipes, the cookbook attempts to communicate an attitude about food, the service of food, the operation of those restaurants, and in its own way, it tells a story about an era in contemporary American culture. It is not like any other cookbook that you own.

I had not always wanted to cook and run restaurants. I grew up in Yonkers, New York in a fairly prosperous and sheltered setting. I came to Philadelphia in 1964 as a freshman at the University of Pennsylvania with a strong desire to be an architect. Fairly early in my undergraduate training I encountered difficulty in a freehand drawing class and concluded that I was not cut out to be an architect. In the very socially conscious period of the mid-sixties, I concluded that my interests lay more in people and the cities they inhabited than in buildings per se, so a change in career direction made some sense.

A key book for me at that time was Jane Jacobs's *Death and Life of Great American Cities.* Jacobs wrote about the role neighborhood candy stores played in defining a community. It was often the neighborhood candy store that provided people with a way to define and connect with their neighborhood. The candy store was symbolic of numerous small elements that helped break down the anonymity of cities. I graduated from Penn with a sociology degree and a strong interest in contributing to the kind of positive urban life that Jacobs presented.

During my college years, I developed an interest in cooking. My mother was a very good cook, and at an early age I came to appreciate good food and the pleasure that can result from serving it. Without my mother's cooking in college, I had both the need and opportunity to learn how to cook. A summer's long trip provided extraordinary exposure to the wonderful food of France, Spain, and Italy and whetted my appetite to be able to produce such food. I subscribed to the then new Time-Life Series of International Cookbooks and began experimenting.

My love of cooking and a vision of contributing to urban life was coming together as an idea for a restaurant that could serve the same role as Jane Jacobs's neighborhood candy store. It would be the sort of restaurant where people would come together over good food and wine and discuss the great issues of the day. The restaurant would provide a sense of place for people. I would do the cooking.

I knew that I needed experience before I could open a restaurant, so after a brief stint in the Peace Corps and peace movement, I answered a newspaper advertisement for a busboy. I was offered the job if I agreed to cut off my beard. I did. For the next six months, I was the busboy and glass polisher at La Panetière, then Philadelphia's most elegant French restaurant.

I really wanted to cook. A position opened up in La Panetière's kitchen. I peeled carrots and potatoes, cleaned mussels, pulled feathers out of pheasants, shaped turnips, chopped parsley, and eventually got to sauté vegetables on the cooking line. I was now doing some serious cooking. I invested in Julia Child's *Mastering the Art of French Cooking.* I kept it by my bed and it became my bible.

Much of what I had been cooking, both at La Panetière and at home on my one night off, was very conventional with familiar Western flavors and ingredients. Though my parents' parents were Eastern European Jews, my real culinary heritage was a curiously neutral result of growing up suburban in the postwar assimilationist era of the fifties and sixties. La Panetière's approach to cooking was classic French. The experimentation of Bocuse, Gérard, and the brothers Troisgros that would soon explode as Nouvelle Cuisine and open French cooking to broader influences, was taking place in the isolation of their French kitchens.

The Vietnam War was going on and there were a number of young men from Thailand working in La Panetière's kitchen. The exposure to the exotic tastes of Thailand while sharing the staff dinners that they prepared was a revelation: sweet and fiery, red, green, blue and orange curries; pickled vegetables and preserved radish; lemongrass and fish sauce. The Thais with whom I worked and slurped noodles introduced me to the Orient . . . and a particularly exotic corner of it, at that.

Only in America and only at that time could a Jewish kid from Yonkers, having graduated from the University of Pennsylvania, be working and learning how to cook in a French restaurant alongside a substantial contingent of Thais. And my lack of a strong culinary tradition created an openness to a vast world of ingredients, tastes, textures, and methods of cooking. *The Frog/Commissary Cookbook* is very much a result of this new heritage, whose origin was in the kitchen of La Panetière. Its recipes and spirit continued to be influenced by a long list of young cooks whose parents were Italian, Irish, German, Japanese, Chinese, Vietnamese, or Iranian. We have all worked together, sharing culinary traditions in evolving a rich, new, and curiously friendly multicultured cuisine. We never sought originality for its own sake nor were we ever limited by adherence to tradition. Our simple guiding principle was "Does it taste good?" The recipes evolved this way and have been refined in the crucible of the highly competitive, very sophisticated, and greatly appreciative restaurant market of Philadelphia over the past twelve years.

Anne Clark was our test chef when the commitment to go ahead with a cookbook was made. In my strongest early recollection of Anne, she sat at table 25 at Frog with one of her twin sons and curled chocolate to garnish a peanut butter pie she had baked for us at her home. Anne was one of a corps of home bakers who prepared desserts for Frog in the early days. Anne loved to bake.

As Frog got busier and Anne's twins got older, she came to work in our kitchen as a baker. When The Commissary opened, she was head baker. It was she who developed the tradition of great desserts in all our restaurants. Anne developed our Carrot Cake, Strawberry Heart Tart, Chocolate Mousse Cake, and numerous other now classic desserts. Today, The Commissary employs ten bakers to keep up with the demand.

One night over dinner in Chinatown, Anne asked if there might be a role for her outside of the bakery. While she loved to bake, she also loved to cook. The Commissary had been running a series of loosely organized but successful cooking classes that I thought could stand some order and expansion. In addition, because the kitchen staff was constantly experimenting with new dishes, I was worried about quality control. I offered Anne the position of our first testing chef. She went on to become the general manager of The Commissary.

From the outset we made serious commitment to the testing process for the cookbook. We knew that all dishes selected for the cookbook were good because we had served all of them in the restaurants. Translating those dishes into recipes that work for you in your kitchen was very much another matter. Simply reducing the size of a recipe designed to produce fifty portions by dividing rarely works. Even when a dish we were using was recorded in a restaurant-size recipe, we began from the beginning in constructing the recipe in a way that we knew it would work for you in your home.

viii

It was Anne who brought discipline to our recipe-development program. Before she came to work for us she had worked in the test kitchen of *Farm Journal*. At The Commissary she was always admonishing staff in the warmest and gentlest way to measure, measure, measure. Anne understood that if you're just producing a dish once you can work by feel—a little of this, a pinch of that. But a restaurant must constantly reproduce a dish over and over again. Each time a customer has it, it should taste the same. For Anne, the challenge of getting a recipe down was the challenge of capturing creativity. For this you had to measure. You never resented Anne. For her, you wanted to measure.

Along with discipline Anne brought tremendous skill and an unerring sense of taste to the cookbook project. She tested many recipes herself and worked closely with testing chefs Roxanna Petzold and Prilla Rohrer. A small apartment up the street from The Commissary served as our test kitchen. We chose an apartment because we wanted to develop the recipes for the book on the kind of equipment you would be using and not commercial equipment. Customer satisfaction has always driven the restaurants and we had no less a concern for it with the cookbook.

The testing chefs often started with someone's vague outline of a dish. It may have been a mere recollection of something we served over a busy week years ago that was remembered as extra special. Anne coaxed and nursed these recollections through the testing process to what we present here. Each day she recruited a small crew of tasters from the restaurant's staff to judge the results of the day's efforts. When we were having a particular problem with a recipe, she would retest it over dinner with her husband and kids, and often again late into the night until she was satisfied. I shudder to think of the sleepless nights Anne will have should one instruction here be unclear, one ingredient left out, one measurement incorrect. We've tried very hard to prevent any of this from happening.

Becky Roller wrote most of the copy and illustrated the book. Becky was the cashier at The Commissary on May 5, 1977—the day that it opened. She had just graduated from Smith College with a major in art history. She loved food and The Commissary looked like an exciting place to spend a little time while she figured out what she really wanted to do. She had been cashiering for about a year when she quit to go to Europe for an extended wining and dining holiday. I vividly remember the day she walked back into The Commissary. She had come in for breakfast and was bursting with excitement about the glorious meals she had eaten and wines she had drunk. I had been thinking that I might need an administrative assistant of sorts, I liked Becky's enthusiasm and she still had no career plans. I offered her a loosely defined job then and there and happily she accepted it.

One of Becky's early projects was to put together a newsletter. We had two restaurants at that point and there was always something going on to report about: food festivals, cooking classes, new menus and recipes, future plans. A regular newsletter seemed like a good idea and Becky was a natural. She had studied calligraphy at Smith and had done beautifully illustrated recipes as a class project. (Her rendition of our carrot cake recipe hangs framed in my kitchen at home.) Next Becky undertook to produce what has become an annual Commissary calendar. The calendar and the newsletter laid the graphic basis of the book. Becky worked with Anne and our testing chefs and translated their scratchings into the recipes contained here and tested quite a few herself. She also wrote all of the recipe introductions, gathered the collective expertise of staff members for the boxes, tips, and hints, and then did the illustrations.

At this point the basic purpose of the Introduction has been served. You have a good feel for what this cookbook is about, who the key characters are, and how the food evolved. If you just cannot wait to get into the kitchen and start cooking, proceed to the recipes on page 2 and begin. Have fun. There is, however, a story attached to the book having to do with the creation of these restaurants over the past twelve years. Some of you may find it interesting, so keep reading. The recipes will still be there.

At the age of twenty-six, having spent a year and a half at La Panetière in a variety of positions, I opened Frog on an investment of thirty-five thousand dollars, including liquor license and opening inventory. The restaurant contained mismatched old chairs that my parents scavenged from secondhand furniture stores. (They paid no more than six dollars for a chair and refinished them all themselves.) There were church pews that we cut down into banquettes, and huge old library doors were set on their sides to become our bar front. Slabs of green marble that someone paid me one hundred dollars to remove from an old soda fountain in a defunct drugstore became the bar top. Bright green Formica tables; lots of hanging plants; and assorted artwork from my extended family of amateur artists, including Uncle Herb, Uncle Ralph, my mother, and brother Fred, completed the decor. Frog seated fifty-five.

The kitchen held a new South Bend six-burner commercial stove, grill, and broiler; a small steamtable; a used one-thousand-dollar Jackson dishwasher (our single most expensive piece of equipment, which is running to this day at our 16th Street Bar and Grill); a used refrigerated worktable; a borrowed junked refrigerator from a friend's basement; and a bridge table (borrowed from the same friend) that served as our salad station. We had to tie a leg of the bridge table to something so it would stand up. This is what you call operating on a shoestring. I built the restaurant—such as it was—with the help of friends. It looked it.

Our menus were written on 18″ × 24″ blackboards. In addition to giving us a great deal of menu flexibility, they were a lot cheaper than printing menus. In the beginning I wrote all the menu boards. I print very neatly. We had six boards, the menu was extensive, and it was quite a job. Each day I would write out six lunch boards. Then I would cook lunch. I'd come out to the dining room after lunch, erase the boards, and print six dinner menus. I would return to the kitchen to cook dinner. The next day the process would begin again. It was several months before I figured out that if I just bought six more blackboards, I wouldn't have to reprint the boards for every meal. That's the way things were in the beginning.

Don Falconio was among our opening-night staff. A Purdue graduate, Don had been teaching English at a nearby junior college while doing graduate work and editing a literary magazine. He had been passing the soon-to-be restaurant on his way to work and noted our progress by reading the weekly letters to the neighborhood that I posted in the front window during construction. When the HELP WANTED sign went up, Don came in. Don liked restaurants, and thought an extra evening job as a busboy—he had no waiting experience—might be fun, since he wasn't making any fortune teaching in junior college. Don was hired. Today, Don is part owner and proverbial right-hand man, overseeing all of our operations. Over the years, Don's impeccable taste, his sense of style, his ability to put customers completely at ease, the total respect with which the staff regards him, and his own love of food have contributed greatly to our success. Though he has never worked as a chef, he has always played an important role in our menu-planning process.

During Frog's first summer, Carol DeLancey arrived out of Keene, New Hampshire, via Skidmore College. Carol had worked as a waitress all through high school and college and was probably the most experienced among us. She was hired as our first busgirl. With us, Carol went from beer-drinking Skidmore coed to one of the most knowledgeable wine buyers in the industry. Carol's wine-training classes are legendary. She is now proprietor (what we call general manager) of Frog. More than anyone else, Carol has created the esprit de corps that marks our entire organization.

For all its storefront funkiness, Frog became a very successful restaurant. Within a year its seating expanded to eighty-five through the acquisition of an apartment behind the kitchen. In the summer of 1976, I was approached by the local chapter of the American Institute of Architects to cater the final ball of their national convention. The ball was to be held in the dramatic, nearly finished apartment building a few blocks from Frog. They expected fifteen hundred people to attend. And so began what was to become one of the most creative parts of our business—catering.

Nineteen hundred and seventy-seven marked the opening of The Commissary. Several months prior to its opening, I had gathered key staff members to the initial menu planning meeting over lunch at my home. I was renting a small house a few blocks from Frog. Our lunch menu was simple. We had caviar, lobster, and champagne. As I proposed a toast to the adventure on which we were about to embark, I told them that it was our objective to open a restaurant that would be thought of as one of the great restaurants in America. Nothing less. At The Commissary we would produce great food at moderate prices in great quantities. These were heady and exciting times.

The Commissary has evolved over the years into a busy complex of restaurants that include the original one-hundred-seat cafeteria that we planned for that day; The Piano Bar; the USA Cafe, a sixty-five seat table-service restaurant that is balconied over the cafeteria and features an interesting blend of cuisines from the Southwest with a touch of Louisiana; and The Market of The Commissary, a "convenience store for people who care about the quality of their conveniences." The Market features on a take-out basis many of the foods that we prepare in the restaurants. Catering also operates out of The Commissary.

Over the years Frog's menu had evolved into a very sophisticated one that could no longer be accommodated in its tiny kitchen and presented in its original funky setting. Frog moved in 1980 to a beautiful Federal-style building around the corner from its original home. It now seats 140 in three dining rooms, 40 in the bar, and up to another 36 in a private dining room. It is characterized by an understated sort of Japanese-style elegance and cost $1.1 million. We had come a long way in seven years.

Ten months later, we reopened old Frog as the 16th Street Bar and Grill. The location was once again the informal neighborhood restaurant it had started as. It is the sort of place that every neighborhood should have. Great burgers and deep-dish pizza, interesting nightly specials, a phenomenal jukebox, and a group of friendly bartenders.

The most recent addition to our family of restaurants is City Bites. City Bites occupies the entire second floor of a two-story steel-and-glass building between the Society Hill and Olde City sections of Philadelphia overlooking the Delaware River. It's hard to capture in words what City Bites looks like. In my memo on its design to Ed Bronstein (a dear friend and a wonderful architect, who taught me how to hammer together studs when I first built Frog and with whom I have worked with on every project), I suggested that a great restaurant is also a great theatre and that he think of the project not as architecture but stage design. To give a flavor of the space, tables for two are triangular, the host stand and bar are built of black-and-white-striped marble with bright yellow Formica trim. Nestled in a corner is a "Greek

Temple" that seats twenty-four in turquoise booths at fifties dinerlike tables. It has a black-and-white checked vinyl floor and is lighted with Italian "headlights." Chain-link fencing sprayed bright yellow adds texture. Art is everywhere. Daily specials are posted on video display terminals. A ten-foot-long hardwood grill puts out great food.

So there's a brief history and description of the restaurants in which the recipes that fill *The Frog/Commissary Cookbook* evolved. In addition to those mentioned above there are numerous others who have contributed to the life and success of the restaurants and who deserve mention. The late Peter von Starck presided over me and La Panetière with great style and gave me my first taste of caviar. Mitch Eisen joined us in the early years and has played important roles in each of the restaurants. Others include Greg Tobias, Marge Gapp, and Liz Leitner, who anchored Frog's dining room for many years; Kamol Phutlek, who was my first chef and whose Thai heritage became a key ingredient in our success; Bob Maranville, who as Frog's chef for five years made significant refinements in our cooking style; Frog's current chef, Mohamoud Azzizi, whose wonderful Persian heritage helps create menu miracles each night that excite customers and staff alike; Gary Bachman and Hilary Rayvis, who provided so much of the flair and excitement that has been The Commissary's legacy and who were followed by William Quigley, Jill Horn, Ilene Sobel, Jean Orr, Vincent Prudente, Robin Fuoco, Lynn Buono, Pat Cahill, and Elayne Brick; Paul Roller, whose talent and determination brought us through one difficult period; and Joe Mercuri, whose similar qualities are bringing us into the future; John Taylor for building the world's largest cabinet, as he characterized The Commissary's intricate façade; Toby Schmidt for bringing our level of graphic design up to that of our food; Jenny Pearman for following in Becky's special footsteps without losing stride; Frank Conlin for teaching the rewards of hard work and determination; Jack Adler for teaching that it is a business, too; Irv Herman and Jay Baer for hours of professional wisdom and good counsel; Meryl Levitz for hours of personal wisdom and good counsel; my wife, Naomi, who helped teach me that there is more to good food than cream and eggs and has shared the hard times within the good times; to Ella, Jon, Charlie, Maris, Frank, Ellen, Nancy, Saul, Howard, Joe, Ruth, Gerard, Berk, Bill, Diane, Sara, Tex, and Mr. Sumner—all of whom in their own way made unique contributions. There is an emerging generation of great cooks and restaurants who are carrying on and expanding what we started and who will help write the next *Frog/Commissary Cookbook*. A special thanks to my mother not just for many good meals, but for believing in me from the beginning, and my brother, Fred, who helped me start and in a very important way helps me continue. Thank you, one and all, and finally, thank you to the people of Philadelphia and to customers from around the country and around the world without whom we wouldn't have had a reason to do it.

Every day we serve about three thousand people in our various emporiums, and while I wouldn't trade places with anyone, it isn't easy. The restaurant business requires great discipline. Yes, talent is important, but so much of running a continually successful restaurant is psychological. Being a great basketball fan, I marvel through the NBA basketball season at the ability of the great players to keep playing great. The season is clearly a grind. Only by sheer force of will can even a great player play great night after night. It's just like that in the restaurant business, where you're only as good as your last meal. The issue isn't whether you have the talent to produce one great meal or a great evening. The question is, can you do it night after night, year after year.

We have tried night after night, year after year to serve great food in warm surroundings. We hope that this book helps you do the same. And if you find yourself in the neighborhood, come say hello.

Steven Poses
January 10, 1985

Authors' Note

Because this book is the result of a living organization, should you have a problem with any recipe in the book, just call us at 215-592-7401, and we will find someone who can help you.

Wherever the name of a recipe is capitalized (Creamy Curried Dressing, for example, or Spinach-Walnut Pesto), the recipe is included elsewhere in the book; the page number may be found by consulting the Index.

Postscript

Twenty-eight years have passed since we opened Frog and sixteen years since the original publication of *The Frog/Commissary Cookbook*. We have served more than 15 million guests. If you live in or around Philadelphia, you probably know what's happened with us over the years. For those outside our area, allow me to give a quick update.

This is a difficult business. Restaurants go through natural life cycles. After long and successful runs, both Frog and The Commissary restaurants ran their course and closed, as did our other restaurants. But that's not the end of the story. Since 1976 we have operated a catering company named for our two flagship restaurants. Today at 15,000 events and counting, Frog Commissary Catering continues to serve a wide range of clients in their homes, offices, and at sites throughout our region, including the Franklin Institute and Independence Seaport Museum. We even have a kosher division, Noah's Kitchen, named for my now fourteen-year-old son. In addition, we operate the food services at Philadelphia's premier outdoor entertainment venue, the Mann Center for the Performing Arts. So, though the cast of characters has changed, the story continues. We're still busy imagining, creating, and serving interesting, flavorful, and stylish food.

With the republication of *The Frog/Commissary Cookbook*, we have made modest changes in a handful of recipes. But the recipes feel as fresh and contemporary as when we first served them. Maybe one day we'll do another cookbook, but for now, here's a new copy to replace your worn-out one or a gift to yourself, a friend, or a loved one.

Thank you for years of support. Enjoy.

Steve Poses
September 26, 2001

Dedicated to all the people
who have worked for us over the years
and have contributed so much
to our success.

Hors d'oeuvre s

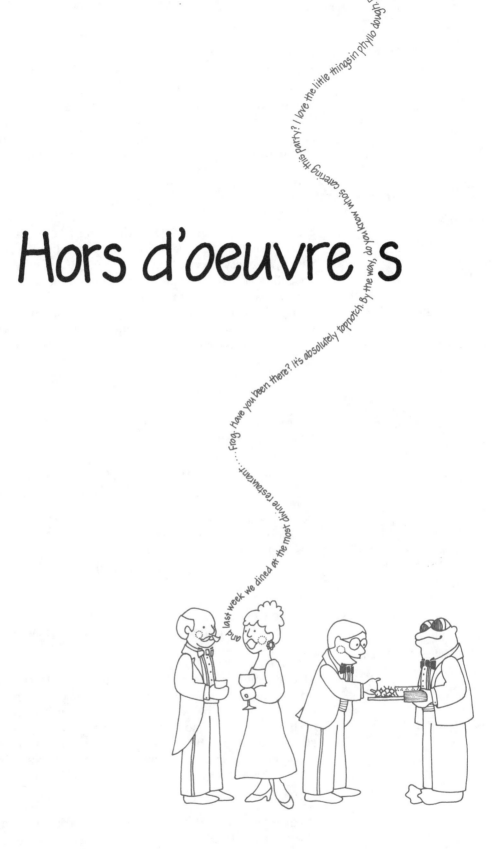

...Frog. Have you been there? It's absolutely topnotch. By the way, do you know who's catering this party? I love the little things in phyllo dough don't... and last week we dined at the most divine restaurant...

Crabmeat can be purchased frozen, pasteurized, vacuum-packed or simply plain cooked. We prefer the plain cooked, which seems to have the best flavor and texture, although it is also the most perishable. This kind is generally available in the following grades:

LUMP • large solid pieces of white meat mostly free of shell. It is used where appearance is important, as in cocktails and salads.

BACKFIN or FLAKE • smaller pieces of white meat. Always pick through for missed pieces of shell before using.

CLAW • small brownish pieces that can be used where appearance isn't important. Crabmeat should be used within 2-3 days of purchase or thawing. Freeze it if you can't use it within that time span. Defrost frozen crabmeat slowly in the refrigerator... allowing at least one day.

BUYING CRABMEAT

CRAB AND BRIE IN PHYLLO DOUGH

Makes about 25–30 triangles

In the spring, when balmy weather beckons us all outdoors, some of our kitchen staff barely get to see the light of day, for they are working (seemingly round the clock) to ready the food for the frenzy of catered parties that crowd the schedule in April, May, and June.

It was just one such spring that Paul, then Frog's lunch chef, was prepping away deep in the recesses of old Frog's basement for a particularly elegant private dinner we were catering. Hors d'oeuvres were called for but not specified other than that they be, once again, "totally new, innovative . . . very special." Remembering how popular hot, crisp little phyllo-wrapped hors d'oeuvres always were, Paul looked for something new to use as a filling other than our customary mixture of spinach, feta cheese, and pine nuts, which, though delicious (see following recipe), seemed a bit too plebeian for this party. Hmmmmm . . . crab! Ummmmm . . . gooey Brie! Sounded good. Today, it is still one of the most requested items on our catering menus.

FILLING
1 tablespoon butter
2 tablespoons minced shallots
½ pound crabmeat, well picked over for shell (see box on buying)
¼ teaspoon salt
¼ teaspoon pepper
2 teaspoons minced parsley
OPT. Tabasco to taste
½ pound Brie cheese, cut into thin slices

ASSEMBLY
15 sheets of phyllo dough (about ½ pound)
¾ cup clarified butter (see p. 124 for how to make)

FILLING
Melt the butter in a skillet. Add the shallots and sauté until golden. Add the crab and heat through. Season with the salt, pepper, parsley, and Tabasco. Spread the slices of Brie over the crab and keep over low heat without stirring until the Brie softens enough to be stirred in without breaking up the lumps of crab. When the mixture is fairly homogeneous, set aside and let cool a bit.

ASSEMBLY
Preheat the oven to 375°. Unroll the package of phyllo sheets. Lift off 15 sheets of phyllo and set them aside covered with plastic wrap topped with a dish towel to

2

help prevent them from drying out. Reroll the remaining phyllo, wrap well in plastic wrap, and either refrigerate or freeze. Remove the covering from the 15 sheets you are using and, with a very sharp knife, carefully cut the stack in half lengthwise. Replace the covering.

For each packet, lay out 1 strip of phyllo with the short end toward you and brush the strip very lightly with melted butter. Fold in half lengthwise and butter again. Put about 1½ teaspoons of the filling at the bottom of the strip, off to one corner. Fold up the strip as you would a flag (see diagram) so that you end up with a neat little triangular packet. Set the packet on a buttered baking sheet and brush once again with the butter. Repeat with all the strips of phyllo, laying out 2 or 3 at a time and keeping the rest covered. If you are not planning to serve the triangles immediately, cover the baking sheets with plastic wrap and refrigerate. Otherwise, bake as needed for 20–25 minutes until crisp and golden. Serve hot.

HOW TO FOLD....

Finished Triangle

Filling

NOTES
This recipe (as well as the following 3 fillings) can be doubled.

These hors d'oeuvres freeze very successfully. To do so, arrange the *unbaked* packets in a single layer on plastic-wrap-lined baking sheets. Brush the packets with butter, wrap each baking sheet tightly with plastic wrap and put in freezer. When frozen, repackage the packets more conveniently in layers (with plastic wrap between the layers) and return to the freezer. To bake, preheat the oven to 375°. Take the packets from freezer, arrange on baking sheets, and put directly into the oven. Bake until crisp and golden.

VARIATIONS
In the summer, minced fresh herbs make a fine addition to this filling.

Use the crab and Brie mixture in other ways, too . . . as a filling for omelets, quiche, or stuffed mushrooms; or spread it while still warm on crackers, black bread, or toast points.

Strudel These make up very quickly and so are useful when time is of the essence, as when you are doing hors d'oeuvres for a crowd. For each strudel roll, lay out 1 full sheet of phyllo, butter it lightly, top with a second sheet and butter again. Spread about ⅓ of the filling along one of the longer edges of phyllo and roll up as you would a jelly roll, tucking in the ends as you go. Set the rolls on buttered baking sheets seam side down. Brush the rolls with butter and lightly score them into bite-size pieces with a sharp knife. Bake as for the triangles, then cut into pieces and serve hot. (Makes about 3 strudels.)

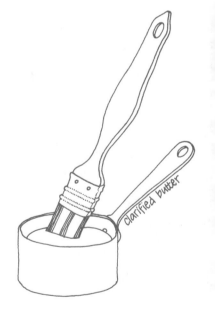

Clarified butter

3

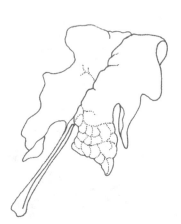

• Phyllo freezes very well, which makes it easy to keep on hand. To defrost, leave it unopened overnight in the refrigerator so that it thaws slowly & evenly.
• Fresh or defrosted phyllo keeps about 5 days in the refrigerator.
• When working with phyllo, keep the leaves you aren't actually using that second covered with a sheet of plastic wrap topped with a dish towel to prevent the phyllo from drying out and becoming brittle ... which it does quickly.

Wontons Instead of the phyllo and butter, have ready about 3 dozen wonton wrappers (available in oriental groceries) and a deep-fryer filled with vegetable oil. For each wonton, put 1–2 teaspoons of filling in the center of a wonton square. Brush the edges with water and bring the corners together in the center. Pinch the edges together to form ribs. Heat the vegetable oil to 360° and fry the wontons, several at a time, until lightly browned, about 2–3 minutes. Drain on paper toweling and serve with a bowl of soy sauce and sliced scallions for dipping. (Makes about 36 wontons.)

Appetizer-size Make larger packets by using one full sheet of phyllo per packet. Butter each sheet and fold in half lengthwise. Butter again and fold up as for the smaller packets but using about ¼–⅓ cup filling for each. Finish and bake as directed.

SPINACH, FETA, AND PINE-NUT FILLING   *Filling for about 25–30 triangles*

1 (10-ounce) bag fresh spinach
6 tablespoons butter
1 cup finely chopped onion
⅓ cup finely chopped scallions
¼ cup finely chopped dill
⅓ cup finely chopped parsley
¼ cup toasted pine nuts
½ pound feta cheese, crumbled
¼ teaspoon salt
½ teaspoon pepper

Wash the spinach well and remove any thick, coarse stems. With water still clinging to its leaves, put the spinach in a large pot. Cook and stir over medium high heat until just wilted. Rinse under cold water, squeeze very dry and finely chop. Heat the butter in a small sauté pan. Add the onion and sauté until golden. Combine with the spinach and remaining ingredients. Proceed with recipe for making phyllo packets using about 1½ teaspoons per packet.

VARIATIONS
Substitute lightly toasted chopped walnuts for the pine nuts and goat cheese for the feta cheese.
See other variations under Crab and Brie in Phyllo Dough.

HONEYED LAMB AND
RAISIN FILLING

Filling for about 30 triangles

Sweet, hot, and spicy all in one. A tantalizing surprise!
Serve them, if you like, with a dipping sauce of plain
yogurt mixed with chopped fresh mint.

¼ cup raisins
¼ cup olive oil
2 cups finely chopped onion
1 tablespoon minced garlic
1 pound ground lamb
1½ teaspoons salt
½ teaspoon pepper
½ teaspoon cinnamon
⅛ teaspoon cayenne pepper
¼ cup tomato paste
1 cup chopped fresh tomato
⅓ cup honey

Cover the raisins with hot water, let sit 10 minutes, then
drain and set aside. Heat the olive oil in a skillet. Add the
onion and garlic, sauté over medium heat until tender and
golden, transfer to a bowl, and set aside. Add the lamb to
the skillet and cook until no longer pink. Drain off any
excess oil. Add the salt, pepper, cinnamon, cayenne, tomato
paste, chopped tomato, honey, the sautéed onions, and
the reserved raisins. Sauté 5–7 minutes over medium-high
heat to blend the flavors and evaporate any liquid. Cool
to room temperature. Proceed with making the phyllo
packets, using about 2 teaspoons of filling for each.

VARIATIONS
See Variations following Crab and Brie in Phyllo Dough.

MUSHROOM, WALNUT, AND GRUYÈRE FILLING   *Filling for about 25–30 triangles*

OTHER FILLINGS FOR PHYLLO…

- Ham, Cheddar, chutney
- Brie, sautéed mushrooms
- Roquefort, walnuts, cream cheese
- Chicken, walnuts, raisins, cream cheese
- Avocado, Monterey Jack, salsa
- Prosciutto, Fontina, sautéed mushrooms
- Smoked salmon, cream cheese, dill
- Smoked trout or bluefish, cream cheese, horseradish, chives
- Mozzarella, sautéed spinach, sun-dried tomatoes
- Swiss cheese, corned beef, sauerkraut

3 tablespoons butter
2 tablespoons finely chopped shallots
1 pound mushrooms, chopped
1 teaspoon salt
1 teaspoon pepper
OPT. 1–2 teaspoons minced fresh herbs (tarragon, marjoram, oregano, chives, etc.)
½ cup dry white wine
½ cup finely chopped scallions
⅓ cup minced parsley
1 tablespoon lemon juice
1⅓ cups walnuts, lightly toasted and finely chopped
½ pound Gruyère cheese, grated (about 2 cups)

Melt the butter. Add the shallots, mushrooms, salt, pepper, and fresh herbs. Cook over medium heat until most of the liquid has evaporated. Add the wine and cook until evaporated, stirring occasionally. Remove from the heat and put into a bowl. Stir in the scallions, parsley, and lemon juice. Let cool, then add the walnuts and cheese. Blend thoroughly. Proceed with making the phyllo packets using about 2 teaspoons of filling for each triangle.

VARIATIONS
See Variations following Crab and Brie in Phyllo Dough.

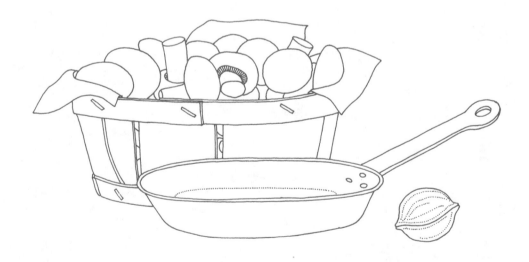

6

ORIENTAL BARBECUED CHICKEN WINGS

Serves 20 as an hors d'oeuvre or 5 as an appetizer

the chicken-wings-in-trash-cans saga

These chicken wings are a delicious result of our predilection for oriental seasonings, and they should leave you happily licking your fingers clean. Pass them with plenty of napkins as an hors d'oeuvre or serve them on shredded greens as an appetizer or with rice for an inexpensive entrée. Imagine, too, what this sauce would do for ribs!

We once prepared a full ton of these wings to sell at one of the Philadelphia Restaurant Sundays on the Parkway. It rained, the festivities were canceled, and we had eight forty-gallon trash cans fulls of chicken wings to deal with . . . literally a TON! We froze them until the following week for Restaurant Sunday's rain date, but the momentum had been lost and business was slow. The six hundred pounds that were still left became staff lunch for the next three weeks as well as the giveaway hors d'oeuvres in the Piano Bar.

¼ cup Chinese fermented black beans
½ cup soy sauce
¼ cup sesame oil
¼ cup unseasoned rice vinegar
½ cup brown sugar
¼ cup molasses
⅔ cup hoisin sauce
¼ cup horseradish
¼ cup Dijon mustard
1 tablespoon minced garlic
½ cup ketchup
4 pounds chicken wings (about 28–36)

Combine all the ingredients except for the chicken wings. Toss the sauce with the wings and let marinate in the refrigerator overnight or for at least 6 hours. **Preheat the oven to 400°.** Arrange the wings, with their sauce, in a single layer on foil-lined rimmed baking sheets and bake 45 minutes, basting every 10 minutes, until well glazed and a deep, rich, reddish-brown color. Serve hot or at room temperature.

CHINESE FERMENTED BLACK BEANS

Heavily salted and dried black beans are an intriguing Chinese seasoning product that is at the same time both subtle and strong. Potent on their own, fermented black beans become flavor-accenters when used in cooking. Chicken and seafood are natural hosts for these beans as are dishes flavored with garlic. Experiment with adding them to such Western dishes as country pâté and scrambled eggs.

7

BROCHETTES OF SWEET AND SPICY ORANGE DUCK

Makes about 45 pieces

DUCK AND GLAZE
1 (4½-pound) duck
2 tablespoons grated orange rind
2 cups orange juice
2 packets of green Thai curry paste (see box on p. 129)
1 teaspoon sriraja (Thai hot sauce) or Tabasco
2 teaspoons minced garlic
½ teaspoon salt
1 cup honey

ASSEMBLY
25 snow peas, stemmed, stringed, and halved crosswise
2 tablespoons corn oil
1 teaspoon salt
1 teaspoon pepper
1 large red pepper cut into ½" cubes

DUCK AND GLAZE
Preheat the oven to 425°. Trim any excess fat from around the cavity of the duck. Put the duck in a roasting pan and roast for 45 minutes. Meanwhile, put the orange rind, orange juice, curry paste, sriraja, garlic, and salt in a saucepan and reduce the mixture to ⅔ cup. Remove from the heat and stir in the honey. After 45 minutes, brush the duck lightly with the reduced glaze and bake 10 minutes more. Let the duck cool. Remove the duck meat from the bones, leaving the skin on the meat. Cut the meat into 1½" strips ¼" thick and try to let each piece have some of the skin. Toss the pieces with half of the remaining glaze.

ASSEMBLY
Preheat the oven to 450°. Toss the snow peas and the red peppers with the oil, salt, and pepper. For each brochette, skewer a piece of the red pepper with a wooden sandwich pick and follow the pepper with a strip of the duck and half a snow pea. Set the assembled brochettes on a baking sheet and bake for 3–5 minutes. Brush the brochettes with the remaining glaze and bake 1 minute more. Serve at once.

NOTE
The duck can be roasted a day ahead and cooled, wrapped, and refrigerated. Similarly, the glaze can be made in advance.

SCALLOP AND BACON BROCHETTES WITH DILL-HORSERADISH MAYONNAISE

Makes about 32 brochettes

DILL-HORSERADISH MAYONNAISE

2 egg yolks
1⅓ cups corn oil
2 tablespoons vinegar
1 teaspoon salt
1½ teaspoons pepper
2 tablespoons Dijon mustard
4 teaspoons minced dill
2 tablespoons horseradish
4 teaspoons lemon juice

BROCHETTES

1 pound sea scallops (cut up large ones to make a total of 32 pieces)
16 bacon slices, halved crosswise (about 1 pound regular thickness)

MAYONNAISE

Follow the procedure for making Basic Mayonnaise on p. 100 using the ingredients listed above. Flavor with the dill, horseradish, and lemon juice.

BROCHETTES

Preheat the oven to 350°. Arrange the bacon in a single layer on a rimmed baking sheet. Bake until the bacon has given off most of its fat but will still be very pliable even when cool. Drain on paper toweling and let cool to lukewarm. Wrap a piece of bacon around each scallop and secure with a wooden toothpick or small skewer. Turn the oven to 400°. Arrange the brochettes on a foil-lined baking sheet and bake 8 minutes. Drain on paper toweling and serve hot with the mayonnaise as a dipping sauce.

NOTES AND VARIATIONS

The brochettes can be assembled in advance, refrigerated, and then baked as needed during the hors d'oeuvres period.

Use any extra mayonnaise on sandwiches, chicken or seafood salads, or with smoked fish or cold shrimp.

PUTTING TOGETHER AN HORS d'OEUVRES SELECTION

For a 1½ hour cocktail party, 6 different hors d'oeuvres make a good selection. For a 3-hour party, serve 9...2 of which should be fairly substantial, like mini-sandwiches or pâté, since many people will probably regard the party as their dinner. ☺ The number of hors d'oeuvres to prepare per person depends on the time of day and whether dinner is to follow. As a basic guide, though, figure 1-2 of each hors d'oeuvres per person. ☞ If you have kitchen help, serve more hot hors d'oeuvres than cold since people really do prefer the hot ones. However, if you don't have help, do just 2 or 3 hot items. ("Cold" hors d'oeuvres are really at room temperature since few things are best cold.) For a very simple assortment, stick to crudités, dips, and spreads with toasted pita triangles, flavored nuts, a cheese board and the like. ☞ As for balance, offer a mixture of vegetable, fish, shellfish, light meat, poultry, cheese and fried hors d'oeuvres. The fried items are always very popular, but they're also very heavy (as are cheeses) when served prior to a dinner. When dinner does follow, try to keep the hors d'oeuvres in a lighter vein and balance their flavors with those of the dinner.

CHICKEN SATAY
WITH SPICY PEANUT SAUCE *Makes about 50 pieces*

Sometimes it is hard for us to imagine a Frog/Commissary catered cocktail party without Chicken Satay. Not that we always serve it, but it is certainly one of the most requested hors d'oeuvres in our repertoire and, for some reason, is a particularly complementary accompaniment to cocktails . . . maybe it's the peanuts.

The Satay Sauce is wonderful—a sophisticated outlet for us closet peanut butter freaks, who find fingerfuls of this sauce nearly as good as the tender little pieces of chicken we're supposed to dip in it. The catering staff also relies on the sauce as a quick "pick-me-up" to be scooped up on chunks of French bread and inhaled in the frenzied midst of a catered party.

This recipe was originally developed years ago as a luncheon entrée at Frog. An offshoot in the guise of skewered pork, beef, and chicken on a bed of orange-flecked rice with Satay Sauce often appears these days as The Commissary's plat du jour.

CHICKEN
1¼ pounds boneless, skinless chicken breast
2 tablespoons sesame oil
2 tablespoons corn oil
¼ cup dry sherry
¼ cup soy sauce
2 tablespoons lemon juice
1½ teaspoons minced garlic
1½ teaspoons minced ginger
¼ teaspoon salt
¼ teaspoon pepper
Dash of Tabasco

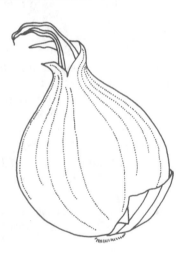

SATAY SAUCE
4 teaspoons corn oil
2 teaspoons sesame oil
½ cup minced red onion
2 tablespoons minced garlic
1 teaspoon minced fresh ginger
1 tablespoon red wine vinegar
1 tablespoon brown sugar
⅓ cup peanut butter, smooth or chunky
½ teaspoon ground coriander
3 tablespoons ketchup
3 tablespoons soy sauce
1 tablespoon lime or lemon juice
½ teaspoon pepper
Dash of Tabasco

10

⅓–½ cup hot water
OPT. ½ teaspoon turmeric for color

CHICKEN
Cut the chicken into strips ½" wide by 3" long. Combine with the remaining ingredients and leave to marinate in the refrigerator for anywhere from 1–12 hours.

SATAY SAUCE
Heat the corn and sesame oils in a small saucepan. Add the onion, garlic, and ginger and sauté over medium heat until softened. Add the vinegar and sugar and continue to cook and stir until sugar dissolves. Remove from the heat and stir in the remaining ingredients (or combine in a food processor for a completely smooth sauce). Feel free to adjust seasonings to taste. (Every person here who makes this sauce seems to do it a little differently.)

TO SERVE
Preheat the oven to 375°. Thread each piece of chicken onto a wooden toothpick or small skewer and arrange on baking sheets. Bake for 5–10 minutes or until just cooked. Serve hot with a bowl of the room temperature sauce for dipping.

VARIATIONS AND NOTES
Substitute beef, lamb, shrimp, pork, or scallops for the chicken.

Since the sauce can be made in advance, it may thicken or separate before you use it. In that case, whisk in a little hot water until the sauce is the consistency you desire.

SETTING UP BAR FOR 50
This is a lot of liquor to buy but people's tastes vary, and you don't want to be caught short. Besides, the stuff won't go bad. We'd get:

liquor is in fifths
- 3 scotch • 3 gin
- 3 vodka • 2 bourbon
- 1 blended • 1 light rum
- 1 sweet vermouth
- 1 dry vermouth
- 5 magnums white wine
- 1 magnum red wine
- 1 Lillet Blonde
- 1 medium dry sherry
- 1 case champagne (OPT.)
- 4 club soda • 4 tonic

soda is in quarts
- 1 bitter lemon
- 1 ginger ale • 1 7-Up
- 1 cola • 1 diet soda
- 4 Perrier

1 lb. ice per person
(more if you're icing wine at bar, it's very hot or the refrigerator is full)

- 8 limes • 6 lemons
- 1 orange • 10 cherries
- 15 olives
- 1 small jar onions
- 1 qt. sour mix
- 1 qt. Bloody Mary mix (4 qts. at brunch)
- 3 qts. OJ (brunch)
- 40 highball glasses
- 25 old-fashioned glasses
- 35 wine glasses
- 1-2 cases beer
- 1 bartender
- corkscrew • stirrers
- cocktail napkins
- containers for storing ice and chilling wine

11

GRILLED MALAYSIAN SHRIMP

Makes 25–30 hors d'oeuvres

Shrimp hors d'oeuvres are usually the first to disappear, and we predict that this particularly dramatic (yet easy to prepare) presentation will barely make it out of the kitchen before being gobbled up. Butterflied shrimp are threaded on small wooden skewers (the skewers prevent the shrimp from curling up as they cook), given a bath in a spicy Southeast Asia–inspired marinade and then grilled or broiled briefly.

½ teaspoon crushed red pepper flakes
1 teaspoon minced garlic
¾ cup very finely minced red onion
2 teaspoons turmeric
2 teaspoons ground coriander
1 teaspoon ground cumin
4 teaspoons grated lemon rind
1 tablespoon lemon juice
1 tablespoon nam pla (Thai fish sauce) or soy sauce
⅓ cup peanut or corn oil
1 pound medium-size shrimp in the shell (26–30 per
   pound)

Combine all the ingredients except the shrimp and set aside. Peel the shrimp, leaving the tails on. Butterfly each shrimp by cutting halfway through along the vein on the outer curve. Remove the vein, open the shrimp, and thread a wooden sandwich pick or skewer lengthwise through it. Toss the shrimp with the marinade and refrigerate for an hour. To cook the shrimp, shake off any excess marinade and grill them quickly over glowing coals or mesquite, or broil them 3" from the heat source for 2 minutes without turning. Remove the wooden picks if you wish and arrange in a spoke-wheel pattern. Serve hot.

MESQUITE

Grilling with mesquite charcoal or chips gives rich, woody overtones to foods. Mesquite is a hardwood indigenous to the Southwest and Mexico. It produces a hotter fire than other fuels and thus is great for searing foods and sealing in the natural juices. Because the heat is so intense, be careful not to let your food overcook. ☆ We prefer to mix mesquite with other hardwood charcoal so that the mesquite's flavor isn't overpowering. Briefly soak a handful of chips in water and then throw them on your glowing charcoal just before putting the food on the grill.

TARAMASALATA

Makes about 2 cups

This recipe of Greek extraction has been a favorite at Frog staff parties for years, since it was the frequent contribution of Prilla, who first came as a waitress, moved on to Dining Room Manager, and was last seen doing the second testing of the recipes for the book. Her version uses potatoes (others call for bread or all olive oil) for a light, fluffy texture. For that reason, avoid using a food processor, since it tends to make potatoes gluey instead of fluffy. Caviar it isn't, but with its good "fishy" flavor highlighted by lemon, this Taramasalata always disappears quickly when scooped up by crudités or bits of pita, French, or black bread.

½ pound red or spring potatoes
⅓ cup lemon juice
1 cup olive oil
4 ounces tarama (carp roe)
⅓ cup finely chopped red onion
¼ cup minced dill or parsley

Peel the potatoes and cook until soft in boiling salted water. Combine the lemon juice and olive oil and set aside. Drain the potatoes and *while still hot* mash them with the tarama using an electric mixer. Gradually add the lemon juice-olive oil mixture to the still warm mashed potatoes until mixture is light and fluffy. Fold in the onions and parsley or dill and put into a serving bowl. Cover with plastic wrap and refrigerate at least 1 hour or up to 3-4 days. Just before serving, garnish with a sprinkling or "wreath" of fresh parsley or dill.

TAILGATE PICNIC

Before retiring to the hearthside for the winter, rally the fans together for one last outdoor feast. A football game doesn't have to be your excuse for this picnic. Take it along, instead, on a ramble through the woods, antiquing in the country, apple-picking, or on a foliage tour by car. The menu is casual, easy to prepare and pack, and hearty enough to provide plenty of energy for cheering on your team (if you do make it to the game).

Taramasalata* with Crudités and Pita Bread Triangles
Thermoses of Scotch Broth with Coriander*
Thinly Sliced Grilled Marinated Flank Steak* on Soft Rolls with Lettuce and Herb Mayonnaise
Curried Red Lentil Salad*
Pears and Apples
Peanut Butter Oatmeal Raisin Cookies*

*see Index for recipe page number.

VANILLA WALNUTS

Makes 4 cups

We defy you to eat just one! Serve them with cocktails, with fruit and cheese as dessert, or include them as garnish on a pumpkin pie decorated with whipped-cream rosettes. These nuts with their counterparts, Curried Walnuts and Bourbon Pecans, are hot sellers in our Market and make especially nice edible gifts.

1 pound walnut halves
½ cup sugar
2½ tablespoons corn oil
1 (4"-long) vanilla bean, pulverized or very finely minced to a paste
¼ teaspoon salt
⅛ teaspoon pepper
¼ teaspoon ground coriander
¼ teaspoon cinnamon
¼ teaspoon nutmeg
¼ teaspoon allspice

Preheat the oven to 325°. Blanch the walnuts for 1 minute in boiling water. Drain well. While still hot, put in a bowl and toss with the sugar and corn oil. Let stand 10 minutes. Arrange on a rimmed baking tray. Bake for 30–35 minutes, turning every 5–10 minutes until nuts are light brown and crispy. Combine the vanilla, salt, pepper, coriander, cinnamon, nutmeg, and allspice. Put the still hot nuts into a bowl and toss with the seasoning mixture. Spread in a single layer to cool. Store in an airtight container.

VARIATION
Instead of a vanilla bean, substitute 1 tablespoon vanilla extract, blending it first with the corn oil before tossing with the nuts.
   This is also very good with pecans.

ZINFANDEL - CRANBERRY PUNCH

Heat together until hot (but NOT boiling): one fifth of zinfandel, 1 quart cranberry juice, ⅓ cup brown sugar, the peel of 2 oranges, 15 cloves, 6 cinnamon sticks, 10 cardamom pods and ½ cup applejack. Boil ½ cup cranberries in ¼ cup water for a minute or so until they pop. Serve the hot wine in mugs or heatproof glasses and divide the cranberries among the servings. Makes eight 1-cup servings.

CURRIED WALNUTS

Makes 4 cups

Sweet and savory all at once. We used to call these "Chinese" walnuts because the recipe we originally started with was for Chinese deep-fried walnuts. With time, however, the seasonings were changed, making them less Chinese; we also found that baking the nuts worked just as well as deep-frying them—*and* also spared us the wrath of the chef in whose domain the fryer was located and who accused us of constantly dirtying his frying oil in our effort to meet The Market's demand for these nuts.

14

1 pound walnut halves
½ cup sugar
2½ tablespoons corn oil
½ teaspoon salt
¼ teaspoon pepper
¼ teaspoon cayenne pepper
1¼ teaspoons ground cumin
¼ teaspoon coriander
½ teaspoon ginger
¼ teaspoon ground cloves
½ teaspoon chili powder

Preheat the oven to 325°. Blanch the walnuts in boiling water for 1 minute and drain well. While still hot, put in a bowl and toss with the sugar and corn oil. Let stand 10 minutes. Arrange in a single layer on a rimmed baked tray. Bake for 30–35 minutes, turning every 5–10 minutes. When nuts are brown and crispy, put them into a bowl. Combine the seasonings and toss with the still warm nuts. Spread the nuts in a single layer to cool completely. Store in an airtight container.

BOURBON PECANS

Makes 4 cups

1 pound pecan halves
3 ounces bourbon, reduced by ½ to 3 tablespoons
½ cup sugar
½ teaspoon Angostura bitters
1 tablespoon Worcestershire sauce
1 tablespoon corn oil
½ teaspoon cayenne pepper
½ teaspoon salt
¼ teaspoon pepper
1 teaspoon ground cumin

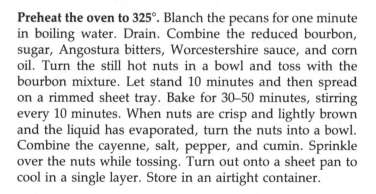

Preheat the oven to 325°. Blanch the pecans for one minute in boiling water. Drain. Combine the reduced bourbon, sugar, Angostura bitters, Worcestershire sauce, and corn oil. Turn the still hot nuts in a bowl and toss with the bourbon mixture. Let stand 10 minutes and then spread on a rimmed sheet tray. Bake for 30–50 minutes, stirring every 10 minutes. When nuts are crisp and lightly brown and the liquid has evaporated, turn the nuts into a bowl. Combine the cayenne, salt, pepper, and cumin. Sprinkle over the nuts while tossing. Turn out onto a sheet pan to cool in a single layer. Store in an airtight container.

GIFTS FROM THE KITCHEN

Vanilla or Curried Walnuts
Bourbon Pecans
Herb-Garlic Cheese
Chicken Liver Pâté
Deep-fried Brie
Szechuan Shrimp
Country or Nutmeat Pâté
Vegetarian Chili
Frog's Mustard Dressing and Croutons
Oriental Salad Dressing
Cider Vinaigrette
Roquefort Herb Dressing
Crème Fraîche (and a pint of fresh raspberries)
Basic Oriental Stir-fry Sauce
Walnut Butter Sauce for pasta
Spinach Walnut Pesto
Caponata
Any of our breads and muffins
Commissary Carrot Cake
Linzer Torte
Oatmeal Chocolate Chip Walnut Cookies
☆ Pack your gift in a decorative, reusable container and include directions/suggestions for serving.

SEE INDEX TO LOCATE RECIPES

A FEW THOUGHTS ON CRUDITÉS

We have a standing house joke of sorts that claims the reason crudités are nearly always included on our catering menus is that Don, former Catering Manager and now company Vice President, invented crudités and thus receives a royalty each time we serve them.

Crudités, a cocktail-hour fixture of assorted raw and barely blanched vegetables, are most frequently accompanied by a dipping sauce or two. For all their visibility they need never be tiresome. After all, crudités can be as simple or as elaborate as you wish—anything from a rustic basket of just-picked radishes and sugar snap peas to a harvest table overwhelmed with all manner of vegetables and dips in fantastical containers. Crudités are a light, colorful, inexpensive, easy-to-prepare inspiration for the artistic spirit—*and* they don't spoil the appetite.

Let the seasons be your guide in selecting vegetables. Include fennel, red peppers, and endive in your winter lineup; asparagus, of course, in the spring; and go absolutely haywire in summer with all the fresh-from-the-garden choices. Consider colors and shapes too. Carrots, cherry tomatoes, radishes, and red and yellow peppers can all be relied on to relieve monotony. Don't overlook the sophistication of an all-green-and-white presentation. Mingle groupings of stalks, strips, and pods with gatherings of flowerets, wedges, spheres, and the like. Tuck sprays of fresh herbs here and there for lightness.

Some vegetables such as broccoli, carrots, cauliflower, asparagus, green beans, and snow peas are best if briefly blanched. This not only makes them a little less obviously "raw" but also sets their colors brilliantly. Be careful, though, not to overdo the blanching (it can be as brief as a few seconds for snow peas) so that the crispness is lost. It helps to have a bowl of ice water ready to transfer the vegetables into immediately from the boiling water. When they are thoroughly cooled, drain the vegetables, pack them in plastic containers lined with paper toweling, and refrigerate.

On the matter of how to present crudités, our favorite presentation for small cocktail parties is to hollow out a red cabbage (see diagram) for the dip, and place it in the center of a tray or basket lined with the outer cabbage leaves. Generous groupings of vegetables are then arranged around the cabbage "rose." For larger parties, we enjoy creating fanciful crudités tables literally spilling over with produce. Another idea is to use an arrangement of crudités as the table centerpiece for a casual dinner and invite your guests to help themselves.

The idea is to be generous, abundant, and overflowing with crudités. Don't worry about leftovers. At The Com-

CABBAGE ROSE
for holding dips

Remove the full outer leaves of a head of red or green cabbage and use them to line the tray or basket for the crudités. Cut off the stem end to make the cabbage stand flat. With a sharp knife, cut a wavy line about ⅓ of the way down from the top and all the way around the cabbage. Remove the top and scrape out the insides to form a bowl. Fill with dipping sauce.

missary, any crudités that return from a catering party are quickly cooked up for pasta sauces, omelet fillings, and soups.

Bugs Bunny may prefer his carrots straight, but we can't resist a good dip. The following are three of our favorites.

TAPENADE MAYONNAISE   *Makes about 1¾ cups*

Tapenade, that pungent, soul-warming Provençale black olive spread, is here transformed into a mayonnaise to work its wonders on crudités.

2 egg yolks
⅔ cup olive oil
⅔ cup corn oil
2 tablespoons red wine vinegar
1½ teaspoons pepper
2 tablespoons lemon juice
⅛ teaspoon Tabasco
1½ teaspoons minced garlic
1 (2-ounce) can anchovies, drained and finely chopped
¼ cup small capers, drained
¼ cup pitted and finely chopped imported Greek or
   French olives

Follow the procedure for making Basic Mayonnaise on p. 100 using the ingredients listed above. Stir in the anchovies, capers, and olives by hand at the end.

VARIATIONS
We've found other applications for this wonderful mayonnaise. Drizzle it over summer's best tomato-basil salad, use it to bind a fresh vegetable salad for stuffing in pita bread, energize a tuna salad with it, or toss it with tiny pasta shells and green pepper bits and fill hollowed tomatoes.

PACKED IN PURE OLIVE OIL
PRODUCT OF PORTUGAL
☆ANCHOVY FILETS ☆

SETTING UP A RAW BAR

This is a major undertaking but makes a stunning centerpiece for a cocktail party. ☆ A rectangular table (6 ft. minimum) is best because the person shucking the clams and oysters can stand behind it to replenish the display. We also like to add a tier to give the table some height and drama. For the seafood, you'll need plastic buspans or other waterproof containers not more than 8" deep. Arrange them on the table and fill each ¾ with ice. Use mustard greens or kale to cover the table and hide the buspans. Garnish the leaves with bright fresh vegetables. On the ice, arrange oysters, clams, cooked shrimp, mussels, and crab claws. Sushi, seviche, and sashimi as well as crudités are nice additions. Put dipping sauces in seashells or bowls and nestle in the ice. Add lemon wedges, soy sauce, and wasabi (Japanese horseradish) around the table. Plates, cocktail forks, and napkins are essential. ☆ For the amount of seafood to prepare, figure per person: 2 oysters, 2 clams, 2 shrimp, ¼ cup seviche, 1 oz. raw fish for sashimi, 1 mussel, 2 pieces of sushi and 3-4 pieces of crudités. One type of passed hot hors d'oeuvres would then round out the selection appropriately.

17

PIMENTO MAYONNAISE   *Makes 1¾ cups*

An unusual mayonnaise with a bright, piquant flavor. Don't overlook the fact that it also is delicious with cold roast beef, poached fish, Cold Poached Mussels, shrimp, Eastern Shore Crab Cakes, and other dishes.

2 egg yolks
1⅓ cups corn oil
3 tablespoons vinegar or lemon juice
1 teaspoon salt
1½ teaspoons pepper
2 tablespoons Dijon mustard
½ cup finely chopped pimentoes, drained well
2 tablespoons finely chopped scallions
½ teaspoon minced garlic

Follow the procedure for Basic Mayonnaise on p. 100 using the ingredients listed above. Stir in the pimentoes, scallions, and garlic by hand at the end.

TUNA-CAPER MAYONNAISE   *Makes 1¾ cups*

Shades of vitello tonnato and Salade Niçoise . . . a little tuna and a few capers turn mayonnaise into a Mediterranean wonder that is sensational with crudités; on a salad of roast veal, zucchini, and black olives; over sliced tomatoes and the like.

2 egg yolks
⅔ cup olive oil
⅔ cup corn oil
3 tablespoons vinegar or lemon juice
1 teaspoon salt
1½ teaspoons pepper
2 tablespoons Dijon mustard
¼ cup sour cream
⅔ cup crumbled tuna fish, drained
¼ cup chopped capers

Follow the procedure for making Basic Mayonnaise on p. 100 using the ingredients listed above. Fold in the sour cream, tuna, and capers by hand at the end.

HERB AND GARLIC CHEESE   *Makes about 2 cups*

This is so easy to make (and deliciously potent) that we think it puts its prepackaged counterparts to shame. We find ourselves using it in a zillion different ways: piped onto cucumber or zucchini disks or into hollowed cherry tomatoes or raw mushroom caps, spread on burgers, thinned with cream and served as a dip, slathered on baked potatoes, used as a sandwich spread with tomatoes or with roast beef and watercress on French bread, served as part of the cheese course, and so on.

16 ounces cream cheese at room temperature
1 tablespoon heavy cream or milk
½ teaspoon minced garlic
¼ cup minced parsley
¼ cup minced dill
⅓ cup minced scallions
½ teaspoon salt
½ teaspoon pepper
OPT. ¼ teaspoon Tabasco

In a food processor or in a mixer fitted with a paddle attachment, cream the cream cheese with the cream. (Using a food processor will make the cheese greener.) Add the remaining ingredients and process until smooth. This keeps for several days if well covered and refrigerated. Bring to room temperature before using.

ASSEMBLING A CHEESE BOARD

Five different cheeses is a generous amount but also the minimum for an interesting selection. Include one triple crème, one hard, one blue, one goat, and one mild semisoft. Figure on at least a total of 2 lbs. of cheese for 10 people. Serve the cheeses at room temperature with an assortment of good breads and crackers. (Avoid overly salty crackers.) Some tangy mustard is a nice touch, and the ubiquitous apples, grapes, and pears add color. Be sure there is a knife and cutting board for the fruit. If you have baskets, use them for the breads and crackers. We like to set the cheeses on grape leaves in flat basket trays. For a special addition, serve a warm deep-fried cheese such as our recipe for Deep-Fried Brie (or its Camembert with Pesto variation) on page 31.

SMOKED SALMON AND PARMESAN CREAM CANAPÉS

Makes 32

These rich little mouthfuls rank high on the list of catering hors d'oeuvres favorites. For catering, we usually bake the mixture in tiny pastry barquettes which The Commissary's bakery routinely produces by the hundreds. For serving at home, however, we find that decoratively piping the mixture onto toast canapés and then baking them is easier and just as delicious.

8 ounces cream cheese, softened
¾ cup grated Parmesan cheese
½ teaspoon Worcestershire sauce
¼ teaspoon Tabasco
8 slices finely textured white bread, trimmed of crusts
⅓ cup butter, softened
3 ounces thinly sliced smoked salmon
32 sprigs fresh dill

Combine the cream cheese, Parmesan, Worcestershire sauce, and Tabasco in the bowl of a food processor and whiz 30 seconds. **Preheat the oven to 350°.** Spread each slice of bread on each side with 1 teaspoon of butter. Cut each slice into quarters (you can make fingers, squares, or triangles) and arrange in a single layer on a baking sheet. Bake for 3–5 minutes until lightly browned, remove from the oven, flip all the pieces over, and bake 1–2 minutes more. Top each piece of toast with a small piece of smoked salmon. Put the cream cheese mixture in a pastry bag fitted with a number 5 open star tip and pipe rosettes of the cream cheese over the smoked salmon. Bake for 5 minutes. Garnish each canapé with a sprig of dill and serve hot.

NOTE
The cream cheese mixture can be made up to 4 days in advance and kept refrigerated. Bring to room temperature before using.

LEMON CROWN GARNISH

Cut off the ends of a lemon. With a sharp paring knife, cut a sawtooth pattern around the middle, inserting the knife as far as the center. Pull the halves apart. Set each crown on a nest of watercress or parsley.

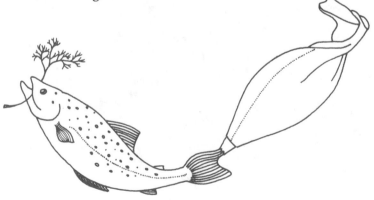

CHICKEN LIVER PÂTÉ WITH
BRANDY, BACON, AND HERBS   *Makes 5 cups*

No run-of-the-mill chicken liver pâté this. Even people who normally won't get near a chicken liver love our version, which is mellowed by brandy and bacon and perfumed with herbs.

½ pound bacon, diced
2 cups chopped onion
⅛ teaspoon ground cloves
¼ teaspoon ground nutmeg
¼ teaspoon cayenne pepper
¼ teaspoon coriander
½ teaspoon dried marjoram
½ teaspoon dried oregano
½ teaspoon dried basil
1 teaspoon dried rosemary
1 teaspoon dried thyme
1 teaspoon dried tarragon
2 bay leaves
1 teaspoon pepper
¼ teaspoon salt
2 tablespoons minced garlic
3 tablespoons minced shallots
1 pound chicken livers
¼ cup brandy
¼ cup heavy cream
¾ pound butter, at room temperature

In a large skillet, partially cook the bacon until its fat has been rendered. Add the onion, spices, herbs, pepper, salt, garlic, and shallots. Sauté for 3–5 minutes until the onion has softened. Add the chicken livers and brandy and sauté, stirring frequently, until the livers are cooked but still pink in the middle. (Be careful not to overcook or they will develop an unpleasant color and texture.) Let cool until lukewarm. Remove the bay leaves. Purée the mixture in batches in a food processor or blender. Add the cream. Add the butter bit by bit until the mixture is smooth and well blended. (Mixture will seem soupy, but don't worry.) Pack into small 1-cup crocks or into a single large one. Cover flush with plastic wrap and chill. Serve with toast points or black bread.

NOTES AND SERVING SUGGESTIONS
For cocktail parties, bring the pâté to room temperature and, using a pastry tube fitted with a star tip, pipe rosettes of pâté onto toast points or croutons. Anne went one further for a party and cut her croutons from bread slices using a small chicken-shaped cookie cutter. These surrounded a crock of the pâté.

Make small individual molds of pâté to serve as first course by lining ramekins with cheesecloth, filling with pâté, chilling, and then unmolding just before serving.

If the finished product is grainy, it may be because the butter was not soft enough when it was added. To remedy, whisk the pâté mixture over very low heat just to melt the butter, then whisk over ice to bring it back to room temperature. This way the butter should smooth out and then be reabsorbed.

25 QUICK HORS D'OEUVRES AND APPETIZERS

Wrap cubes of melon with strips of thinly sliced prosciutto or Westphalian ham, top with mint leaves, and skewer with toothpicks.

Fill miniature biscuits with Black Forest ham, Cheddar cheese, and fruit chutney.

Spread paper-thin slices of raw fillet of beef with a seasoned horseradish–cream-cheese mixture and wrap around blanched asparagus spears.

Spread thin slices of French bread with olive oil and pesto, top with slivers of sun-dried tomatoes and mozzarella, and run under the broiler briefly.

Brush mushroom caps with olive oil, fill with pieces of Brie cheese, top each with a partially cooked piece of bacon, and bake for 10 minutes at 350°.

Halve cherry tomatoes, scoop out the centers, fill with seasoned ricotta cheese, and top with a dab of pesto or black olive spread.

Blend fresh goat cheese with minced fresh herbs of choice, roll in more herbs or coarsely cracked peppercorns, drizzle with olive oil, and serve with a loaf of whole grain bread.

Wrap stalks of blanched asparagus with thinly sliced prosciutto and pass Herb Vinaigrette as a dipping sauce.

Set out an impromptu hors d'oeuvres array: baskets of radishes and sugar snaps, a dish of coarse salt, a sliced loaf of crusty bread, herb butter in a crock, a bowl of Niçoise olives, and a plate of thinly sliced salami.

Brush thin slices of raw salmon with sesame oil, arrange them on a tray and sprinkle with snipped chives. Serve with bowls of soy sauce and wasabi (Japanese horseradish).

Marinate bay scallops in lime juice for two hours, drain and combine with Crème Fraîche, salt and pepper to taste, and minced dill or mint. Serve on greens.

Serve small wedges of a summer frittata at room temperature: Fry sliced zucchini in olive oil in a small skillet. Pour on eggs beaten with salt, pepper, Parmesan cheese, and minced basil. Cook until brown on the bottom, then run under the broiler until the top is set.

Dip small chunks of vegetables in extra virgin olive oil and sprinkle with salt and pepper. Thread the vegetables on skewers and grill.

Make canapés of black bread spread with Herb and Garlic Cheese and topped with thin slices of rare fillet of beef.

Make a mixture of smoked whitefish and cream cheese, put into pastry bag, and pipe into gladiola blossoms (with stamens removed) that have been gently rinsed and shaken dry.

Top crackers or fingers of whole grain bread with a mild creamy cheese (such as stracchino) or fresh goat cheese and garnish with slivers of sun-dried tomatoes.

Wrap cubes of mozzarella with strips of roasted red peppers, skewer with toothpicks, and serve with slices of Italian bread and extra virgin olive oil for dipping.

Present a big platter of blanched asparagus spears surrounded by bowls of several different dipping sauces.

Brush mushroom caps with olive oil, fill each with mozzarella and a dab of pesto, and bake at 350° for 10 minutes.

Top cucumber disks with a horseradish–cream-cheese mixture, smoked bluefish, and sprigs of dill.

Put a smoked mussel in a radicchio leaf and nap half the mussel with a curried mayonnaise.

For an appetizer, cut green beans, carrot strips, and red pepper strips to equal lengths. Blanch and chill the beans and carrots and arrange with the red peppers in individual piles on each plate. Nap with Basic Vinaigrette or the dressing of your choice.

Arrange blanched green beans and sliced baked beets on individual plates and nap with Aioli.

Top oysters on the half shell with crumbled Stilton and pieces of partially cooked bacon. Run under the broiler until the bacon is crisp.

Cut toast rounds the diameter of a log of Montrachet. Top each round with a slice of Montrachet and a slice of kiwi.

Appetizers

and we'd like to order a selection of appetizers...the Salmon, Scallop and Spinach Pâté; Chicken in Romaine Leaves...is that hot or cold? Deep-Fried Brie with Apple-Pear Purée, and...let's see...the Mussels with Avocado Mayonnaise

THREE-NOODLE APPETIZER   *Serves 6–8*

This is one of the classic Frog appetizers from those earliest days. We can easily recall how delightfully intriguing its name looked printed ever so neatly on the blackboard menus we used at old Frog. Still just as popular today, this fun-to-eat ensemble of three different oriental noodles, each seasoned separately, bears heavily the influence of the Thai cooks who worked at Frog and often concocted some fabulous noodle dish for a staff meal. The use of a little sugar or honey in these otherwise savory dishes is a distinctive trait of Thai cooking and adds an extra flavor dimension while actually underscoring the savory qualities.

Though you can use other methods, this dish is best prepared with the aid of a microwave oven. Each noodle mixture is prepared ahead of time, and then all are reheated just prior to serving. Because the noodles are fragile (and the broccoli darkens), they don't reheat as well in the oven or on top of the stove. We recommend using the microwave to reheat them as we do at Frog. If you don't have a microwave, at least try serving one of the noodles. Any of them alone would make a good entrée for two.

BEAN THREADS WITH CHINESE MUSHROOMS AND EGGS
½ ounce dried Chinese mushrooms (4–6 mushrooms)
2 (2-ounce) packages bean threads (cellophane noodles)
⅓ cup corn oil
1½ teaspoons minced garlic
3 eggs, lightly beaten
¼ teaspoon pepper
½ teaspoon salt
1 teaspoon sriraja (Thai hot sauce) or Tabasco
1½ tablespoons sugar

RAMEN WITH BROCCOLI AND PEANUTS
2 (3½-ounce) packages ramen noodles with seasoning
    packets (we use the Ichiban brand)
2 tablespoons corn oil
2 cups broccoli flowerets
¼ cup lemon juice
¼ cup honey
1 teaspoon salt
½ teaspoon pepper
1 cup finely chopped roasted unsalted peanuts

SOMEN WITH THAI CURRIED BEEF
2 (3-ounce) bundles somen, broken in half
2 tablespoons corn oil
¾ pound ground chuck beef
½ cup finely chopped onion
1 package red or green Thai curry paste (see box on p. 129)
⅓ cup soy sauce
⅓ cup honey
¼ teaspoon pepper

BEAN THREADS
Soak the mushrooms in hot water until soft (about 20 minutes). Drain the mushrooms, discard the stems, and slice the caps into thin strips. Cook the noodles in boiling salted water for 1 minute. Refresh under cold running water, and drain well. Cut the noodles into 6″ lengths. Heat the oil in a skillet. Add the garlic and sauté briefly. Add the noodles, sliced mushrooms, eggs, pepper, salt, sriraja or Tabasco, and sugar. Stir lightly so as to scramble the eggs, but watch carefully so the noodles don't burn. Cool, cover, and refrigerate until ready to reheat.

RAMEN
Cook the noodles (*without* the seasoning packets that accompany them) according to package directions (about 2 minutes in boiling salted water). Drain and rinse with cold water. Drain well and toss with the corn oil.

Blanch the broccoli for 1 minute in boiling salted water. Refresh under cold running water and drain well. Blend the lemon juice, honey, and seasoning packets. Combine the noodles with the broccoli, salt, pepper, and lemon-honey mixture. Cool, cover, and refrigerate. Stir in the peanuts just before reheating.

SOMEN
Cook the somen in boiling salted water for 2–3 minutes. Refresh under cold water and drain well. Toss with the corn oil and refrigerate until serving time. Sauté the beef with the onion until beef is cooked and the onion tender. The meat should be well broken and crumbly. Drain most of the fat from the pan. Add the curry paste to the meat in the pan and stir and cook another minute. Turn the heat to high and add the soy sauce, honey, and pepper. Cook until the liquid becomes a glaze. Cool, cover, and refrigerate until ready to serve.

TO SERVE
Preheat oven to 175°. Have ready 6–8 microwave ovenproof appetizer plates. Arrange a small pile of each of the noodle mixtures on each appetizer plate. Heat the beef mixture

ORIENTAL NOODLES
We have great fun with oriental noodles. The Thais who have worked in our kitchens introduced them to us way back. There are so many different kinds... of wheat, rice, buckwheat, mung beans... in thick, thin, squiggly, transparent, soft, brittle shapes. Most of them cook in no time and are an easy way to make what you're doing a little different. Use them in soups and salads, as the basis for a pasta dish, or with an entrée instead of potatoes or rice. ☆ For a quick side dish use a 3-ounce packet of instant oriental noodle soup mix. Cook the noodles according to directions but without the seasoning packet. Serve the noodles hot or cold sprinkled with sesame oil, chopped scallions, and the contents of the seasoning packet. Serves 2.

for the somen in a pan on top of the stove. Heat the plates of noodles in the microwave oven until just hot. Top the somen noodles with the hot beef mixture and keep in the warm oven until all the plates of noodles have been reheated. Serve at once.

SPRING ROLLS WITH SWEET AND SOUR SAUCE
Makes 12 spring rolls

The peanuts and brine-cured radish (Thai touches) in these spring rolls make them distinctive and quite different from anything we've ever had in Chinatown.

SWEET AND SOUR SAUCE
2 cups sugar
1 cup white vinegar
1 teaspoon salt
¼ cup finely grated carrots
¼ cup very finely minced red pepper

FILLING
1 (2-ounce) package bean threads (cellophane noodles)
1 cup brine-cured radish
3 tablespoons water
6 tablespoons corn oil
1 tablespoon minced garlic
½ pound ground pork
1 cup unsalted roasted peanuts, finely ground
⅓ cup sugar
½ teaspoon pepper
⅔ cup chopped scallions
1⅓ cups bean sprouts

ASSEMBLY
12 spring-roll wrappers (7"–8" squares)
1 egg yolk, beaten
Vegetable oil for deep frying

SAUCE
Combine the sugar, vinegar, and salt in a large saucepan and reduce to 1½ cups. Add the carrot and red pepper and cool to room temperature.

FILLING
Soak the bean threads in hot water to cover for 20 minutes. Rinse the noodles, drain well, and cut them into 2" lengths. Set aside. Coarsely chop the radish and whiz the pieces

with the water in a food processor for 30 seconds or until very fine. Set aside. Heat the corn oil in a 9″ skillet. Add the garlic and sauté until it just begins to turn light brown. Add the pork and stir well over high heat until the pork loses its pinkness. Add the reserved radish, the peanuts, sugar, and pepper. Stir for 2–3 minutes over high heat. Combine the mixture with the bean threads and cook while stirring for 2–3 minutes. Cool to room temperature. Stir in the scallions and the sprouts.

HOW TO FOLD...

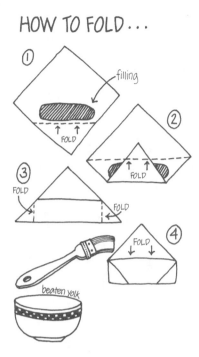

ASSEMBLY

Set one of the spring-roll wrappers in front of you so that it looks like a diamond. Put a generous ⅓ cup of the filling on the wrapper just below the center (see diagram). Fold the bottom point of the diamond over the filling. Fold it up again so the filling is now hidden. Fold over the right-hand point, then fold over the left-hand point. Brush the remaining top point with a little of the egg yolk, and finish rolling up the spring roll firmly. Repeat with the other 11 wrappers. (The spring rolls may be frozen at this point.) Heat vegetable oil to 360° in a deep fryer or deep saucepan. Fry the spring rolls several at a time for 2 minutes or until golden. Drain on paper toweling and serve hot accompanied by the sauce, which should be at room temperature.

VARIATION

Make miniature spring rolls for hors d'oeuvres by cutting the wrapper into 4 squares and using each one to make a little spring roll.

1. asparagus 2. rhubarb 3. country ham 4. scallions 5. spring rolls 6. chives 7. shad & shad roe 8. soft shell crabs 9. new potatoes 10. peas 11. baby carrots 12. strawberries

ARTICHOKES STUFFED WITH SAUSAGE
AND SMOKED MOZZARELLA   *Serves 8*

8 artichokes, 4–4½ ounces each
2 tablespoons lemon juice
1 pound Italian sausage
½ pound smoked mozzarella, grated
1 tablespoon olive oil
¼ cup sliced scallions
¼ cup finely chopped red pepper
1 tablespoon minced shallots
½ teaspoon minced garlic
½ teaspoon dried oregano
½ teaspoon dried basil
½ teaspoon salt
½ teaspoon pepper
¼ teaspoon allspice
¼ cup dry bread crumbs
½ cup grated Parmesan cheese

ARTICHOKE TRIMMING
(for one to be stuffed)
Cut off the stem
so that the arti-
choke will sit solidly
on a plate. Slice off the
top ¼ of the way down.
Rub the cut surface with lemon
juice. Use scissors to cut off
the tips of the leaves,
giving them a squared-off
look. Proceed
with the recipe.

Trim (see box) the artichokes and set them in 1 inch of boiling water in a large pot. Cover the pot and steam the artichokes in simmering water for 25–30 minutes or until tender (leaves should pull off easily). Refresh the artichokes under cold running water. Remove the center leaves and scrape out the chokes. So that they don't discolor, drop the artichokes into a large bowl of cold water with the lemon juice and leave them until ready to stuff.

Remove the skin from the sausage and sauté until cooked through. Drain well, crumble until very fine, and set aside. Pour off the fat from the pan. Add the olive oil to the pan. Add the scallions, red pepper, shallots, and garlic. Sauté briefly to soften. Add the herbs, seasonings, and the sausage and cook 2 minutes more. Turn into a bowl and combine with the bread crumbs and mozzarella.

Preheat the oven to 350°. Drain the artichokes upside down. Loosely stuff the centers with the filling. Pack the remaining filling inside each of the outer leaves. (They may be made ahead to this point.) Set in a baking pan just large enough to hold them all, or tie each one with string so it holds its shape while baking. Bake 15 minutes, or until hot in the center. Sprinkle each with 1 tablespoon of Parmesan cheese and run under the broiler until lightly browned. Serve hot.

DEEP-FRIED BRIE IN ALMOND CRUST WITH APPLE-PEAR PURÉE

Serves 8

What is it that is so addictive about warm, gooey melted cheese? Whether it be a familiar, quickly made grilled cheese sandwich or Frog's elegant presentation of deep-fried Brie, we shall never tire of comforting, satisfying melted cheese in any of its guises. This recipe, however, has to be one of our favorite presentations. A thin, crisp nutted crust encases a wedge of oozing, mellow Brie, which is further enhanced by being served with a cool, pretty pink purée of spiced apples and pears. Add a basket of water biscuits on the side, and we're in heaven.

APPLE-PEAR PURÉE
Makes 2 quarts

3 cloves
1 orange, quartered
6 tart red-skinned apples, cored and quartered
6 ripe pears, cored and quartered
3 cups dry white wine
⅓ cup brown sugar
1 cinnamon stick
1 tablespoon minced fresh ginger or 1 teaspoon ground

BRIE

1½ cups whole toasted blanched almonds, finely ground
1 cup dry bread crumbs
1 (1½-pound) piece of Brie, chilled
1 cup flour
3 eggs, beaten
Vegetable oil for deep frying

PURÉE

Stick the cloves into the skin of the orange. Combine with the other ingredients in a large pot. Bring to a boil and allow to simmer until the fruit is tender—about 15 minutes. Let cool. Remove the cinnamon stick and orange. Purée the apple-pear mixture through a food mill, let cool, and refrigerate.

BRIE

Combine the almonds with the bread crumbs. Cut the Brie into 8 wedges. Coat each piece with flour, dip in the egg, and roll in the crumbs. Dip in the egg and roll in the crumbs again. Set on a tray covered with plastic wrap and refrigerate until ready to use.

Preheat the oven to 350°. Heat the vegetable oil to 360° in a deep pan or deep fryer. Deep-fry the cheese, 1 or 2 pieces at a time, for about 1½ minutes, turning once. Drain on paper toweling and put in the oven for 3–5 minutes to finish melting the centers. (Cheese may leak if left too long in the fryer or the oven.)

To serve, spoon a pool of the cold Apple-Pear Purée on each plate and top with the hot cheese. Garnish, if desired, with a fan of apple and pear slices and a sprig of watercress. Serve with water biscuits.

NOTES AND VARIATIONS

Coated, unfried cheese will keep 1 day in the refrigerator. You could also deep-fry the cheese, cool and chill it and then reheat it in the oven the next day.

For catering, we deep-fry the Brie for 1–2 minutes, let it drain and cool, and then reheat it in the oven just before serving.

You will have leftover purée—we purposely made a lot because it is so good. Try it for breakfast or in any recipe that calls for applesauce.

Experiment with other cheeses and nuts. A Market variation splits a small Camembert, sandwiches it back together with pesto or fresh herbs, coats it with herbed or nutted crumbs, and then deep-fries the whole thing. Customers then reheat the cheese at home in a 325° oven for 10–15 minutes or until the cheese begins to ooze out a bit.

The Commissary's upstairs restaurant has offered a delicious rendition, too, using Cheddar cheese served with an apple-cranberry chutney.

BOUQUET of HERBS

A bouquet of herbs from your garden makes a novel… and fragrant… summertime arrangement. Purple basil adds great color. You could also tuck in a few stems of some of the more delicate-looking flowers like coreopsis and coralbells. Keep a second vase of herbs on the kitchen counter where they will be handy to snip from when you are cooking.

GRILLED GOAT CHEESE WITH TOMATO CHUTNEY
Serves 4–6

Tangy goat cheese is here imbued with a fragrant coating of fresh summer herbs and a delicate smokiness that only a hickory-chip-laced fire can give. At its side is a bold tomato chutney that also shouts of summer. Because the cheese needs time to cool and set up again after grilling, please plan accordingly.

TOMATO CHUTNEY

1½ cups cider vinegar
2 tablespoons brown sugar
1½ teaspoons dry mustard
1¾ teaspoons salt
½ teaspoon whole cloves
1 cinnamon stick
¼ teaspoon ground ginger
¼ teaspoon pepper
1 cup diced onions (⅛" dice)
½ teaspoon minced garlic
½ cup diced green peppers (¼" dice)
3½ cups diced tomatoes (½" dice) (about 1½ pounds)
1 tablespoon minced fresh coriander (or add ½ teaspoon
   dry with the spices)

GOAT CHEESE

2 cups hickory chips
1 log Montrachet goat cheese, with or without the ashes
½ teaspoon ground cumin seed
2 tablespoons minced parsley
1 teaspoon each minced fresh oregano, chives, thyme,
   and marjoram (or combination of your choice)
½ teaspoon pepper
1 cup olive oil
Romaine leaves
Homemade melba toast, thinly sliced black bread, or
   water crackers
OPT. Sprigs of fresh herbs for garnish

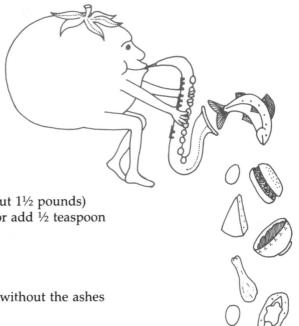

CHUTNEY

In a nonaluminum 9" saucepan, combine the vinegar, brown sugar, dry mustard, salt, cloves, cinnamon stick, ginger, and pepper. Stir until mixture comes to a boil. Over medium heat, reduce to ⅓ cup. Remove the cloves and cinnamon stick. Add the onion and garlic to the liquid and cook 3 minutes. Add the peppers and tomatoes, increase the heat to high, and cook 2–3 minutes. Pour the mixture into a sieve set over a bowl to catch the liquid and let drain 10 minutes. Return the liquid to the saucepan and reduce over medium-high heat to ⅓ cup. (Stir it as it begins to thicken so that it doesn't burn around the edges.) Combine this reduction with the tomato mixture and let cool. Stir in the coriander. (Refrigerated, this will keep for at least a week.)

CHEESE

Soak the hickory chips for ½–1 hour in 3 cups water. Meanwhile, in a hibachi or grill, start a charcoal fire. When it reaches the glowing coal stage, scatter on the hickory chips and leave them about 10 mintues or until they also

CHUTNEY CAN JAZZ UP:

- a ham and cheese omelet
- curry or onion dip
- fried flounder or other fish
- baked potatoes with sour cream
- a hamburger
- any deep-fried cheese (see recipe for Brie on page 31)
- fried chicken
- potato salad or egg salad
- mayonnaise to serve with cold meat, fish or chicken
- Country Pâté or Nutmeat Pâté (see pages 42-44)
- Canapés - mix with cream cheese, spread on canapés, and top with ham, shrimp or avocado.

begin to smolder.

Prepare the cheese by rolling the log of Montrachet in a mixture of the cumin, parsley, herbs, and pepper. Wrap the log in a piece of cheesecloth (about 12" × 14") and secure with twine as you would a roast. Soak this bundle well in the olive oil. When the coals are ready and the chips are smoldering, set the log on the grill for about 25 minutes. Occasionally turn the cheese gently with a spatula and try to keep it off direct flame. (The cheesecloth will probably become charred anyway.) Carefully transfer cheese to a plate and refrigerate for several hours.

To serve, untie and unwrap the log and slice it into 12 medallions. Line appetizer plates with romaine leaves, arrange 2–3 medallions accompanied by melba toasts and a small serving of the chutney on each plate. Garnish with sprigs of herbs.

CHICKEN IN ROMAINE LEAVES
WITH LIME HOT SAUCE *Serves 8*

From the files of The Commissary's second-floor restaurant, we have drawn this unusual appetizer: small green bundles of blanched romaine leaves enclosing a spicy chicken-walnut filling and set aswim in a pale sauce composed of a curious but delicious blend of cream, lime, and orange juice. Execution is uncomplicated, and we recommend assembling the dish earlier in the day and then reheating it just before serving.

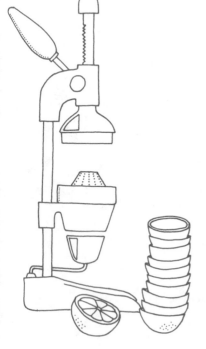

LIME HOT SAUCE
1 cup water
1 tablespoon dried lemongrass
½ teaspoon red pepper flakes
1 tablespoon soy sauce
1½ tablespoons sugar
¾ teaspoon salt
1½ teaspoons nam pla (Thai fish sauce)
1 cup orange juice
½ cup heavy cream
OPT. 1½ teaspoons plum sauce
2 tablespoons lime juice
2 tablespoons cornstarch
2 tablespoons cold water

34

MARINADE

2 tablespoons water
1 tablespoon cornstarch
1 teaspoon sugar
3 tablespoons soy sauce
¼ cup rice wine or dry sherry
1 pound boneless skinned chicken breast, cut into ½"
  cubes

FILLING AND ASSEMBLY

16 large unblemished romaine leaves
⅓ cup corn oil
2 teaspoons crushed Szechuan peppercorns
2 teaspoons minced ginger
2 tablespoons minced garlic
1 cup chopped walnuts
1 tablespoon sesame oil
1 teaspoon red pepper flakes
½ cup finely sliced scallion
½ cup finely sliced celery
½ cup finely julienned red cabbage
½ teaspoon salt
2 tablespoons finely julienned scallions (1" lengths) for
  garnish

SZECHUAN PEPPERCORNS

From the Szechuan province in China, these peppercorns are rust-brown in color and have a pungent, spicy aroma. Less hot, actually, than black pepper, their flavor "numbs" more than it burns. Buy them with their husks broken open and the seeds (which have little flavor) removed. Grind them or use whole in your cooking. They're particularly good for flavoring an oil for stir-frying.

LIME HOT SAUCE

In a saucepan, combine the water, lemongrass, red pepper flakes, soy sauce, sugar, salt, and nam pla. Bring to a boil, cover, and simmer for 10 minutes. Strain and discard the solids. Add the orange juice, cream, plum sauce, and lime juice. Dissolve the cornstarch in the water and then add to the sauce. Bring to a boil and stir until thickened. Simmer 1 minute. Remove from the heat. Just before serving, reheat the sauce.

MARINADE

Whisk together the water, cornstarch, sugar, soy sauce, and rice wine or dry sherry. Add the chicken and toss together. Let sit 2 hours.

FILLING AND ASSEMBLY

Blanch the romaine leaves, 3–4 at a time, in boiling water for 10–15 seconds. Refresh immediately under cold water and lay flat on paper toweling. Pat dry.

Drain the chicken, reserving the marinade. Heat the corn oil in a skillet until very hot but not smoking. Add the peppercorns and sauté 10–15 seconds. Add the chicken with the ginger and garlic. Stir-fry for 30 seconds. Add the walnuts and stir-fry 30 seconds more. Add the marinade liquid and stir-fry a minute. Combine with the remaining ingredients, excluding the scallion garnish.

HOW TO FOLD...

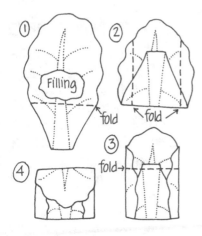

To assemble each packet, lay out a romaine leaf wrong-side-up and put about ¼ cup of the filling in the center. Fold up the leaf like an envelope (it's okay if the rib down the middle of the leaf cracks) tuck in the sides, and set seam side down on a baking tray. Repeat with all the leaves. If not serving right away, cover with plastic wrap and chill until ready to reheat.

To serve, **preheat the oven to 350°**. Have the sauce hot. Put the packets in the oven for 8 minutes (you can also reheat them in a steamer on the stove or in a microwave). Arrange the packets 2 to a plate and pour some of the hot sauce over each portion. Garnish with the julienned scallions.

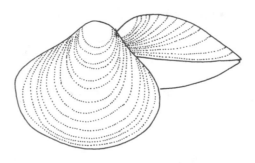

CHINESE PICKLED VEGETABLES consists of
shredded or chopped celery cabbage and/or turnips and cucumbers that have been pickled with garlic, salt and other seasonings. The effect is that of a crispy, salty sauerkraut, and it often comes packaged in great crocks. Try chopping the vegetables and stirring them into mustard to serve with hamburgers, hot dogs and other sandwiches. Adding the vegetables to sour cream with a touch of sesame oil and soy sauce makes a good dip.

BAKED SESAME CLAMS WITH CHINESE PICKLED VEGETABLES   *Serves 4*

20 cherrystone clams on the half shell
¼ cup Chinese Tientsin pickled vegetables, chopped
½ cup lime juice
¼ cup plus 2 tablespoons sesame oil
1 tablespoon minced garlic
1 teaspoon minced ginger
3 tablespoons toasted sesame seeds
¼ cup soy sauce
1 teaspoon crushed red pepper flakes

Preheat the oven to 500°. Loosen each clam in its shell. (This will facilitate eating them.) Arrange the clams in 4 individual ovenproof dishes or in 1 shallow baking pan (lined with foil for easy cleaning). Combine the remaining ingredients. Spoon 1 tablespoon of the filling mixture over each clam and distribute any remaining filling over them. Bake for 7–10 minutes. Serve hot.

36

SZECHUAN SHRIMP

Serves 8–10

Look out! Szechuan Shrimp, as the name implies, are spicy and exotic. A much-in-demand item at The Market, they make a striking appetizer served on a bed of shredded greens, or include them as the surprise star attraction in your next picnic basket.

1 teaspoon chili oil
1 tablespoon sesame oil
2 tablespoons corn oil
1 tablespoon Szechuan peppercorns
1 tablespoon minced garlic
2 teaspoons minced fresh ginger
2 pounds medium-size shrimp in shell (26–30 per pound)
1 tablespoon nam pla (Thai fish sauce)
3 tablespoons soy sauce
3 tablespoons rice wine or dry sherry
2 tablespoons unseasoned rice vinegar
1 teaspoon crushed red pepper flakes
1 cup thinly sliced scallions
¾ cup broken walnut pieces
1 tablespoon lemon juice
½ teaspoon sriraja (Thai hot sauce) or Tabasco
Shredded greens

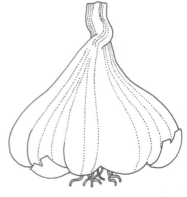

A quick, efficient way to peel garlic is to first cut off the bottom of the head of garlic, as close to the roots as possible. This helps you to break up the head into cloves. With the flat side of a knife or cleaver, smack the cloves just to crush them a little and break the skins. Peeling the cloves should be easy now. (You might also want to look for heads with larger, and thus easier to peel, cloves.)

In a large skillet, combine the chili oil, sesame oil, corn oil, peppercorns, garlic, and ginger. Sauté 30 seconds. Add the shrimp and sauté 1–2 minutes. Add the nam pla, soy sauce, rice wine, wine vinegar, and pepper flakes. Stir and sauté over medium-high heat for 2–3 minutes more, or until the shrimp are cooked through. With a slotted spoon, remove the shrimp to a bowl. Reduce the liquid in the skillet to ¼ cup and remove from the heat. Combine with the scallions, walnuts, lemon juice, and sriraja and let cool to room temperature. Peel the shrimp, leaving tails intact. Toss them with the walnut-scallion mixture and serve on a bed of shredded greens.

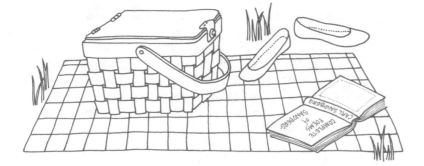

MUSSELS WITH AVOCADO MAYONNAISE

Serves 8–10

AVOCADO MAYONNAISE
1 egg yolk
⅔ cup corn oil
2 tablespoons lemon juice
1¼ teaspoons salt
¾ teaspoon pepper
2 cups puréed very ripe avocado (about 3 medium)
2 teaspoons red wine vinegar
½ teaspoon Tabasco
1 teaspoon minced garlic
2 tablespoons minced red onion
½ cup minced watercress

MUSSELS
1 cup dry white wine
1 quart water
1 tablespoon minced shallots
1 tablespoon peppercorns
1 bay leaf
5 pounds mussels (about 64–80)
OPT. Red caviar for garnish

AVOCADO MAYONNAISE
Follow the procedure for Basic Mayonnaise on p. 100 using the ingredients listed above. Add to the food processor the avocado purée, the wine vinegar, Tabasco, salt, garlic, onion, and watercress. Whiz to combine.

MUSSELS
In a large pot, combine the white wine, water, shallots, peppercorns, and bay leaf. Bring to a rapid boil and add the mussels. Cover and steam the mussels, stirring once or twice, for 3–5 minutes, until they open wide. Remove to a colander and pour ice over to cool mussels quickly. (Save poaching liquid for another use.) Chill until ready to serve.

To serve, remove the completely cooled mussels from their shells. Scrape the "foot" muscle (which attaches the mussel to its shell) from each shell. Dry the shells and lightly oil the outsides with corn oil so that they glisten. Replace the mussels in the shells and just before serving, top each with a bit of avocado mayonnaise. If desired, sprinkle several red caviar eggs on each. Arrange 8 on a plate and garnish with watercress.

VARIATIONS AND NOTES
Substitute parsley or spinach in the mayonnaise if watercress is not available.

GARNISHES
The idea behind a garnish for the plate is to balance color and spaces with taste. It is better to have no garnish than one that will camouflage the food or be incompatible with the flavor of the dish. In the restaurants, we traditionally use a few sprigs of watercress and half a cherry tomato. Sprigs of fresh herbs that echo the flavorings in the food are especially nice, and don't forget chive blossoms, marigolds, and nasturtiums, all of which are edible

Avocado Mayonnaise is also a good sandwich spread—
Try it on Walnut-Mushroom-Onion Bread with slices of
bacon and Cheddar cheese and then broil.

The mayonnaise and mussels may be prepared a day in
advance. Store the mussel meats separately covered with
their poaching liquid. Refrigerate the shells also.

ORIENTAL SMOKED SWORDFISH AND VEGETABLE SALAD

Serves 8

We smoke a lot of different foods at both Frog and The
Commissary—chicken, duck, bluefish, turkey, eggplant,
beef sirloin, and swordfish, to name a few. Smoking
imparts intriguing overtones to food, and we have long
been fascinated by its possibilities. If you have a smoker
(we use a Little Chef), do try this recipe.

DRESSING
1 teaspoon minced garlic
1 teaspoon minced fresh ginger
2 teaspoons Dijon mustard
¼ cup cider vinegar
¼ cup sesame oil
½ cup corn oil
1 teaspoon soy sauce
½ teaspoon salt
½ teaspoon pepper

SWORDFISH
2 tablespoons soy sauce
1 teaspoon minced fresh ginger
1 tablespoon lemon juice
½ teaspoon sesame oil
1 teaspoon minced garlic
1 tablespoon honey
1 pound skinned and boned swordfish

SALAD
1½ cups thinly sliced mushrooms
1 cup julienned zucchini in 1" matchsticks
1 cup julienned snow peas in 1" matchsticks
1½ cups julienned red peppers in 1" matchsticks
1½ cups julienned carrots in 1" matchsticks
1 tablespoon minced parsley

DRESSING

Whisk together all the ingredients and refrigerate for at least 2 hours to bring out the flavors.

SWORDFISH

Make a marinade by combining the soy sauce, ginger, lemon juice, sesame oil, garlic, and honey. Coat the sword-fish with this mixture and refrigerate the fish in the marinade for an hour.

Meanwhile, **preheat your oven to 400°** and get your smoker going according to the manufacturer's instructions. Bake the fish for 5 minutes in the oven or until it is almost but not quite done. (Time will depend on the thickness of the fish.) Transfer the fish to the smoker and smoke for ½ hour. Let the fish cool, chill it, and then cut into ½" cubes.

SALAD

The vegetables for the salad can be readied up to 4 hours in advance and refrigerated.

Fifteen minutes before serving, strain the dressing and combine ⅓ of it with the cubed swordfish. Set aside to marinate. Just before serving, toss the mushrooms and julienned vegetables with the remaining dressing and divide among 6 salad plates. Arrange the swordfish with its dressing over the vegetables and dust with parsley.

Hot Water Bath

SALMON, SCALLOP, AND SPINACH PÂTÉ

Serves 10–12
using a 5–6 cup rectangular mold

Delicately pink, with an emerald green "heart" of spinach, this seafood pâté is the ethereal, pretty cousin of our earthy Country Pâté. With the aid of a food processor, it can be concocted in no time—and as much as three days in advance.

SALMON-SCALLOP MIXTURE
¾ pound bay or sea scallops, rinsed
¾ pound salmon fillet
3 egg whites
¼ teaspoon nutmeg
1¼ teaspoons salt
½ teaspoon pepper
⅛ teaspoon cayenne
2 tablespoons brandy
1¾ cups heavy cream

40

SPINACH-SCALLOP MIXTURE
1 tablespoon butter
1 tablespoon minced shallots
2 cups packed fresh spinach
⅜ teaspoon salt
¼ teaspoon pepper
2 tablespoons minced dill
¼ pound bay or sea scallops, rinsed
¼ cup heavy cream

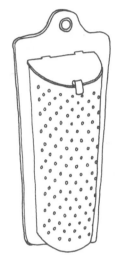

SALMON-SCALLOP MIXTURE
Put the salmon and scallops in the bowl of a food processor and whiz for 1 minute. Scrape down the sides. Add the egg whites, nutmeg, salt, pepper, cayenne, and brandy. Blend 10 seconds. Transfer to a mixing bowl. Whisk in half the cream. Blend in the rest until smooth. Refrigerate.

SPINACH-SCALLOP MIXTURE
Melt the butter in a very small pan. Add the shallots and sauté over low heat until tender—about 5 minutes. Cool.

Wash and stem the spinach. With water still clinging to the leaves, put the spinach in a sauté pan and stir over high heat until it is completely wilted. Refresh under cold running water, squeeze very dry, and coarsely chop. Put the spinach in a food processor with the sautéed shallots, salt, pepper, and dill. Whiz 10 seconds. Add the scallops and whiz until completely smooth—about 30 seconds. Transfer to a bowl and stir in the cream. Refrigerate.

ASSEMBLY
Preheat the oven to 350°. Butter a 5–6 cup rectangular mold and spread 2½ cups of the salmon-scallop mixture in the bottom. With the back of a wet spoon, make a trough down the center for the spinach mixture. With your hands, arrange the spinach mixture down the center in the trough and cover with the remaining salmon-scallop mixture. Smooth the surface, top with wax paper, and cover with foil or a lid. Set in a hot water bath at least 2" deep and bake for 55 minutes (or to an internal temperature of 135°). Cool completely to room temperature, unmold, wrap well, and refrigerate until thoroughly chilled. To serve, cut ½"-thick slices, being sure to wipe off the knife between slices or the green center will streak.

SERVING SUGGESTIONS AND VARIATIONS
Serve each slice with Tomato Coulis or with an herbed mayonnaise.

Bake the pâté in individual timbale molds set in a water bath for about 20 minutes or until the centers are puffed. Let rest 5–10 minutes, then unmold while still hot. Serve at once with Beurre Blanc or serve cold with either of the above suggestions.

Add 2–3 tablespoons of minced fresh herbs such as dill, chives, or tarragon to the salmon-scallop mixture, or fold in 2 ounces finely chopped smoked salmon.

COUNTRY PÂTÉ

Makes two 9" × 5" × 3" loaves
Or one 4 quart loaf

Cut yourself a slice of this pâté, add crusty French bread, butter, mustard, cornichons, and a glass of Beaujolais on the side and for a moment imagine yourself tucked away in a charming little Parisian bistro where you've gone for a bite of lunch while you decide which *arrondissement* to explore next.

Other types of pâtés come and go at The Commissary, but we've always served this Country Pâté. We like its somewhat coarse texture and well-balanced seasonings, although we have to laugh when we remember the grossly underseasoned seventy-pound batch that instead of being discarded was cubed, combined with vegetables, and dressed with a highly seasoned vinaigrette for a "pâté salad." You will want to make it over a period of several days, as the chicken and ham need time to marinate and the finished pâté is best left to chill overnight. But, once made, the pâté will keep at least a week in the refrigerator. It's a very fine thing to have on hand.

A small electric coffee grinder is terrific for pulverizing whole spices. You will want to have a separate grinder, though, just for your coffee beans, so that you don't end up with strange, spicy coffee.

¼ cup brandy
½ pound boneless skinned chicken breast, cut into ½"–¾" pieces
¼ pound ham, cubed ½" cubes (about ¾ cup)
1 pound chicken livers
2 tablespoons butter
1¼ pounds ground veal
1 pound unsalted fatback or pork fat, ground
1¼ pounds lean ground pork
4 teaspoons dried rosemary
4 teaspoons dried thyme
2 teaspoons dried marjoram
2 teaspoons pepper
2 teaspoons salt
1½ teaspoons ground allspice
2 teaspoons ground bay leaf (use a spice grinder or blender)
¾ cup pistachios, toasted 10 minutes at 300°
¾ cup dry bread crumbs
2 beaten eggs
2 tablespoons plus 2 teaspoons minced garlic

2½ cups heavy cream

¼ cup sherry, port, or Madeira

2 pounds of unsalted fatback cut into ⅛"-thick strips for lining the pans

Combine the brandy, chicken, and ham and let marinate overnight. Sauté the chicken livers for 2–3 minutes in the butter so that they are still pink in the center. Combine the veal, ground fatback, pork, herbs, and spices. Add the chicken-ham-brandy mixture, pistachios, bread crumbs, eggs, garlic, cream, and sherry.

Preheat the oven to 350°. Line two 9" × 5" × 3" pans (or other containers that will hold 4 quarts) with the strips of fatback, reserving some for the top. Spread half the pâté mixture in the pans, arrange chicken livers down the centers, and cover with the remaining pâté mixture. Smooth the top of each pâté and top with the reserved strips of fatback. Cover the pans tightly with foil and set in a hot waterbath. Bake for 65–70 minutes or until the internal temperature is 145°. Let cool, then weight with a cookie sheet topped with heavy cans and refrigerate overnight.

TO SERVE

The classic presentation is to cut the pâté in slices and serve it with black or French bread, cornichons, and Pommery mustard or caper mayonnaise. For hors d'oeuvres, cut thin slices into triangles and serve on black bread with seasoned mayonnaise and slices of cornichons. Team a pâté sandwich on a croissant with a beautiful setting for a memorable picnic. Even the "pâté salad" idea can be quite delightful: Try cubes of pâté (it doesn't have to be underseasoned!), boiled new potatoes, blanched green beans, and cherry tomatoes in our Herb Vinaigrette.

NUTMEAT PÂTÉ

Makes one 8″ × 4″ × 3″ loaf
Or other 5-cup mold

1½ cups cooked drained white beans (¼ pound raw),
   whizzed until smooth in a food processor
2 cups walnuts (½ pound), lightly toasted and finely
   ground
2 cups pecans (½ pound), light toasted and finely
   ground
1 cup grated Gruyère cheese (¼ pound)
1 cup grated Parmesan cheese
⅓ cup minced scallion
⅓ cup minced parsley
¼ teaspoon ground cumin
½ teaspoon dried thyme
½ teaspoon dried marjoram
½ teaspoon crumbled dried rosemary
1¾ teaspoons salt
¾ teaspoon pepper
⅓ cup heavy cream
1½ teaspoons minced garlic
6 tablespoons butter, softened
2 eggs
1 tablespoon brandy
1 cup shelled pistachios
1 ounce dried mushrooms, reconstituted in warm water,
   drained and sliced

In a large bowl, combine all the ingredients well. **Preheat
the oven to 350°.** Grease a 8″ × 4″ × 3″ pan (or other 5-
cup mold) and line it with parchment paper. Fill the pan
with the pâté mixture and cover it tightly with tin foil. Set
in a larger baking pan filled with hot water an inch deep.
Bake for 1 hour. Let cool 10 minutes and then invert the
baking pan onto a serving plate and unmold the pâté.
Remove the parchment paper. The pâté can be served
either hot or cold.

AVOCADO WITH TAHINI-YOGURT DRESSING

Serves 6

This is an old Frog recipe that is still a crowd pleaser. Beautiful, creamy avocados come to life under this tangy, nutty dressing, which would also be delicious for chicken-bacon-avocado salad, as a dip for crudités, or with a mixed vegetable salad in pita bread.

8 ounces plain yogurt
⅓ cup tahini
⅜ teaspoon ground cumin
⅛ teaspoon ground coriander
¼ teaspoon minced garlic
1 tablespoon lemon juice
¼ teaspoon salt
¼ teaspoon pepper
⅛ teaspoon cayenne pepper
3 ripe avocados
⅜ cup slivered almonds, toasted

Whisk the yogurt gradually into the tahini until well combined. Add the remaining ingredients and blend well. Just before serving, peel the avocados. Halve them lengthwise and remove the pits. Thinly slice each half lengthwise and fan out the slices on individual salad plates. Spoon the dressing over each serving and sprinkle with the toasted almonds.

Soup's

Good morning, all. Welcome to this Frog cooking class on soups. Today, I will demonstrate for you... AHEM! Ladies, if you please! I will begin with Broccoli and Cheddar Soup... a very simple

MUSHROOM BARLEY SOUP   *Makes 3½ quarts*

When the weather turns raw, a good, thick, simple soup such as Mushroom Barley can be as necessary to one's well-being, both physically and psychologically, as a beloved old teddy bear can be in a lonely moment. This particular soup originated in old Frog's kitchen, but made its really grand debut at Philadelphia's first Restaurant Festival Sunday where we dispensed sixty gallons of it in a few short hours to crowds buffeted by the day's blustery weather.

3 tablespoons butter
1½ cups chopped onions
1 cup chopped carrots
1 cup chopped celery
2 teaspoons minced garlic
1 pound mushrooms, sliced
3 quarts chicken broth
1 teaspoon salt
½ teaspoon pepper
⅛ teaspoon nutmeg
1 teaspoon thyme
1 cup pearl barley
2 tablespoons minced dill
2 tablespoons chopped parsley

In a large stockpot, melt the butter. Add the onions, carrots, celery, and garlic and sauté until tender but not browned. Add the mushrooms. Cook until just soft. Add the broth, seasonings, and barley. Bring to a boil. Simmer 2 hours or until barley is tender. Just before serving, stir in the dill and parsley.

NOTES
Cut down on the cooking time by soaking the barley for 2 hours before beginning the soup; then it need only simmer about ½ hour.

The soup can be made up to 2 days in advance, refrigerated, and reheated. If it becomes too thick, thin with additional broth.

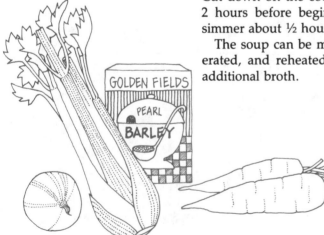

GOLDEN FIELDS

PEARL
BARLEY

BROCCOLI-CHEDDAR SOUP   *Makes 2 quarts*

3 cups broccoli in ⅜″ dice
¼ cup butter
1 cup chopped onions
1 teaspoon minced garlic
2 tablespoons flour
2 cups half-and-half
3 cups chicken broth
¾ pound sharp Cheddar cheese, grated
½ teaspoon nutmeg
¾ teaspoon salt
½ teaspoon pepper
2 tablespoons Dijon mustard
OPT. ¼ cup dry sherry

Blanch the broccoli in boiling salted water, refresh under cold water, drain, and set aside. Melt the butter in a large saucepan, add the onions, and sauté until tender and translucent. Add the garlic and sauté 30 seconds. Add the flour and cook and stir 2 minutes. Whisking hard, add the half-and-half and chicken broth. Bring the mixture to a boil. Reduce to a simmer and stir in the cheese. Add the seasonings, mustard, and sherry. Lower the heat to be sure soup doesn't boil again or it may curdle. Add the broccoli and heat through. Garnish with additional shredded Cheddar, if desired.

VARIATIONS
Substitute cauliflower for the broccoli and garnish the soup with bits of red pepper and lots of minced parsley.

If you prefer a smooth soup, purée the broccoli with some of the liquid and stir into the rest of the soup.

BASIC CHICKEN STOCK
In the restaurants, we will use 70 pounds of chicken backs, 140 quarts of water, 20 peeled and chunked onions, 5 bags of carrots in chunks, 5 bunches of parsley, 5 celery bunches in chunks, and some thyme, bay leaves, and peppercorns for our chicken stock. We let it simmer over a very low flame all night. ☆ For home purposes, however, try 6-7 pounds of chicken parts, 7 quarts of water, 2 onions, ½ bunch of celery, ½ bunch of parsley, ½ bag of carrots, 2 bay leaves, ½ teaspoon of thyme, and ½ teaspoon of peppercorns. Bring to a boil, then keep to a bare simmer about 3 hours. Strain and skim off the fat. Freeze or refrigerate as desired. (This will make about 5-6 quarts.)

FROZEN CHICKEN STOCK 1/8

MEXICAN CORN SOUP
WITH CHEESE AND CHILIES   *Makes 1¾ quarts*

This is an incredibly soothing soup with here and there the surprising bite of green chilies. It was added to our repertoire when we were developing some dishes for a Mexican Day of the Dead Festival held one Halloween at The Commissary.

CROUTONS
⅛ teaspoon cayenne pepper
1 teaspoon ground cumin
¼ teaspoon salt
¼ cup melted butter
1½ cups cubed French or Italian bread (½" cubes)

SOUP
5 large ears of fresh corn or 3 cups kernels
1 cup water
¼ cup butter
2 tablespoons minced onions
3⅓ cups half-and-half
1 teaspoon salt
½ teaspoon Tabasco
¼ teaspoon pepper
3 tablespoons diced roasted hot green chilies
½ pound Monterey Jack or Cheddar cheese, shredded

CROUTONS
Preheat the oven to 325°. Combine the seasonings with the butter and toss with the bread cubes until they are well coated. Spread the cubes in a single layer on a baking sheet and bake for 10–15 minutes, stirring once midway through, until golden brown.

SOUP
Cut the kernels from the corn cobs. Whiz the kernels with the water in a food processor or blender to make a coarse purée. Melt the butter in a large saucepan. Add the onions and sauté until soft and translucent. Add the corn purée and cook over medium heat for 5 minutes, stirring occasionally. Add the half-and-half, salt, Tabasco, and pepper. Gently heat through, but do not allow to simmer.

To serve, ladle the soup into 5 deep soup bowls. Sprinkle each serving with some of the cheese and chilies. Garnish with the croutons.

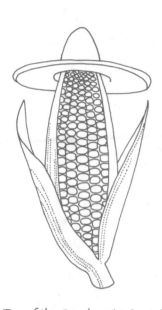

Day of the Dead, or All Souls' Day, is a traditional Mexican celebration somewhat akin to our Halloween. Once a year, on November 2, the dead are said to return to visit. It is not a solemn occasion, but a fiesta to which the dead are welcomed with bonfires, flowers, food and other festivities.

Omit the chilies and croutons; garnish instead with minced fresh chives and bits of crisp crumbled bacon.

Frozen or canned corn can be substituted when fresh is not available.

VEGETARIAN CHILI

Makes 1¾ quarts

Can chili be chili without meat? With this recipe in hand, we can give a resounding "Yes!" A hot take-out item in The Market, this hearty, spicy chili is so good that you may never notice that bulgur has replaced the usual ground beef. While the ingredient list may seem intimidatingly long, most of the items are kitchen-shelf staples, and it can be made and served within the hour!

⅓ cup olive oil
2 cups finely chopped onions
¾ cup chopped celery
1 cup chopped green peppers
1 cup chopped carrots
1 tablespoon minced garlic
2 cups chopped mushrooms
¼ teaspoon red pepper flakes
1 tablespoon ground cumin
¾ teaspoon dried basil
2 tablespoons chili powder
¾ teaspoon dried oregano
2 teaspoons salt
½ teaspoon pepper
2 cups tomato juice
¾ cup bulgur wheat
2 cups chopped tomatoes
2 cups (1 20-ounce can) undrained kidney beans
½ teaspoon Tabasco
2 tablespoons lemon juice
3 tablespoons tomato paste
1 tablespoon Worcestershire sauce
¼ cup dry red or white wine
2 tablespoons chopped canned green chilies or to taste

Have all the ingredients ready. Heat the olive oil in a large skillet. Over high heat, add the onions, celery, green peppers, carrots, garlic, mushrooms, spices, salt, and pepper. Cook, stirring, for 1–2 minutes. Add the remaining ingredients. Bring to a boil, stirring. Reduce the heat and simmer for 20 minutes, uncovered. If too thick, the chili can be thinned with additional tomato juice.

TO SERVE
Turn this chili into a full meal by serving it with cornbread or one of our breads (see Index), a green salad, and perhaps some beer.

GINGERED CARROT VICHYSSOISE

Makes about 5 cups, serving 5–6

A beautiful soup from Frog's files, with certainly more color and, to our minds, more character than the traditional vichyssoise. It seems just the thing to start off an elegant picnic, not to mention a special dinner.

1 cup thinly sliced leeks (about 2 large)
2 tablespoons butter
¼ cup chopped onions
¾ pound carrots, peeled and thinly sliced (about 3 medium)
2½ teaspoons minced fresh ginger
½ pound all-purpose potatoes, peeled and thinly sliced (about 1 medium)
½ teaspoon salt
½ teaspoon pepper
OPT. 1–3 teaspoons sugar if carrots themselves are not particularly sweet
1½ cups chicken stock
3 cups half-and-half
OPT. Minced chives or slivered candied ginger for garnish

Soak the sliced leeks in cold water to remove any grit, then rinse well under running water. Melt the butter in a medium-size saucepan. Add the drained leeks and onions and sauté until wilted and translucent. Add the carrots, ginger, and potatoes. Sauté and stir several minutes. Add the salt, pepper, optional sugar, and chicken stock. Cover and let simmer until the vegetables are very tender and can be easily mashed with a fork (about 10–15 minutes). Purée in a food processor or through a food mill and then strain through a fine sieve. Chill thoroughly. Blend in the half-and-half. To serve, ladle into chilled small soup bowls or cups. Garnish each serving, if desired, with minced fresh chives or slivers of candied ginger.

Serve the soup hot instead of chilled. Heat it gently without boiling and garnish with crisp, buttery croutons and chives.

For an unusual vegetable purée, drain off any excess stock, purée the vegetables, omit the half-and-half, heat gently, and swirl in some butter just before serving. Season to taste.

GUACAMOLE SOUP

Makes about 7 cups

Because we adore guacamole, this soup seemed a natural extension. (Or did it really evolve, as some claim, from an enormous amount of guacamole left over from a catering party?) Regardless of its origins, this creamy, green, spicy yet cool liquid will surely awaken the mouth to whatever is to follow.

1½ cups avocado purée (2–3 ripe avocados)
¼ cup lime juice
1¾ teaspoons salt
½ teaspoon pepper
1¼ teaspoons ground cumin
½ teaspoon Tabasco
1 teaspoon chili powder
1 teaspoon minced garlic
¼ cup minced red onions
1¾ cups sour cream
3 cups water
¾ cup peeled, seeded, finely chopped, and drained
  tomatoes (see p. 102 for how to peel)

Peel the avocados and purée with the lime juice in a food processor/blender or through a sieve. Turn into a bowl and stir in the spices, seasonings, garlic, and onions. Fold in the sour cream. Stir in the lime juice and water. Chill thoroughly, and just before serving, stir in the tomatoes.

SERVING SUGGESTIONS
This soup looks well served in brightly colored bowls.

Garnish, if desired, with watercress and cooked, peeled shrimp or diced roasted green chilies.

PEA SOUP WITH STAR ANISE   *Makes 6 cups*

A beautiful starter for any party, this lovely cold soup was developed for a catered dinner where the menu, though not strictly Japanese or Chinese, was to have oriental overtones. As the party took place in the spring, Steven, in creating this recipe, chose to play with a variation on fresh pea soup and substituted shellfish stock and dashi (a Japanese soup stock) for the base and seasoned the soup with that intriguing Eastern spice, star anise.

Dashi is the basic stock and one of the most characteristic flavors in Japanese cooking. It is made from dried bonito flakes and dried seaweed cooked in water. Instant dashi (often containg MSG) is available in packets or jars and is a good product.

1 tablespoon crushed star anise or 2 teaspoons ground
6 cups water
1 cup dry vermouth
¼ cup dry sherry
Shells from ½ pound shrimp (use shrimp elsewhere or save for garnish)
6 ounces sea scallops
1 cup coarsely chopped celery tops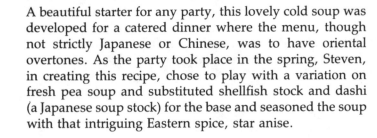
2 tablespoons sesame oil
2 cups chopped onions
¾ cup chopped celery
2 bags dashi, or enough to flavor the 6 cups of water
3 pounds frozen peas, defrosted
1 teaspoon salt
1 teaspoon white pepper
OPT. 1 teaspoon nam pla (Thai fish sauce)
12 snow peas, blanched and very finely julienned, for garnish
6 cooked shrimp, butterflied with tails on, for garnish

Combine and bring to a boil the star anise, water, vermouth, sherry, shrimp shells, scallops, celery tops, sesame oil, onions, and celery. Cover and simmer until vegetables are completely tender, about 20 minutes. Strain the liquid and discard the solids. (Use the scallops in a salad if you can't stand to throw them away, but they will be very overdone.) Return the liquid to the pot and bring to a simmer. Add the bags of dashi and simmer 10 minutes more. Remove the dashi bags. Add the peas and cook until the peas are tender *but still bright green*. Strain, saving the liquid. Purée the peas in a food processor or through a food mill and then push them through a sieve to remove all pieces of skin. Add the salt, pepper, and nam pla. Stir in the reserved liquid. Chill thoroughly. Serve cold with a garnish of julienned snow peas and butterflied shrimp.

THAI SHRIMP AND LEMONGRASS SOUP

Makes about 2½ quarts

This is one of the most popular soups with the staff at Frog. The lunch chef, who worked out the recipe, swore it was the perfect hangover cure. Whatever its effect, it is deliciously different—a dark broth full of shrimp, slippery noodles, and all sorts of intriguing seasonings.

2 quarts chicken stock
½ ounce dried lemongrass
2 packages cellophane noodles (2 ounces each)
2 teaspoons minced garlic
1¼ teaspoons minced fresh ginger
2 teaspoons sesame oil
3 tablespoons soy sauce
⅛ teaspoon dried red pepper flakes
1½ tablespoons nam pla (Thai fish sauce)
½ teaspoon sriraja (Thai hot sauce) or Tabasco
3 tablespoons rice wine or dry sherry
1 tablespoon cornstarch
3 tablespoons water
½ pound small mushrooms, quartered
2 tablespoons fermented black beans, rinsed
½ pound peeled shrimp, coarsely chopped
¾ cup sliced scallions
2 teaspoons lime juice

The flavor of lemongrass infuses much of Thai cooking, giving a haunting lemony edge to soups, salads, curries and the like. It can be found fresh (with a white, bulbous base), dried, and powdered. Dried lemongrass should be soaked first or cooked in a liquid, and pieces should always be strained from the final product. Lemon peel can be used as a substitute, but the flavor will be stronger.

Simmer the stock with the lemongrass in a covered saucepan for ½ hour. Meanwhile, soak the noodles in water to cover for 20–30 minutes, then drain and, if desired, cut into 2" pieces. Set aside. To the stock, add the garlic, ginger, sesame oil, soy sauce, red pepper flakes, nam pla, sriraja, salt, and rice wine. Cover and simmer 10 minutes. Strain off the solids. Combine the cornstarch and water. Bring the soup to a boil and whisk in the cornstarch mixture. Return to a boil and add the noodles and simmer 5 minutes (can be made ahead to this point). Add the mushrooms, black beans, shrimp, and scallions. Return to a boil and cook 1 minute. Remove the soup from the heat, stir in the lime juice, and serve.

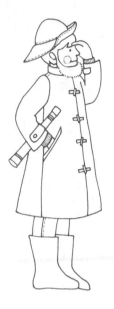

CORN AND CLAM CHOWDER
WITH BACON

Makes about 3 quarts

A real all-American soup, this one. We worked out this recipe for a cooking class on soups, and Eden later borrowed it for its own menu.

For us, a bowl of this soup inspires dreams of cozy weathered cottages nestled along the rocky New England coastline, of invigorating, blustery days by the sea, and of friends and family gathered round to break bread together and trade a few tales.

2 dozen cherrystone clams or 1¼ cups minced clams
2 cups dry white wine
4 teaspoons minced garlic
½ pound bacon, diced
¼ cup butter
1 cup chopped onions
1 cup fresh or canned corn
2 cups minced carrots
¼ cup minced celery
¼ cup flour
1 cup water
½ teaspoon nutmeg
¼ teaspoon dried thyme
¼ teaspoon pepper
⅛ teaspoon cayenne pepper
½ teaspoon salt
¾ pound new potatoes, peeled and cut into ¼" dice
   (about 1¾ cups)
1 quart half-and-half
¼ cup sherry or Madeira
2 tablespoons minced parsley

Scrub the clams. Discard any open ones that don't close when you tap the shell. Put them in a deep pot with the wine and garlic. Cover and steam for 10–15 minutes over high heat. Remove the clams with a slotted spoon to a bowl as they open. Discard any that don't open. Strain the remaining liquid through a filter or cloth into another bowl. Measure the liquid and, if necessary, add water to make 3 cups. Set aside. Let clams cool, then remove from their shells and finely chop them. Refrigerate until ready to use.

Sauté the bacon until crisp. Drain on paper toweling. Melt the butter in a clean saucepan. Add the onions, corn, carrots, and celery. Stir and sauté over medium-high heat until vegetables are slightly browned. Add the flour. Cook and stir 3–4 minutes more. Add the reserved clam broth, water, nutmeg, thyme, pepper, cayenne, salt, potatoes, and bacon. Bring to a boil, reduce heat, cover and cook 10 minutes. Add the clams and half-and-half. Bring just to a boil, stir in the sherry or Madeira, and serve at once, garnished with minced parsley.

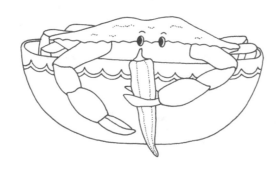

NOTE
If using canned minced clams, use 8 ounces of bottled clam juice and 2 cups of white wine for the necessary 3 cups of liquid.

CRAB GUMBO
Makes 4 quarts

It is not always an easy task to produce a home-size recipe from a restaurant-size recipe that was designed to serve ten times as many or more. In addition, recipe cards used in our kitchens are not always as explicit as we might wish, since it is often assumed that the professional cook doesn't need a lot of direction.

This is one recipe, for instance, that we initially had trouble reducing for some reason; but a number of tests later, we are proud to hereby present our Crab Gumbo—a thick, aromatic, and above all "crabby" soup that could easily be the main course for a meal. We like it best when made a day or two ahead so that the flavors really have time to develop. It freezes quite well, too.

Gumbo. The name is believed to have come from an African word, "kingumbo," meaning okra. Gumbo, in fact, is traditionally thickened with okra. From there, the recipe is subject to variation but usually includes roux (browned flour and oil), vegetables, and meats and/or seafood.

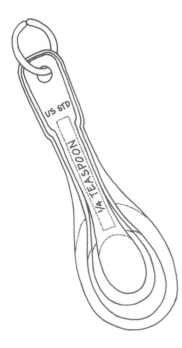

ROUX
¾ cup butter
¾ cup flour

GUMBO
3 tablespoons butter
1 tablespoon minced garlic
½ cup finely chopped celery
1¼ cups finely chopped green peppers
½ teaspoon red pepper flakes
2 teaspoons chili powder
1 (15-ounce) can tomato tidbits/purée
2 quarts water
½ pound okra, sliced ¼" thick (2 cups)
1½ teaspoons Worcestershire sauce
1 teaspoon dried thyme
1 teaspoon dried marjoram
¾ teaspoon dried oregano
¾ teaspoon rubbed sage
3½ teaspoons salt
1 teaspoon pepper
1 teaspoon sugar
1 pound chopped fresh tomatoes (2½ cups)
½ cup lemon juice
1 teaspoon Tabasco
2 pounds claw crabmeat
¾ cup chopped scallions

ROUX
Melt the butter in a heavy saucepan and blend in the flour. Cook and stir occasionally over low heat until the color of peanut butter. Set aside.

GUMBO
Melt the butter in a stockpot. Add the garlic, celery, green peppers, red pepper flakes, and chili powder. Sauté about 5 minutes until the vegetables have softened. Vigorously whisk in the roux, making sure that it doesn't lump. While whisking add the remaining ingredients except for the crabmeat and scallions. Let the soup simmer 30–40 minutes. Add the crabmeat and scallions and simmer 5 minutes more.

VARIATION
You can substitute frozen okra for fresh, but first drop the frozen okra into boiling water for 1 minute. Drain and slice it ¼" thick if it has not already been cut.

TOMATO, SAUSAGE, AND
EGGPLANT SOUP

Makes 3 quarts

Anne helped develop this soup for Eden when it opened
in February 1981. It was so good that we couldn't resist
serving it at The Commissary, too, where we now make
it in 180-quart batches to last three days. Thick and hearty,
the soup is nearly a meal in itself, needing only the company
of some fine crusty bread and a green salad.

⅓ cup plus 2 tablespoons olive oil
4½ cups cubed unpeeled eggplant (½" cubes)
1½ teaspoons salt
1½ cups chopped onions
½ cup chopped fennel or celery
2 tablespoons minced garlic
2 teaspoons ground or crushed fennel seed
½ teaspoon pepper
4 bay leaves
1 teaspoon dried basil
1¼ teaspoons dried thyme
1 pound sweet Italian sausage with casing removed
1½ cups chicken stock
1 29-ounce can heavy tomato purée
1 28-ounce can whole peeled tomatoes, chopped

Heat the ⅓ cup of olive oil in a 4–5 quart saucepan. Add
the eggplant and ½ teaspoon of the salt. Sauté over
medium-high heat, stirring frequently, for 4–5 minutes or
until just tender. Transfer the eggplant to a bowl. In the
same pan, heat the remaining 2 tablespoons of olive oil.
Add the onions, fennel or celery, garlic, fennel seed,
pepper, bay leaves, the remaining teaspoon of salt, basil,
and thyme. Cook over medium-high heat, stirring frequently, for 5–6 minutes. Add the sausage and sauté 5–6
minutes, breaking up the meat into small pieces with a
spoon. Add the chicken stock, tomato purée, chopped
tomatoes with their juice, and the eggplant. Cover and
simmer 10–15 minutes. If the soup seems too thick, add
more chicken stock. Remove the bay leaves before serving.

59

SCOTCH BROTH WITH CORIANDER

Makes 4 quarts

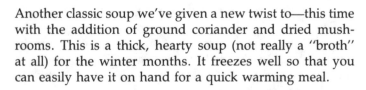

Fresh coriander, alias cilantro and Chinese parsley, usually takes some getting used to. Its parsley-like (in appearance only) leaves are much used in Latin American, Asian, Arabic, and Indian cuisines where they combine well with the often spicy dishes. Once you learn to love it, you'll find yourself using coriander like parsley... but with much more dramatic results. Try it especially on fish, in eggplant dishes, in cornbread, on potatoes, in eggs, and so on.

Another classic soup we've given a new twist to—this time with the addition of ground coriander and dried mushrooms. This is a thick, hearty soup (not really a "broth" at all) for the winter months. It freezes well so that you can easily have it on hand for a quick warming meal.

½ ounce dried imported mushrooms (we use Japanese dried shiitake mushrooms)
2 tablespoons butter
1½ pounds boneless lamb shoulder cut into ½" cubes (about 3 pounds with bone)
1 onion, chopped
2 cups peeled, diced yellow turnips (¼" dice)
1⅓ cups diced carrots (¼" dice)
¼ cup thinly sliced celery
1 teaspoon dried thyme
2 teaspoons minced garlic
⅔ cup pearl barley
2½ quarts water
5 teaspoons salt
1 teaspoon pepper
4 teaspoons ground coriander
2 cups cream
OPT. 2 tablespoons minced fresh coriander or parsley for garnish

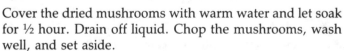

Cover the dried mushrooms with warm water and let soak for ½ hour. Drain off liquid. Chop the mushrooms, wash well, and set aside.

In a 12" saucepan or soup pot, melt the butter. Add the lamb cubes and brown on all sides. Remove to a plate. To the same pan, add and brown the onions, turnips, carrots, celery, and thyme. Toward the end of the browning, add the garlic, barley, and lamb. Stir in the water, salt, and pepper along with the ground coriander and reserved mushrooms. Simmer, covered, for 1 hour and 20 minutes until the barley is very tender. Add the cream, heat just to boiling, and check the seasoning. If too thick add milk to desired consistency. Serve garnished with the fresh coriander or parsley.

Salads

"...half that case of peppers...or at least 6 sour creams worth of 2" strips. Jill, we'll need a gallon of herb mayonnaise. While I get these croutons started, you chop and wash the romaine, Joe, and then julienne"

ROMAINE

CALIFORNIA PEPPERS

FROG MIXED SALAD WITH MUSTARD DRESSING

Serves 6

This recipe dates back to Frog's infancy and, as a sure sign of its appeal, has not left the menu since. The mustard dressing in particular has become a sort of classic hereabouts. We use it lavishly in many other ways, too. It's unbeatable on cold blanched asparagus spears, as a dip for crudités, and on an entrée salad sporting ham and cheese, to name a few.

FROG'S MUSTARD DRESSING
½ cup Dijon mustard
2 tablespoons red wine vinegar
¼ teaspoon salt
¾ teaspoon pepper
1 cup corn oil

CROUTONS
4 (½"-thick) slices fine-textured white bread
4 tablespoons butter
1 teaspoon dried thyme
⅛ teaspoon salt
⅛ teaspoon pepper
2 tablespoons minced parsley

SALAD
3 quarts loosely packed torn romaine leaves (about 1 large head)
12 cherry tomatoes, halved
⅓ cup pitted oil-cured black olives, quartered
3 marinated artichoke hearts, quartered
1½ cups broccoli flowerets, blanched

MUSTARD DRESSING
Whiz in a food processor or whisk together by hand the mustard, vinegar, salt, and pepper. Gradually add the corn oil.

CROUTONS
Preheat the oven to 350°. Trim crusts from bread and cut slices into ½" cubes. Spread in a single layer on a sheet tray and bake 10–15 minutes until dry and lightly browned. Heat the butter in a skillet. Add the croutons and the remaining ingredients and toss well. Sauté for 1–2 minutes over medium heat and then cool.

SALAD
Wash and dry the romaine. Chill until ready to use. Just before serving, whisk the dressing well and toss the salad

CRISPING GREENS
An easy way to get your salad greens ready for dressing if you don't have a salad spinner is to tear them into bite-size pieces, wash well, shake a bit in a colander to drain, and then spread out on a dry dish towel. Roll up the towel, fold the roll in half and tuck it in the refrigerator. When you're ready to serve the salad, you will have dry, crisp, chilled greens to toss in the dressing.

ingredients and the croutons with ¾–1 cup of the dressing. Serve at once.

CURRIED RED LENTIL SALAD   *Serves 8–10*

Steven's mother was in attendance at the tasting session the day this salad was tested, and she declared, "This salad cannot be improved upon!" We tend to agree. It has great color, texture, and flavor; keeps extremely well; and is a wonderful way to use those pretty (and nutritious) little red/orange beans that most of us had never used for anything more than decorations in our kitchens. (This salad is best started the night before.)

CLEAR CURRIED VINAIGRETTE
¾ cup corn oil
½ cup wine vinegar
2 tablespoons sugar
2 teaspoons salt
2 teaspoons pepper
1 teaspoon ground cumin
1 teaspoon dry mustard
½ teaspoon turmeric
½ teaspoon mace
½ teaspoon coriander
½ teaspoon cardamom
¼ teaspoon cayenne pepper
¼ teaspoon ground cloves
¼ teaspoon nutmeg
¼ teaspoon cinnamon

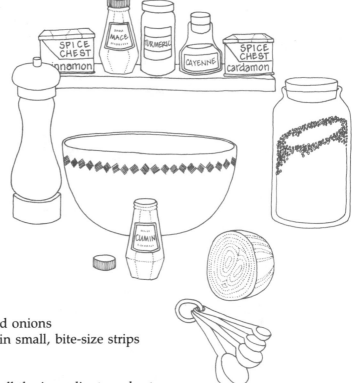

SALAD
1 pound dried red lentils
1 cup currants
⅓ cup capers
1½ cups very finely chopped red onions
OPT. 2 cups cooked leg of lamb in small, bite-size strips

DRESSING
In a large bowl, whisk together all the ingredients and set aside.

SALAD
Wash lentils. Cook them in boiling water for 5–6 minutes or until just tender. (Test after 2 minutes.) Rinse and drain well, combine with the dressing and let sit overnight. At least 2 hours before serving, add the currants, capers, and onions to the lentils. Let marinate several hours.

MIXED VEGETABLE SLAW

Serves 6

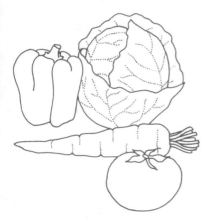

This clean, crisp, confettilike medley of bright vegetables in a light sweet-sour dressing is the perfect foil for fried foods like our Eastern Shore Crab Cakes, not to mention an ideal companion for your favorite hearty sandwiches.

¾ pound cabbage
¼ cup tarragon vinegar
2 teaspoons sugar
2 teaspoons salt
2¼ teaspoons pepper
½ cup corn oil
3 small carrots, peeled and grated (2½ cups)
1 red or green pepper, cut in thin strips
2 tomatoes, cut into 6 wedges each

In general, we "overseason" our salad dressings since the flavors will be diluted when the dressing is combined with the other salad ingredients.

Thinly slice the cabbage and, if necessary, soak briefly in ice water to crisp it (in which case, drain well, wrap in dish towel to dry, and refrigerate). Whisk together the vinegar and seasonings. Whisk in the corn oil. Combine the cabbage, carrots, and peppers and toss with the dressing. Garnish with tomato wedges and serve.

MINESTRONE SALAD
WITH BASIL-GARLIC MAYONNAISE

Serves 6–8

BASIL-GARLIC MAYONNAISE
2 egg yolks
1½ cups corn oil
⅓ cup wine vinegar
1½ teaspoons salt
1½ teaspoons pepper
⅓ cup minced fresh basil or 1 tablespoon dried
1 teaspoon minced garlic

SALAD
¼ pound uncooked ditalini
1 cup drained canned chickpeas
1 cup each of the following all in ⅜"–½" dice: zucchini, carrots, celery, cooked red-skinned new potatoes
½ cup diced red onions (⅜"–½" dice)
1 cup blanched green beans cut into ½"-long pieces
2 tomatoes, cut into wedges
Soft greens (Boston, Bibb, Red Leaf)
½ cup or more of grated Parmesan cheese
OPT. Basil leaves for garnish

BASIL-GARLIC MAYONNAISE
Follow the procedure for Basic Mayonnaise on p. 100 using the ingredients listed above and flavor with the basil and garlic.

SALAD
Cook the ditalini according to package instructions until *al dente*. Drain, refresh under cold running water, drain again, and toss with a little corn oil to prevent sticking. Combine the pasta with the chickpeas, zucchini, carrots, celery, potatoes, onions, and green beans. Fold in 1 cup of the mayonnaise or to taste. Check the seasoning. Serve on a bed of greens and garnish with tomato wedges. Sprinkle each serving with Parmesan cheese and tuck in a few fresh basil leaves, if available.

VARIATION
This salad can be made heartier with the addition of 1 cup diced and sautéed ham, pepperoni, or salami.

ORZO SALAD WITH FRAGRANT SESAME DRESSING
Serves 8

Perhaps this salad is best described as a "fun to eat" hodgepodge of tender slippery orzo, bright crisp carrot shreds, sweet chewy raisins, and crunchy nuts in a fragrant, sesame-oil-based dressing.

FRAGRANT SESAME DRESSING
1 teaspoon salt
¾ cup corn oil
¼ cup sesame oil
½ cup rice vinegar or cider vinegar
2 tablespoons rice wine or dry sherry
½ teaspoon grated orange rind
1 teaspoon soy sauce
2 tablespoons thinly sliced scallions
1 teaspoon minced ginger
½ teaspoon minced garlic
¼ teaspoon crushed red pepper flakes
1 teaspoon pepper
1 tablespoon sugar
2 tablespoons minced fresh coriander or parsley

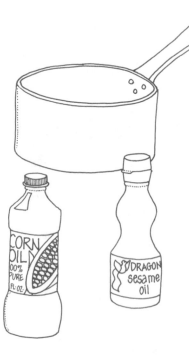

SALAD
1 pound uncooked orzo
1 tablespoon sesame oil
3 cups julienned or shredded carrots
2 cups raisins
1 cup unsalted sunflower seeds or pine nuts, lightly
  toasted

FRAGRANT SESAME DRESSING
Combine all the ingredients by hand or in a food processor
and set aside.

SALAD
Cook the orzo in rapidly boiling salted water until tender—
about 7–10 minutes or according to package instructions.
Refresh under cold water, drain well, and let rest 2–3
minutes to finish draining. Toss with the sesame oil. Cool
completely. Combine with the carrots, raisins, sunflower
seeds, and dressing.

VARIATIONS AND NOTES
Substitute rice for the orzo, but do make the effort to find
the orzo, because that is what makes this fun to eat.

Add other blanched vegetables, if desired. The dressing
would also be good on chicken and oriental vegetables.

This salad will keep quite well for several days in the
refrigerator, although if you make it in advance, add the
carrots and sunflower seeds only just before serving, so
they will be crunchy.

SPINACH AND FRIED TOFU SALAD WITH WARM HERBED SESAME DRESSING

Serves 6

WARM HERBED SESAME DRESSING
⅓ cup sesame oil
2 tablespoons olive oil
¼ cup corn oil
⅓ cup wine vinegar
2 teaspoons soy sauce
1 tablespoon lemon juice
¼ teaspoon dried oregano
½ teaspoon dried basil
½ teaspoon salt
½ teaspoon pepper

SALAD
1 (10-ounce) bag of spinach
½ cup finely julienned carrots
½ cup finely julienned snow peas
1½ cups bean sprouts
6 ounces tofu, cut into ½" cubes (about ¾ cup)
1 egg, beaten
¾ cup dry bread crumbs
¼ cup clarified butter (see p. 124 for how to make) or
    vegetable oil
OPT. 1 tablespoon toasted sesame seeds for garnish

WARM HERBED SESAME DRESSING
Combine the ingredients for the dressing until well homogenized. Heat in a saucepan and keep warm, but not too hot.

SALAD
Wash, stem, and tear the spinach into bite-size pieces. Spin-dry or wrap in dish towels to dry. Have the spinach, carrots, snow peas, and bean sprouts ready in a mixing bowl. Heat the butter or oil in a sauté pan. Dip the cubes of tofu in the beaten egg and then roll in the bread crumbs. Sauté the tofu in the butter until golden and crisp. Remove the cubes with a slotted spoon and immediately add to the salad along with the warm dressing. Toss quickly, divide among salad plates, sprinkle with sesame seeds, and serve at once.

CLASSIC CHICKEN SALAD WITH HORSERADISH–JUNIPER BERRY MAYONNAISE
Serves 5–6

We don't know how the adjective "classic" became attached to this salad, especially since it is generally not our style to use so pretentious a title. Perhaps we called this salad "classic" because it was the first chicken salad we served at The Commissary, or maybe it was because we wanted to distinguish it from our other two basic chicken salads—Oriental and Curried. At any rate, the name has stuck, and Commissary's "Classic" it is.

    While chicken salad with grapes and walnuts may be an old standby in many a Junior League cookbook, the horseradish-juniper berry mayonnaise in our version is anything but traditional and adds an unusual, piquant touch that contrasts deliciously with the sweetness of the grapes. Ideally, this chicken salad should not be made too

JUNIPER BERRIES

Infamous as the pungent and piquant flavoring in gin, juniper berries add an intriguing peppery tartness when used in cooking game, sauerkraut, pork, poultry and other hearty dishes. Juniper itself is a decorative shrub, and its berries need 2-3 years to fully ripen. ☆ Add crushed juniper berries to butter for basting a roasting chicken or duck. They are also good in pork sausage or pâté.

KITCHEN↓
WATCH STEPS

far in advance because you want to avoid having to refrigerate it, which would cause the chicken to firm up and lose its juicy tenderness.

HORSERADISH–JUNIPER BERRY MAYONNAISE
2 egg yolks
1⅓ cups corn oil
¼ cup vinegar
1 teaspoon salt
1 teaspoon pepper
1 teaspoon Dijon mustard
2 tablespoons prepared horseradish
2 teaspoons pulverized juniper berries

SALAD
2 pounds skinned, boneless chicken breast (for 3½–4 cups cooked and cubed meat)
1¼ cups seedless green grapes
1¼ cups sliced celery
¾ cup broken walnuts, toasted at 350° for 5–8 minutes

HORSERADISH–JUNIPER BERRY MAYONNAISE
Follow the method for making Basic Mayonnaise on p. 100 but use the ingredients listed for Horseradish–Juniper Berry Mayonnaise. Flavor with the horseradish and juniper berries.

SALAD
Preheat the oven to 350°. Lay the chicken breasts on a rimmed baking sheet and cover tightly with foil. Bake for 20–25 minutes until cooked through but still moist and juicy. Cool to room temperature.

Cut the room-temperature chicken into bite-size pieces. Combine with the grapes, celery, walnuts, and mayonnaise. Serve on a bed of romaine or other greens and garnish, if desired, with watercress.

SERVING SUGGESTIONS AND VARIATIONS
For a festive presentation, serve each portion on a round slice of cantaloupe on a bed of greens. The salad also makes a great filling for pita-bread sandwiches. To wash it down, try minted ice tea or a light fruity wine such as a Chenin Blanc or Johannisberg Riesling.

Substitute diced, unpeeled Granny Smith apples for the grapes, toasted blanched whole almonds for the walnuts, crushed green peppercorns for the juniper berries, or roast duck or turkey for the chicken.

68

ORIENTAL CHICKEN SALAD

Serves 6

Number two in our trio of not-to-be-missed basic Commissary chicken salads. The Oriental Dressing in particular has become an invaluable part of our salad repertoire, as it teams well with so many different things, such as blanched vegetables, beef, pork, lamb, seafood, and cold noodles. Let your imagination have some fun with it.

ORIENTAL DRESSING
1 egg
¼ cup sesame oil
¾ cup corn oil
1 teaspoon sugar
½ teaspoon pepper
3 tablespoons vinegar (unseasoned rice vinegar, if you
    have it)
1 teaspoon minced garlic
½ teaspoon salt
2 teaspoons minced fresh ginger
3 tablespoons Dijon mustard
2 tablespoons soy sauce
1 teaspoon lemon juice

SALAD
2 pounds boneless, skinless chicken breasts (for 3½–4
    cups cooked and cubed meat)
2 cups bok choy, ¼" slices
1½ cups bean sprouts
⅔ cup scallions in ¼" slices
⅓ cup sliced bamboo shoots
½ cup sliced water chestnuts
Romaine leaves
2 cups finely sliced red cabbage
¾ cup whole blanched almonds, toasted

ORIENTAL DRESSING
Whiz the egg in a food processor or blender or whisk by hand until light-colored. Gradually add the sesame and corn oils until well homogenized. Add the remaining ingredients.

SALAD
Bake and cool the chicken as described in the preceding recipe for Classic Chicken Salad. Cut into bite-size pieces and combine with the sprouts, bok choy, scallions, snow peas, bamboo shoots, and water chestnuts. Toss with the dressing and arrange on romaine. Garnish with the red cabbage and almonds.

Substitute cashews or ¼ cup toasted sesame seeds for the almonds.

Shrimp and/or scallops are nice in place of the chicken.

For extra color and interest, add fresh pineapple or blanched broccoli or carrots.

CURRIED CHICKEN SALAD   *Serves 5–6*

Last but not least—number three in The Commissary chicken salad triumvirate. Sensations are sweet, salty, crunchy, chewy, savory, spicy—all happily running riot in the mouth. Rather than rely on commercial curry powders, we've used our own concoction of spices in the dressing with what we think are truly superior results. The fresh sweet pineapple and macadamia nuts are delightful in this salad, but at The Commissary, we also often substitute crisp apples and cashews or walnuts.

CREAMY CURRIED DRESSING
1 egg
1 cup corn oil
¼ cup vinegar
1½ teaspoons salt
1 teaspoon pepper
1 teaspoon minced garlic
½ teaspoon sugar
½ teaspoon turmeric
½ teaspoon coriander
¼ teaspoon cinnamon
¼ teaspoon nutmeg
¼ teaspoon dry mustard
¼ teaspoon cardamom
¼ teaspoon ground ginger
⅛ teaspoon ground cloves
⅛ teaspoon ground cumin
⅛ teaspoon cayenne pepper

SALAD
2 pounds boneless, skinless chicken breast (for 3½–4
    cups cooked and cubed meat)
1¼ cups celery, sliced ¼" thick on the diagonal
2 cups cubed fresh pineapple
½ cup dark raisins
¾ cup salted roasted macadamias, cashews, or walnuts
Mixed greens or romaine leaves

CREAMY CURRIED DRESSING
Whiz the egg in a food processor or blender or whisk by hand until light-colored. Gradually add the corn oil so that it is well homogenized. Add the remaining ingredients.

SALAD
Bake the chicken as described in the recipe for Classic Chicken Salad on p. 67. Let cool and cut into bite-size pieces. Combine the chicken with the celery, pineapple, raisins, and nuts. (It is best to add the pineapple just before serving, because if it sits with the chicken for more than a few hours, the acid from the pineapple will turn the chicken mushy.) Serve on greens.

SERVING SUGGESTIONS AND VARIATIONS
Serve in pita bread as a sandwich or on round melon slices for a special presentation.

Add diced red or green peppers and garnish with toasted coconut.

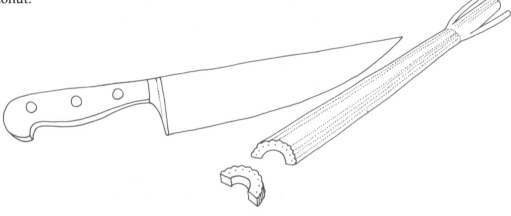

INDIAN CHICKEN SALAD WITH RAITA DRESSING
Serves 6

One of the most exciting features about The Commissary is its ever changing menu which, in turn, has provided plenty of opportunities over the years for whatever creative spirits are currently lurking in the kitchens. Staff have always been strongly encouraged to contribute ideas, and the result has been a unique menu reflecting a host of different cooks and cuisines.

This salad is a fine example of a Commissary-born dish. It was the idea of a salad department head with a penchant for Indian food. The combination of tender chicken, crunchy cashews, and bright crisp vegetables in a spicy yet cooling yogurt dressing is very good, and unlike any chicken salad we've encountered elsewhere.

71

RAITA DRESSING
16 ounces plain yogurt
8 ounces sour cream
1¼ cups peeled, seeded, and grated cucumber
½ teaspoon curry powder
¼ teaspoon ground cumin
½ teaspoon turmeric
¼ teaspoon cayenne
2¾ teaspoons salt
2 teaspoons sugar
½ teaspoon white pepper
OPT. ½ teaspoon grated orange rind

SALAD
2 pounds boneless, skinless chicken breast (for 3½–4
　cups cooked and cubed meat)
1½ cups dried lentils
2 cups broccoli in bite-size pieces, blanched until crisp-
　tender
1 cup scallions cut into ¼″ rounds
1 cup slices halved peeled and seeded cucumbers
1 cup peeled and grated carrots
Mixed greens
1½ cups roasted cashews, coarsely chopped

Raitas are Indian yogurt-based salads or relishes. They make cool, refreshing accompaniments to spicy dishes.

RAITA DRESSING
Combine all the ingredients and refrigerate until ready to use.

SALAD
Cook the chicken breasts as described in the recipe for Classic Chicken Salad on p. 67. Let cool and cut into bite-size pieces.

Cook the lentils for 2–3 minutes or until tender in boiling salted water. Drain well and cool. Combine with the chicken, broccoli, scallions, cucumbers, and carrots. Add the dressing and toss. Serve on greens. Garnish with cashews.

NOTE
The Raita Dressing makes a terrific dipping sauce, or try serving it with a salad of blanched and raw vegetables.

CHICKEN-MELON SALAD WITH ORANGE-TARRAGON DRESSING

Serves 6

A most wonderful summer salad—very refreshing. Note that the salad should be assembled *just* before serving, otherwise the melon will exude juice as it sits and the dressing won't cling as well.

ORANGE-TARRAGON DRESSING

½ cup orange juice
2 tablespoons minced fresh tarragon or 2 teaspoons dried
1 egg
1 cup corn oil
3 tablespoons wine vinegar
1 tablespoon lemon juice
2 teaspoons grated orange rind
¼ teaspoon minced garlic
1 teaspoon salt
1 teaspoon pepper

SALAD

2 pounds boneless, skinless chicken breast (for 3½–4
    cups cooked and cubed meat)
2 cups cubed cantaloupe or crenshaw melon
1½ cups cubed honeydew melon
1 cup sliced celery
1½ cups seedless grapes, purple or green
Mixed greens or watercress
¾ cup toasted hazelnuts, coarsely chopped

ORANGE-TARRAGON DRESSING

In a very small pan, reduce the orange juice with the tarragon to 2 tablespoons. Whiz the egg in a food processor or whisk by hand until light-colored. Gradually add the corn oil to blend well. Add the remaining ingredients and the orange-tarragon reduction. Refrigerate.

SALAD

Cook the chicken as described in the recipe for Classic Chicken Salad on p. 67. Cool and cut into bite-size pieces. *Just* before serving, combine the chicken with the melon, celery, grapes, and dressing. Serve on mixed greens or watercress. Garnish with the nuts.

VARIATIONS

Substitute turkey for the chicken, walnuts or pecans for the hazelnuts, and/or thyme for the tarragon.

The dressing can also be made with a blender or egg beater.

DUCK SALAD WITH CURRIED VINAIGRETTE

Serves 4

We love the elegance that duck gives to a salad. This simple jewel-like creation happily mates the rich, tender duck meat and crisp, brilliant vegetables with the clean sweetness of fresh pineapple and a clear, spice-laden dressing.

CURRIED VINAIGRETTE

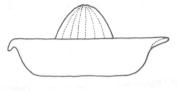

½ cup olive oil
⅔ cup corn oil
6 tablespoons lime juice
¼ cup cider vinegar
1 tablespoon salt
1½ teaspoons pepper
½ teaspoon nutmeg
1½ teaspoons ground cumin
½ teaspoon minced fresh ginger
¼ cup honey
¼ teaspoon cayenne
1 teaspoon curry powder
½ teaspoon ground cardamom
1 teaspoon cinnamon
1½ teaspoons ground coriander
2 tablespoons minced garlic

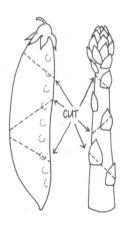

SALAD

1 (4½-pound) duck
¾ cup snow peas (see diagram for how to cut)
6 stalks asparagus, blanched and cut (see diagram)
1 cup julienned red peppers
1 cup cubed fresh pineapple (1" cubes)
1 quart loosely packed Boston lettuce (about 2 heads) or
    other soft greens
1 quart loosely packed watercress, stems removed (2–3
    bunches)
½ cup slivered almonds, lightly toasted
2 large carrots, finely julienned and crisped in ice water

CURRIED VINAIGRETTE

Whisk all ingredients together and refrigerate.

SALAD

Preheat the oven to 425°. Cut the excess neck skin from the duck and remove any loose interior fat. Rinse the duck and pat dry. Prick the skin all over with a fork, being careful not to pierce the meat. Put in a roasting pan and roast for 1 hour. Let cool completely. Remove the skin. Pull the meat from the bones and cut into bite-size pieces. One hour before serving, combine the duck with ¾ cup of the dressing and leave to marinate.

Prepare the vegetables and pineapple. If the pineapple is not particularly sweet, toss it with a little honey.

Add the vegetables and pineapple to the duck and toss. Combine ½ cup of reserved dressing with the lettuce and watercress. Divide among individual plates. Top with the salad and sprinkle with toasted almonds. Garnish with a border of the julienned carrots.

THAI BEEF SALAD WITH SPICY PEANUT DRESSING

Serves 5–6

When Steven asked to have a beef salad with peanut dressing put on the menu at The Commissary, this was the kitchen's response. Light, spicy, and crunchy, it's a great vehicle for leftover beef of any cut.

SPICY PEANUT DRESSING
½ cup unseasoned rice wine vinegar
⅓ cup corn oil
1 teaspoon salt
1 tablespoon sugar
¾ teaspoon minced garlic
½ teaspoon crushed red pepper flakes
1¼ teaspoons soy sauce
1¼ teaspoons sriraja (Thai hot sauce) or Tabasco
1¼ teaspoons minced fresh ginger
2 tablespoons lime juice
⅓ cup coarsely chopped salted roasted peanuts

SALAD
1½ pounds cooked, rare roast sirloin or fillet of beef, cut
    into 1½" × ¼" strips (about 4 cups)
2 medium-large cucumbers, peeled, seeded, and sliced
    into ¼"-thick crescents (about 2½ cups)
¼ pound snow peas, stemmed, blanched 20 seconds
½ pound bean sprouts
1¾ cups julienned red peppers (about 2 medium)
2 cups finely sliced red cabbage
1 cup thinly sliced scallions
Romaine leaves
½ cup chopped salted roasted peanuts

SPICY PEANUT DRESSING
Whisk together all the ingredients (except the peanuts). Refrigerate. Stir in the peanuts just before serving.

SALAD

Just before serving, combine the beef, cucumbers, snow peas, bean sprouts, peppers, cabbage, and scallions with the dressing. Serve on romaine or other greens and sprinkle with the peanuts.

WARM LAMB SALAD WITH PINE NUTS, RAISINS, AND SWEET ONION VINAIGRETTE

Serves 4

Not only is this a different way to serve lamb, but it is also a different kind of salad—a warm one.

SWEET ONION VINAIGRETTE
⅓ cup olive oil
⅓ cup corn oil
1½ teaspoons salt
1½ teaspoons pepper
½ teaspoon minced garlic
¼ cup wine vinegar
2 tablespoons sugar
½ cup minced red onion

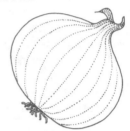

SALAD
4 quarts loosely packed mixed greens of the more
    assertive varieties, such as spinach, arugula,
    watercress, dandelion, radicchio, or mustard greens
1 cup julienned red peppers in 1″ matchsticks
2 tablespoons olive oil
1 pound raw lamb trimmed, from the leg or loin, cut
    into bite-size strips ¼″ thick
¼ cup raisins
¼ cup pine nuts, toasted

SWEET ONION VINAIGRETTE
Whisk together all the ingredients and refrigerate. This can be done up to 2 days in advance.

SALAD
Wash and dry greens. Tear them into bite-size pieces and set them aside in a bowl with the red peppers. Heat the olive oil in a 9″ skillet until very hot but not smoking. Add the lamb in a single layer and let it cook 1 minute. Stir and turn it for 15 seconds. Turn off the heat and at once add the raisins, pine nuts, and dressing. Stir 15 seconds to let the dressing heat through. Immediately pour the contents of the skillet over the greens, toss well, and serve at once.

76

SALADE NIÇOISE WITH ANCHOVY HERB DRESSING

Serves 5–6

We've given our Salade Niçoise Italian overtones by substituting pasta for the usual potatoes and tossing the whole with a wonderful creamy dressing heady with anchovies and herbs. It is one of our best salads.

ANCHOVY-HERB DRESSING

1 egg
1 cup corn oil
¼ cup wine vinegar
1 teaspoon minced garlic
1 teaspoon sugar
2 tablespoons minced dill
2 tablespoons minced parsley
1 teaspoon dried basil
½ teaspoon salt
1½ teaspoons pepper
1 (2-ounce) can anchovies in oil, drained and finely
  chopped

SALAD

½ pound green beans
½ pound uncooked medium-size pasta shells, rigatoni,
  or penne
2 tablespoons olive oil
2 (7-ounce) cans of white meat tuna
1 red pepper cut into ¼" × 1½" julienne strips
1½ cups halved cherry tomatoes
½ cup pitted and quartered large imported black olives
½ cup scallions in ¼"-thick slices
3 hard-cooked eggs, halved
Romaine leaves

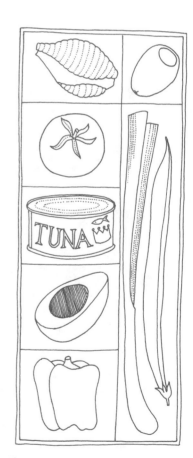

ANCHOVY-HERB DRESSING

Whiz the egg in a food processor or blender or whisk by hand until light-colored. Gradually add the corn oil until well homogenized. Add the remaining ingredients except for the anchovies and whiz until smooth. Stir in the anchovies. Refrigerate.

SALAD

Stem the green beans, cut them into 2"-long pieces, and blanch in boiling salted water until just crisp-tender. Refresh in cold water, drain well, and chill until ready to use. Cook the pasta in boiling salted water until *al dente*. Drain *well* and toss with the olive oil. Let cool. Drain the tuna and chunk or flake it. Combine the green beans, pasta, tuna, red pepper, tomatoes, olives, and scallions with the dressing or to taste. (They benefit from being

77

combined several hours before serving.) Serve on romaine leaves and garnish with the hard-cooked egg halves.

VARIATION
Substitute cooked, quartered red-skinned new potatoes for the pasta.

BOUILLABAISSE SALAD WITH SAFFRON MAYONNAISE

Serves 5–6

Inspired by that divine legendary seafood stew from the South of France, this luxurious salad was an indulgent offering on The Commissary's opening menu. Our intent was for a "solid" seafood salad flavored with the classic bouillabaisse elements of olive oil, saffron, fennel, and parsley. Tenderly poached mussels, shrimp, scallops, and lobster mingle with crisp bits of aniselike fennel in a golden saffron-tinged mayonnaise. Asparagus spears and tomatoes add drama to the final composition. This is a real celebration salad, worth creating a special occasion for if necessary.

SHELLFISH
2 cups dry white wine
2 cups water
2 tablespoons chopped shallots
1 tablespoon chopped garlic
Stems from ½ bunch parsley
3 bay leaves
1 teaspoon black peppercorns
1 teaspoon dried thyme
12 mussels, scrubbed clean
1 (2-pound) lobster or 1 (1-pound) lobster tail
1½ pounds sea scallops
1½ pounds shrimp in the shell

SAFFRON MAYONNAISE
¼ teaspoon powdered saffron
½ cup reduced poaching liquid
2 egg yolks
1⅓ cups corn oil
⅓ cup olive oil
¼ cup lemon juice
¾ teaspoon white pepper
2 teaspoons salt
⅛ teaspoon cayenne pepper

ASSEMBLY

24 asparagus stalks
½ bunch scallions, sliced ¾ of the way up the green
3 cups julienned fennel bulbs
¼ cup minced parsley
2 tomatoes, cut into wedges

SHELLFISH

Combine the wine, water, shallots, garlic, parsley stems, bay leaves, peppercorns, and thyme in a large pot. Simmer 10 minutes. Add the mussels, cover, and bring to a boil. When the mussels open (after about 2 minutes), remove them with a slotted spoon and set aside. Return the poaching liquid to a boil. Add the lobster, cover, and steam until the lobster turns bright red (about 5 minutes). Remove the lobster and let cool until you can easily handle it. Remove the meat from the shell, cut in bite-size pieces, and reserve. Return the poaching liquid to a boil once more, add the scallops, and cook 2–4 minutes or until cooked through. Cut one open to check. Remove the scallops with a slotted spoon and set aside. Repeat with the shrimp. Peel the shrimp after they have cooled sufficiently. Strain the poaching liquid through cheesecloth and return it to a saucepan. Reduce it to ½ cup over high heat. Reserve for use in the mayonnaise.

SAFFRON MAYONNAISE

Combine the saffron and the ½ cup of reduced poaching liquid in a small pan over moderate heat. Simmer 1 minute. Set aside and let cool. Follow procedure for Basic Mayonnaise on p. 100 using the ingredients listed above and adding the saffron liquid when you add the lemon juice.

ASSEMBLY

Trim the asparagus stalks to equal lengths and peel the stems. Blanch in boiling salted water until crisp-tender. Refresh under cold water and drain. Drain the reserved lobster, scallops, and shrimp thoroughly and combine in a large bowl with the scallions, fennel, and 3 tablespoons of the minced parsley. Fold in *half* the mayonnaise. Line a platter or salad bowl with greens. Top with the salad. Loosen the mussels in their shells; dry the shells and lightly coat them with corn oil to make them shine. Arrange the mussels in their shells around the perimeter of the salad alternately with the tomato wedges. Arrange the asparagus spears on top of the salad in a spoke pattern. Sprinkle with the remaining tablespoon of parsley. Pass the rest of the mayonnaise separately.

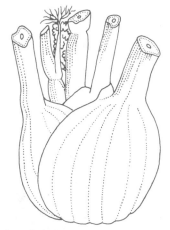

Sprightly, crunchy, anise-flavored Florentine fennel (not to be confused with the herb) is not to be missed when you see it available. Recipes for cooked fennel are many, but do use it raw, too, as part of a crudités selection or instead of celery in a salad. Italians enjoy it in one of the best possible ways: a bulb simple served on its own with salt and a bowl of extra virgin olive oil for dipping into. Another salad we have enjoyed combines sliced fennel, peeled orange sections, greens, and a dressing of olive oil, orange juice and red wine vinegar.

VARIATION
If fresh fennel is not available (as is often the case in the summer, when this salad would be just dandy), you can substitute celery. To compensate for the lost anise flavor, add 2 teaspoons ground fennel seed to the mayonnaise.

PHILADELPHIA SUMMER FOODS

In the spirit of Philadelphia's Century 4 celebration in 1982, we staged a Summer Food Festival to highlight our legacy of regional abundance. Immediately called to mind were towering cones of the smoothest ice cream, fat delicious Jersey tomatoes to cut in thick slabs, steaming ears of sweet corn to slather with butter, buckets of tart blueberries sure to stain teeth and tongue, peaches so juicy they leave chins' dripping, platters of crabs and bowls of clams to attack, roadside stands overflowing with all manner of luscious produce... in fact, we turned the first floor of The Commissary into a veritable produce stand for 3 weeks. It was great, delicious fun.

Philadelphia Summer Foods Festival Logo

BAY SCALLOP AND CORN SALAD WITH DILL MAYONNAISE   *Serves 6*

This recipe was devised for our Summer '82 Food Festival (our contribution to Philadelphia's Tricentennial Celebration), where we highlighted our bounty of local summer foods—corn, tomatoes, herbs, peppers, seafood, and the like.

DILL MAYONNAISE
2 egg yolks
1½ cups corn oil
½ cup tarragon vinegar
1½ teaspoons salt
1 teaspoon pepper
¼ cup minced fresh dill
¼ teaspoon Tabasco

SALAD
4 cups water
1 cup dry white wine
1½ pounds bay scallops or sea scallops
2 cups cooked fresh corn kernels (about 4 ears)
½ cup diced celery (⅜" dice)
1 cup diced red peppers (⅜" dice)
¼ cup finely chopped red onions
3 tomatoes, cut into wedges

DILL MAYONNAISE
Follow the method for making Basic Mayonnaise on p. 100 using the ingredients listed in the Dill Mayonnaise recipe.

SALAD
In a wide saucepan, bring the water and wine to a full boil. Add the scallops and stir them gently over high heat for 1–2 minutes. Drain immediately and let cool to room temperature. (If using sea scallops, cook them 2 minutes, then cut one open to see if it's done. Drain, cool, and then quarter.)

Combine the scallops with the corn, celery, red peppers,

and onions. Add 1½ cups of the mayonnaise or to taste. Check for seasoning. Serve on greens and garnish with tomato wedges and, if available, feathery sprigs of dill.

VARIATION
Substitute cooked crab, shrimp, or chicken for the scallops.

SOUTH AMERICAN SCALLOP SALAD WITH LIME DRESSING
Serves 4–5

The unusual combination of ingredients in this salad blends deliciously in the creamy, lime-brightened dressing for an effect reminiscent of seviche. Small portions of the salad are lovely as a prelude to a summer dinner, or can be included, as we do for catering parties, in a summer buffet lineup.

LIME DRESSING
1 egg
1¼ cups corn oil
1 tablespoon wine vinegar
¼ cup lime juice (about 3 limes)
2 teaspoons salt
2½ teaspoons crushed red pepper flakes
1 teaspoon minced garlic
2 teaspoons grated lime rind

SALAD
1 cup dry white wine
1 cup water
2 bay leaves
1 tablespoon minced shallots
3 sprigs parsley
2 pounds sea scallops
1 (15-ounce) can miniature corn ears, drained and cut
  into 1½" pieces
2 cups julienned red peppers in ¼" strips
1½ cups quartered and thinly sliced red onions
Watercress or greens

LIME DRESSING
Whiz the egg in a food processor or blender or whisk by hand until light-colored. Gradually add the oil so that the mixture is well homogenized. Add the remaining ingredients. Refrigerate until ready to use.

SALAD
In a large saucepan, bring to a boil the wine, water, bay

CROQUET FÊTE
Whether it be a genteel round or a cutthroat match, croquet is a quintessentially summer game and makes a fine reason for a small summer party. There is a leisurely and enviably old-fashioned aura about the game. Let that set the tone for the lovely buffet dinner that follows.

Loin of Veal Stuffed with Spinach and Prosciutto *
South American Scallop Salad *
Pasta and Smoked Mozzarella Salad *
Assorted Breads
Mixed Fruit Bowl with Anisette
Linzer Torte *

* see Index for recipe page number.

81

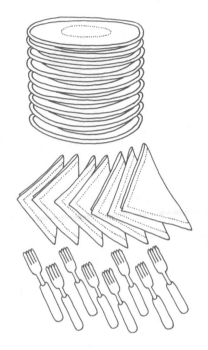

leaves, shallots, and parsley. Reduce heat, cover pan, and simmer 10 minutes. Add the scallops. Cover again and cook for 3–5 minutes or until the scallops are uniformly white (test by cutting into one). Drain the scallops and spread them out in a single layer to cool. When cool, slice horizontally into 2 or 3 pieces each.

Combine the scallops with the corn ears, red peppers, onion, and 1 cup of the dressing. Serve the salad on a bed of greens or watercress and pass the additional dressing. Garnish, if desired, with twisted lime slices.

BUCKWHEAT PASTA SALAD WITH JULIENNED VEGETABLES, SHELLFISH, AND SESAME-GINGER VINAIGRETTE   *Serves 6–8*

Literally a winner—this salad was Steven's entry in a "Best Philadelphia Restaurant Salad" contest sponsored by a local TV station. It took first place!

SESAME-GINGER VINAIGRETTE
½ cup plus 3 tablespoons soy sauce
¾ cup rice vinegar
½ cup corn oil
¼ cup sesame oil
1 tablespoon minced fresh ginger
2 tablespoons sugar
2½ teaspoons pepper
½ teaspoon salt
1 teaspoon minced garlic
½ teaspoon Tabasco

PASTA
1 pound dried buckwheat pasta
3 tablespoons sesame oil

SHELLFISH
12 mussels
1 cup dry white wine
1 cup water
1 tablespoon minced shallots
1 bay leaf
½ pound shrimp, with shells
½ pound bay scallops
⅛ teaspoon salt

VEGETABLES
8 asparagus spears

⅔ cup peeled, julienned carrots in 2″ × ⅛″ strips
4 cups julienned red peppers in 2″ × ⅛″ strips (about 3 peppers)
½ cup quartered canned baby corn ears
16 snow peas, stemmed and halved lengthwise
¼ pound mushrooms, thinly sliced

ASSEMBLY

Romaine leaves or other greens
OPT. Minced parsley or chopped scallions for garnish

SESAME-GINGER DRESSING

Whisk together all the ingredients.

PASTA

Cook the pasta until *al dente* in boiling salted water. Drain, rinse under cold water and drain again. Let rest 3–4 minutes, then toss with the sesame oil. (Pasta can be covered and refrigerated for several hours at this point.)

SHELLFISH

Scrub the mussels. In a 2-quart saucepan, bring to a boil the wine, water, shallots, and bay leaf. Add the mussels, cover, and steam 2 minutes or until mussels open. Remove with a slotted spoon to a plate to cool. Poach the shrimp in the same liquid for 1–2 minutes until just done. Also remove to plate to cool, then peel and devein. Poach the scallops in the same liquid for 1–2 minutes. Transfer to plate to cool. When the shellfish has cooled, remove the mussels from their shells and remove the beard and foot from each mussel. Set aside 8 mussels and 8 shells for the garnish. Cut each shrimp into 4 pieces. Chop the remaining 4 mussels and combine with the shrimp and scallops. Add the salt and 1 cup of the dressing. Refrigerate and let marinate at least 15 minutes or up to 2 hours.

VEGETABLES

Trim and peel the asparagus spears, blanch them, refresh under cold water, and remove and set aside the tips for garnish. Cut the stems into ¾″-long pieces. Have ready the other vegetables.

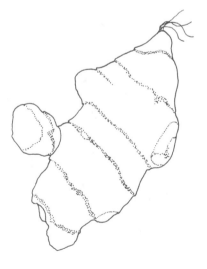

ASSEMBLY

Dry and lightly oil the mussel shells to make them look shiny. Fill each with a reserved mussel and an asparagus tip which have been dipped in the dressing. Combine the other shellfish with the pasta, vegetables, and remaining dressing. Serve the salad on romaine and garnish with the reserved mussels. OPT. Dust with minced parsley or chopped scallion.

NORTHERN ITALIAN RICE SALAD WITH SHRIMP AND CLEAR GARLIC VINAIGRETTE

Serves 6–8

In northern Italy, a cold rice salad studded with bits of seafood or meat often serves as supper when the big meal has been enjoyed at midday. It's a delicious idea that lends itself to variation, holds well if made in advance, and is a wonderful receptacle for leftovers. Our own translation is colorful, piquant, refreshing, and frequently sports chicken and pepperoni rather than shrimp when we serve it in the Downstairs restaurant.

CLEAR GARLIC VINAIGRETTE
1¼ cups corn oil
½ cup white wine vinegar
1¾ teaspoons salt
1¾ teaspoons pepper
1 tablespoon minced garlic
½ teaspoon dried basil
½ teaspoon dried oregano
¼ cup minced parsley

RICE SALAD
6 cups cooked rice (2 cups raw)
¾ pound cooked peeled shrimp, cut in thirds
2 cups finely chopped green peppers
¾ cup finely chopped red onions
1 cup quartered cooked marinated artichoke hearts
¼ cup small capers
⅓ cup minced parsley
⅓ cup minced dill
¼ cup golden raisins
¼ cup dark raisins
Mixed greens

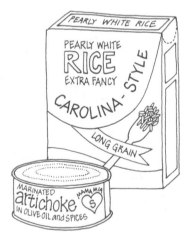

CLEAR GARLIC VINAIGRETTE
Whisk together the ingredients for the dressing and set aside.

RICE SALAD
Combine all the salad ingredients. Toss with the dressing and let marinate several hours. Serve on a bed of greens.

VARIATIONS
As mentioned above, substitute chicken and pepperoni for the shrimp.

Try cooking 1 pound of orzo to use instead of the rice.

Add black olives, peas, red peppers—whatever your heart desires or your refrigerator contains.

PASTA AND SMOKED MOZZARELLA SALAD WITH ROASTED PEPPERS, SPINACH, AND CREAMY PARMESAN DRESSING
Serves 4–6

This salad, because of its colors, would be just the thing to include on a Christmas buffet, but it should not by any means be limited just to that season. A popular item in The Commissary's Market and Downstairs restaurant, it originated as a winner in a pasta recipe contest we held for the staff during our first annual Pasta and Zinfandel Festival.

CREAMY PARMESAN DRESSING
1 egg
½ cup olive oil
½ cup corn oil
⅓ cup wine vinegar
½ teaspoon salt
1½ teaspoons pepper
½ cup grated Parmesan cheese
⅛ teaspoon ground cloves
⅛ teaspoon Tabasco
1½ teaspoons minced garlic

SALAD
½ pound uncooked penne
1 tablespoon olive oil
1 (10-ounce) bag fresh spinach
½ pound prosciutto, thinly sliced and chopped
2 teaspoons vegetable oil
½ cup chopped roasted red peppers
8 ounces smoked mozzarella diced into ½" cubes
Greens
Additional grated Parmesan cheese for sprinkling

CREAMY PARMESAN DRESSING
Whiz the egg in a food processor or whisk by hand until light-colored, gradually add the oils so that the mixture emulsifies, and then add the rest of the ingredients.

SALAD
Cook the penne until *al dente* according to package instructions. Refresh under cold water and drain well. Toss with the olive oil to prevent sticking. Wash the spinach well, put it in a large skillet, and heat, while stirring, until it has just wilted (should not take more than a minute). Refresh under cold water, squeeze dry, and coarsely chop. Briefly fry the prosciutto in the vegetable oil to frizzle it. Combine the penne with the spinach, half the prosciutto, the peppers, mozzarella, and the dressing. Serve on greens,

"AND ADD 2 SOUR CREAMS OF…"
In The Commissary's basement kitchen (the source of an endless parade of enormous bowls of salads, crocks of soup, etc.), the standard of measurement is not the cup, pint, or quart but a sour cream container. We get our sour cream in sturdy plastic 5-pound containers, and way back when Anne was busy trying to record and standardize all the restaurant's recipes she found that these containers were just the thing for measuring out the salads, which were assembled in such large quantities that a 1 cup measure was useless. In addition, the containers had good lids and stacked well, the supply was always being replenished, and exactly 8 "sour creams" filled one salad bowl. It's not surprising, then, that Anne's birthday cake that year was baked to resemble a sour cream container.

Sour Cr
5 pounds

85

ROASTING PEPPERS

If you're only roasting a few peppers, don't want to turn the oven on, and have a gas stove... spear each pepper with an old fork and prop 2 or 3 peppers over each burner. Turn the flame to medium high and leave the peppers 2-3 minutes or until charred and blistered on one side. Using a potholder, turn the peppers and let them blister where they haven't until they are charred in most spots. Put the peppers then in a paper bag. Leave them until they are cool enough to handle. Using a small, sharp knife, peel the peppers and remove the stems and seeds. ☆ If you are doing a lot of peppers, it is easiest to spread them on a rimmed baking sheet and put them in a 500° oven for about ½ hour or until the skins are blistered and charred. Another way would be to put the peppers under the broiler and check them every few minutes, turning as needed.

sprinkle with additional Parmesan cheese, and scatter the remaining prosciutto on top.

VARIATION

Pasta Parmesan Salad Combine the Creamy Parmesan Dressing with 2 cups blanched broccoli flowerets and stems, 6 ounces diced salami, ¾ cup small whole pitted sweet black olives and ½ pound (uncooked) medium-size pasta shells cooked until *al dente*. Garnish with tomato wedges and sprinkle with additional Parmesan cheese.

25 SALAD COMBINATIONS

Greenleaf lettuce, watercress, and sliced peaches with Basic Clear Vinaigrette made with raspberry vinegar and a pinch of sugar

Watercress, sliced crisp apples, and chips of Cheddar cheese with Basic Clear Vinaigrette using walnut oil and sherry vinegar

Cubes of roasted veal, sliced zucchini, black olives, and cherry tomatoes with Tuna-Caper Mayonnaise

Cooked shrimp with pasta shells, blanched broccoli flowerets, julienned red pepper, and Herb Vinaigrette

Summer garden greens dressed with Basic Clear Vinaigrette using walnut oil and sherry vinegar and garnished with marigold petals as a beautiful (and edible!) surprise

Cubed cooked new potatoes, peas, lots of chopped fresh mint, and equal parts sour cream and mayonnaise with salt and pepper

City Bites Salad: spinach, grated fontina cheese, chopped sun-dried tomatoes, julienned roasted red peppers, sautéed cubes of eggplant, sliced mushrooms, toasted pine nuts, crumbled hard-cooked egg with Clear Garlic Vinaigrette

Fresh spinach, crumbled goat cheese, slivers of roasted peppers, and Walnut Vinaigrette

Fresh spinach, small cubes of feta cheese, and cooked turtlebeans in Basic Clear Vinaigrette made with lemon juice and olive oil

Blanched broccoli flowerets, cubes of roast pork, and oriental noodles in Basil, Lime, and Peanut Dressing

Chicken, new potatoes, blanched asparagus, and tomatoes in Basic Mayonnaise flavored with lemon juice

Tortellini, black olives, celery, red onions, and cherry tomatoes in Garlic Vinaigrette

Smoked turkey, brown and wild rice, celery, onions, blanched broccoli flowerets, and Basic Clear Vinaigrette using sherry vinegar

Chicken, avocado, and grapefruit in Rum-Rosemary Dressing

Whole wheat pasta, black olives, cubes of smoked mozzarella, chopped sun-dried tomatoes, and blanched broccoli flowerets in Tomato Vinaigrette

Julienned celeryroot and julienned baked beets with toasted walnuts in Parsley-Shallot Vinaigrette

Cubed roast beef, avocados, tomatoes, green peppers, and onions in Chili Cumin Vinaigrette

Cucumbers, peas, and blanched sliced carrots in Basic Clear Vinaigrette with minced shallots and chopped fresh mint

Bibb lettuce, tangelo slices, seedless red grapes, and Walnut Vinaigrette with grated orange rind

Spinach, sliced tart apples, raisins, and toasted sunflower seeds with Roquefort-Herb Dressing

Spinach, scallions, small cubes of mozzarella, sliced pepperoni, and Creamy Parmesan Dressing

Mixed greens, avocados, orange sections, and Olive Oil–Anise Seed Dressing

16th Street Salad: romaine, spinach, grated Cheddar cheese, carrots, mushrooms, alfalfa sprouts, cherry tomatoes, toasted sunflower seeds, and Parsley-Shallot Vinaigrette

Escarole, romaine, blanched asparagus pieces, and frizzled bits of prosciutto with Basic Clear Vinaigrette using sherry vinegar

Thinly sliced, blanched carrots, sliced scallions, black sesame seeds with Sesame Ginger Vinaigrette. Omit soy sauce and increase salt to 1¼ teaspoons.

Salad Dressings and Sauces

one part vinegar, three parts oil, a pinch of salt, a dash of pepper, a smattering of shallots, a sprinkling of parsley... Ingenious! Salads will

BASIC CLEAR VINAIGRETTE   *Makes 1¼ cups*

This is a basic sketch of a recipe to allow you to take advantage of and experiment with all the wonderful (and often exotic) oils and vinegars that crowd the shelves of fancy food markets these days and are even turning up in our supermarkets.

1 cup oil
⅓ cup vinegar of choice or lemon juice
¾–1 teaspoon salt
1 teaspoon pepper
OPT. Minced garlic, shallots, fresh herbs, or mustard to
    taste

Simply whisk together all the ingredients and chill before using.

VARIATIONS
Vinaigrettes can be flavored in all sorts of interesting ways. Try different oils (nut oils and sesame oil are best "cut" with a bland oil, such as corn oil, so they aren't too overpowering).

Any clear vinaigrette may be made creamy by the addition of raw egg. See procedure for Basic Creamy Vinaigrette on page 94.

TOMATO VINAIGRETTE   *Makes 2 cups*

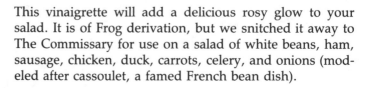

This vinaigrette will add a delicious rosy glow to your salad. It is of Frog derivation, but we snitched it away to The Commissary for use on a salad of white beans, ham, sausage, chicken, duck, carrots, celery, and onions (modeled after cassoulet, a famed French bean dish).

½ pound fresh tomatoes
2 tablespoons olive oil
1 tablespoon minced shallots
1½ teaspoons minced garlic
1 tablespoon tomato paste
2 tablespoons minced parsley
½ teaspoon dried oregano
½ teaspoon dried tarragon
¼ teaspoon dried basil
¼ teaspoon dried marjoram
2 tablespoons rosé or white wine
1 teaspoon salt

1 teaspoon pepper
1 cup corn oil
⅓ cup wine vinegar
1½ teaspoons lemon juice

Peel and seed tomatoes (see p. 102 for how to peel). Finely chop and set aside. In a small pan, heat the olive oil. Add the shallots and garlic and sauté until softened. Add the tomatoes, tomato paste, herbs, wine, salt, and pepper. Let reduce about 5 minutes, stirring occasionally until thickened. Put into a bowl and cool to room temperature. Whisk in the corn oil, vinegar, and lemon juice. Store (in anything but an aluminum container) in the refrigerator.

Chilled salad plates, chilled salad dressing, and chilled, dry greens make for a salad that will stay crisper longer. (Omit any chilled salad fork silliness, though.)

WALNUT VINAIGRETTE   *Makes about 2 cups*

The addition of chopped walnuts to this lovely walnut oil vinaigrette serves to reinforce the delicate nuttiness of the oil and also provides a bit of texture against the soft greens such as Bibb or Boston lettuce to which this dressing is so well suited. A favorite salad combination for this dressing as served at The Commissary combines Bibb lettuce, watercress and thinly sliced tart red-skinned apples. Frog responded with an endive, watercress, and tuna salad.

⅓ cup wine vinegar
1 teaspoon salt
1 teaspoon pepper
1½ tablespoons minced shallots
½ cup walnut oil
½ cup corn oil
½ cup coarsely chopped walnuts, lightly toasted

Whisk together the vinegar, salt, pepper, shallots, and oils until well blended. Refrigerate. Just before serving, stir in the toasted walnuts.

VARIATION
Substitute hazelnuts and hazelnut oil for the walnuts and walnut oil; then, try it on a salad of soft greens and fresh peaches.

SOY-MUSTARD VINAIGRETTE   *Makes 1½ cups*

A contribution from the second-floor kitchen at The Commissary, where it first appeared (and was soundly applauded) on a salad of spinach, feta cheese, and walnuts. May we also suggest that you keep it in mind for the likes of lentil-and-tomato or shrimp-and-vegetable salad.

⅓ cup cider vinegar
1½ tablespoons soy sauce
1 teaspoon minced garlic
2 teaspoons dry mustard
1 teaspoon Dijon mustard
¾ teaspoon salt
1 teaspoon pepper
1 cup corn oil

Combine all the ingredients except the corn oil. When they are well blended, add the oil. Chill before using.

BASIL, LIME, AND PEANUT DRESSING   *Makes about 1¾ cups*

This exotic dressing of Far Eastern influence takes its character from such favorite Thai ingredients as fresh basil, nam pla (fish sauce), chili flakes, coriander, lime, and peanuts. We've loved it on a simple broccoli salad and can imagine it bringing new excitement to chicken, beef, and seafood salads, or even broiled fish.

6 tablespoons lime juice
6 tablespoons nam pla (Thai fish sauce)
½ cup corn oil
1 teaspoon pepper
½ teaspoon salt
4 teaspoons sugar
1 teaspoon crushed red pepper flakes
2 teaspoons minced garlic
2 teaspoons ground coriander
⅓ cup minced fresh basil
⅓ cup minced parsley
½ cup finely chopped roasted peanuts

Whisk together all the ingredients except peanuts, and chill. Just before serving, stir in the peanuts (or sprinkle them over the salad).

CIDER VINAIGRETTE

Makes about 2 cups

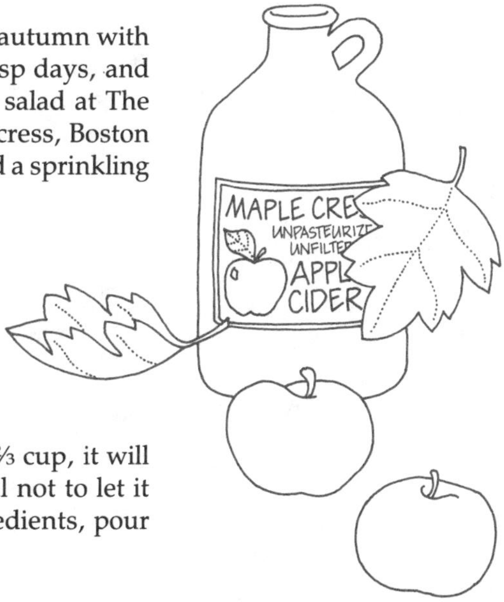

This dressing seems to capture the essence of autumn with all the gloriously colored leaves, snapping crisp days, and the return of heartier appetites. Our favorite salad at The Commissary for this dressing combines watercress, Boston lettuce, slices of crisp unpeeled red apples, and a sprinkling of toasted walnuts.

1 quart clear filtered cider
1 cup corn oil
⅓ cup cider vinegar
1½ teaspoons salt
1 teaspoon pepper

Over medium-high heat, reduce the cider to ⅔ cup, it will look like maple syrup at this point. Be careful not to let it go further and burn. Add the remaining ingredients, pour into a bowl, and let cool. Refrigerate.

VARIATIONS
Substitute ½ cup walnut oil for half the corn oil.
  Heat the dressing slightly before tossing with the salad.

RUM-ROSEMARY DRESSING

Makes about 1⅔ cups

This is a surprisingly refreshing (and admittedly unorthodox) dressing that was first dreamed up to grace a salad at Frog of mixed greens, fresh pineapple, and toasted pine nuts. It would be terrific, too, on a chicken-and-avocado salad.

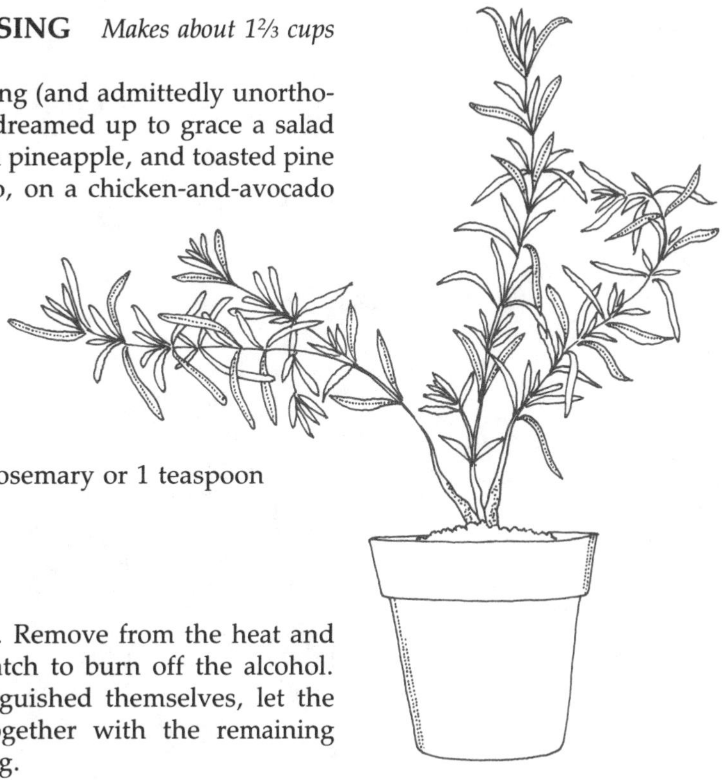

¼ cup dark rum
¼ cup dry white wine
2 tablespoons brown sugar
2 tablespoons lemon juice
½ cup tarragon vinegar
¾ cup corn oil
1½ teaspoons minced fresh rosemary or 1 teaspoon
  crumbled dry
¾ teaspoon salt
¾ teaspoon pepper

Heat the rum in a small pan. Remove from the heat and set aflame with a lighted match to burn off the alcohol. When the flames have extinguished themselves, let the rum cool, then whisk it together with the remaining ingredients. Chill before using.

93

BASIC CREAMY VINAIGRETTE   *Makes 1⅓ cups*

For a basic mixed greens salad blend, we like to combine bibb lettuce, watercress, spinach, and romaine. The quartet makes a fine foil for most any salad dressing. That isn't to say, though, that there isn't a host of other choices out there. We also love a touch of the bitter in a salad... a bit of chicory (pretty and cheap), endive, or mustard greens would do the trick. Leaves of basil or sorrel mixed in add lovely surprise, and for color add one of the red-leafed lettuces or slivers of red cabbage. Don't let us forget arugula, either, whose biting, peppery leaves must surely have been created to set off the simplest dressing of extra virgin olive oil, wine vinegar, and freshly ground pepper.

This is our basic vinaigrette, made creamy and thick by the addition of an egg. We love it for the way it really clings to the greens, but anytime you would prefer a clearer, lighter dressing, don't hesitate to omit the egg from this or any of the following creamy-style dressings.

1 egg
1 cup oil
⅓ cup vinegar or lemon juice
¾–1 teaspoon salt
1 teaspoon pepper

Whiz the egg in a food processor or blender or whisk by hand until light-colored. Gradually add the oil so that it emulsifies well. Add the salt and pepper (and any seasoning of your choice). Chill before using. Store in the refrigerator.

HERB VINAIGRETTE   *Makes about 1½ cups*

This is one of the three regular dressings served daily on the line at The Commissary with our mixed green salad. It is lush and creamy, with a good fresh herb flavor, and its popularity is a sure bet. Try it on potato salad!

1 egg
1 cup corn oil
⅓ cup wine vinegar
1 teaspoon salt
1 teaspoon pepper
½ teaspoon minced garlic
2 tablespoons minced parsley
2 tablespoons minced dill
1 tablespoon minced fresh basil or 1 teaspoon dried

Whiz the egg in a food processor or blender or whisk by hand until light-colored. Gradually add the corn oil so that it is well blended. Add the remaining ingredients. Chill before using. Store in refrigerator.

94

ROQUEFORT-HERB DRESSING   *Makes about 3 cups*

Lovers of blue cheese should find this dressing irresistible.
A simple variation on the preceding Herb Vinaigrette
recipe, this dressing is also one of The Commissary's three
"regulars." (The third "regular" is Frog's wonderful Mustard Dressing.)

1 recipe Herb Vinaigrette (see preceding recipe)
½ teaspoon pepper
1 cup sour cream
4 ounces Roquefort cheese, finely crumbled

Prepare Herb Vinaigrette, adding an additional ½ teaspoon
pepper. By hand, stir in the sour cream and Roquefort.
Chill before using.

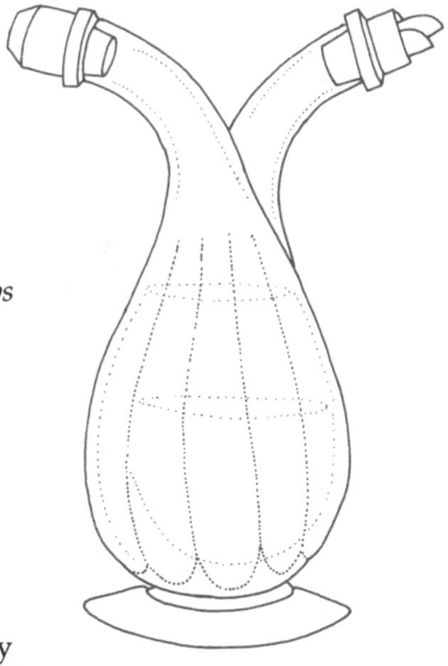

PARSLEY-SHALLOT
VINAIGRETTE   *Makes about 1⅓ cups*

1 egg
1 cup corn oil or olive oil
1 teaspoon salt
1 teaspoon pepper
⅓ cup plus 1 tablespoon tarragon vinegar
2 tablespoons minced parsley
3 tablespoons minced shallots

Whiz the egg in a food processor or blender or whisk by
hand until light-colored. Gradually add the corn oil until
well homogenized. Add the remaining ingredients. Chill
before using.

SERVING SUGGESTIONS
Try with beet-apple-bacon or with beet-celeryroot-walnut
salad. This dressing is also lovely with a simple mixture
of interesting greens such as Bibb, Boston, arugula, radicchio, watercress, mâche, etc.

EXTRA VIRGIN OLIVE OIL

Incredible stuff. Green-gold, the perfume of olives. It is light and sweet with low acidity... the nectar produced from the first pressing of the olives. Its costliness reflects the quality. Summer's tomatoes are incomparable when drizzled with this oil and garnished with basil and cracked pepper. Douse warm blanched vegetables with it and then mop up every last drop with the best crusty peasant bread you can find. Save the lesser grades of olive oil for cooking and use the extra virgin oil where its distinctive flavor can really shine.

OLIVE OIL–ANISE SEED DRESSING

Makes about 1½ cups

The combination of fruity olive oil and anise seeds brings to mind warm, craggy hillsides in the South of France strewn with herbs and gnarled olive trees—with perhaps even a view of the brilliant blue Mediterranean. Set your mind dreaming as you enjoy this dressing with such salad combinations as avocado-tomato, chicken-orange-pepper, seafood-pasta, and greens-grapefruit-red onion.

1 egg
½ cup olive oil (extra virgin, if possible)
½ cup corn oil
⅓ cup wine vinegar
1 tablespoon finely crushed or ground anise seeds
1 teaspoon salt
½ teaspoon pepper

Whiz the egg in a food processor or blender or whisk by hand until light-colored. Gradually add the oils until well homogenized. Add the remaining ingredients. Chill before using.

CREAMY DIJON VINAIGRETTE *Makes about 2 cups*

This tangy, delicately golden dressing was devised to accompany a salad of ham, potatoes, broccoli, and sweet pickles at The Commissary. We also love it with artichokes or on a salad of fresh spinach and Gruyère cheese.

1 egg
1 cup corn oil
⅓ cup wine vinegar
¼ teaspoon sugar
2 teaspoons minced garlic
2 teaspoons dried tarragon
¼ cup Dijon mustard
1 teaspoon salt
1 teaspoon pepper

Whiz the egg in a food processor or blender or whisk until light-colored. Gradually add the corn oil so that it is well homogenized. Add the remaining ingredients. Chill before using.

CHILI-CUMIN VINAIGRETTE *Makes about 1½ cups*

Olé! Transport your mouth to Mexico with this beautiful, spicy, pale pink dressing. We serve it at The Commissary on a salad of roast pork, red cabbage, and baby corn ears and wouldn't hesitate to toss it with the likes of a chicken-avocado or beef, Cheddar cheese, and tomato salad.

1 egg
1 cup corn oil
OPT. ½ teaspoon grated orange rind
½ teaspoon minced garlic
⅓ cup wine vinegar
¼ teaspoon cayenne pepper
1½ teaspoons chili powder
2 teaspoons ground cumin
1 teaspoon salt
1 teaspoon pepper

Whiz the egg in a food processor or blender or whisk by hand until light-colored. Gradually add the corn oil until well homogenized. Add remaining ingredients. Chill before using.

HORSERADISH VINAIGRETTE

Makes about 1½ cups

A Commissary concoction initially destined for an interesting light salad of Chinese cabbage, carrots, snow peas, and Jarlsberg cheese.

1 egg
1 cup corn oil
⅓ cup wine vinegar
2 tablespoons lemon juice
1 teaspoon salt
1 teaspoon pepper
¼ cup drained prepared horseradish
1 tablespoon minced parsley

Whiz the egg in a food processor or blender or whisk by hand until light-colored. Gradually add the oil until well homogenized. Add the remaining ingredients. Chill before using.

Try with any of the following: shrimp, tomato, and avocado salad, corned beef and potato salad, or "Bloody Mary" salad with tomatoes, celery, pepper, pasta, and a dash of Worcestershire sauce.

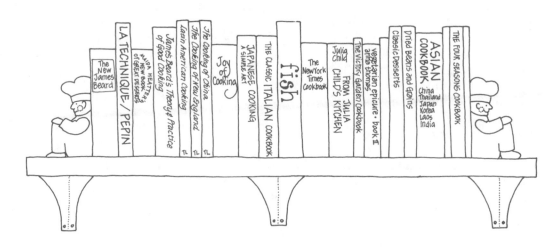

The Commissary's first-floor restaurant sports a cookbook library in the back where customers can sit at a counter and enjoy their meals while perusing the cookbooks from the shelf above them.

ANCHOVY-FETA DRESSING   *Makes about 1½ cups*

Commissary's popular Greek salad, comprised of greens, black olives, tomatoes, green beans, cucumbers, and feta cheese, was the raison d'être for this wonderfully assertive dressing.

1 egg
1 cup corn oil
¼ cup vinegar
¼ teaspoon salt
1 teaspoon pepper
1 tablespoon lemon juice
1 ounce anchovies (about 3 fish), finely chopped
½ cup crumbled feta cheese (about 2 ounces)

Whiz the egg in a food processor or blender or whisk by hand until light-colored. Gradually add the corn oil until well homogenized. Add the vinegar, salt, pepper, and lemon juice. Stir in the anchovies and feta by hand. Chill before using.

WALNUT-YOGURT DRESSING

Makes about 2½ cups

This is delicious on fruit salads of almost any kind. We serve it at The Commissary on our fall fruit salad of greens, pears, apples, oranges, dates, raisins, dried apricots, and walnut halves.

16 ounces plain yogurt
2 tablespoons honey or to taste
2 teaspoons lime juice
¼ cup finely chopped walnuts
¼ cup rosé or white wine

Empty the yogurt into a bowl, but do not whisk it, because if stirred too much it will become watery. Whisk together the remaining ingredients and gently stir them into the yogurt.

VARIATIONS
Substitute chopped dried figs, dried apricots, or toasted almonds for the walnuts.

STRAWBERRY-YOGURT DRESSING   *Makes 4 cups*

Everyone loves this strawberry dressing. It is so pretty, good, and a million times better than any prepackaged strawberry yogurt. We first served it over fresh fruit salad in The Commissary's second-floor restaurant. Equally pleasing partners we've found for this glorious pink stuff are granola, pancakes, and pound cake. Even on its own, this dressing is ambrosia!

16 ounces plain yogurt
1½ pints strawberries, hulled and coarsely puréed
¼ cup orange juice
¼ cup plus 2 tablespoons honey

Empty the yogurt into a bowl, but do not whisk it, because if stirred too much, it will become watery. Whisk together the strawberry purée, orange juice, and honey. Gently stir into the yogurt. Chill before serving.

If your strawberries need to be washed, do so only at the last moment and just before hulling them. Once the stems are gone, the berries absorb water and turn mushy rather quickly.

VARIATION
Strawberry Soup Increase the strawberries to 2 pints and the orange juice to 3 cups. Whisk together with the honey and yogurt and serve very cold.

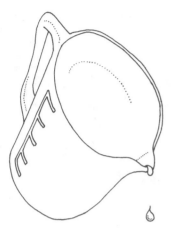

BASIC MAYONNAISE

The making of mayonnaise is just one of those things that couldn't be simpler, once you've overcome an initial trepidation and gotten a feel for how it works. How much better homemade mayonnaise tastes, too!

The following recipe gives proportions and yields for one-, two-, and three-yolk mayonnaises. Decide how much you need to end up with and take it from there. Mayonnaise can be made by hand with a whisk, in a food processor or blender, or with an electic mixer. The one-yolk batch may be too small to get going in a food processor or mixer while the three-yolk batch is most conveniently done in one of those machines.

	1 YOLK	2 YOLK	3 YOLK
YIELD:	*about 1¼ cups*	*scant 2 cups*	*about 2½ cups*
Egg yolks	1	2	3
Oil	¾ cup	1⅓ cups	2 cups
Vinegar or lemon juice	1 tablespoon	2 tablespoons	3 tablespoons
Salt	¾ teaspoon	1 teaspoon	1½ teaspoons
Pepper	¾ teaspoon	1½ teaspoons	2 teaspoons
Dijon mustard	1 tablespoon	2 tablespoons	3 tablespoons

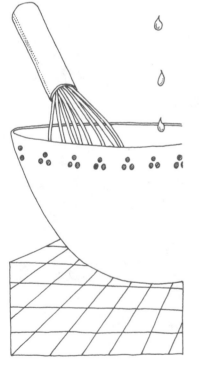

Whisk, whiz, or beat the yolks until light-colored. (If making mayonnaise by hand, you can steady your bowl by setting it on a cloth.) Measure out the oil into a container suitable for controlled pouring, and very gradually (almost drop by drop) add about ⅓ of the oil to the yolks while continuously beating so that the mixture begins to emulsify and thicken properly. At this point, you can begin adding the rest of the oil in a thin trickle, working up to a gradual stream at the end. Your mayonnaise should now be thick, smooth, and glossy. Beat in the vinegar, salt, pepper, and mustard. Cover and refrigerate if not using immediately. It will keep about two weeks.

NOTES

If in the process the mayonnaise "breaks" and becomes curdled in appearance, never mind. Beat another egg yolk in a clean bowl and very gradually begin beating the broken mayonnaise into it. Proceed with the rest of the recipe.

Before using, bring mayonnaise to room temperature and stir to make it creamy again.

Just as with the Basic Vinaigrette recipes, mayonnaise can be flavored in all sorts of interesting ways. Try different oils (most are often best "cut" with corn oil so that they aren't too overpowering). Add minced garlic, shallots, herbs, or try flavored mustards.

CRÈME FRAÎCHE

Makes 2½ cups

This is a wonderful French import that we've come to rely on. Thick, tangy (but not as sharp as sour cream), almost nutty, Crème Fraîche has infinitely more character than heavy cream, and unlike sour cream, it will not separate when boiled. Thus, it is ideal for adding to sauces instead of heavy or sour cream and makes a superb topping for fresh fruits.

2 cups heavy cream
3 tablespoons buttermilk
¼ cup lemon juice

Combine the cream and buttermilk. Heat until just warm (85°). Remove from the heat and stir in the lemon juice well. Cover and let stand in a warm place for 12–24 hours or until thickened. The mixture will separate into 2 layers. Do not use the watery bottom layer. Refrigerate 24 hours before serving. Will keep 1–2 weeks in the refrigerator.

HORSERADISH WHIPPED CREAM

Makes 1½–2 cups

Easy, breezy . . . and just the thing to accompany smoked bluefish or trout or cold roast fillet of beef.

1 cup heavy cream
½ teaspoon salt
⅛ teaspoon pepper
½ cup drained prepared horseradish

Whip the cream to firm peaks with the salt and pepper. Fold in the horseradish. Chill. This can be kept in the refrigerator for several hours before serving.

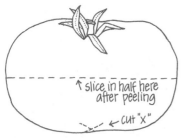

PEELING TOMATOES

Easily done with a paring knife. Cut a small "x" in the skin of the bottom end. Lower the tomato into boiling water to cover. Leave about 30 seconds, then lift out of the water and peel away the now easily removable skin. To remove the seeds, halve the tomato horizontally. Gently squeeze each half and use your finger to help scoop out the seeds.

TOMATO COULIS   *Makes 3⅓–4 cups*

With the "Garden State" just a river away, we really know how good summer tomatoes can be. When the tomato season hits, a good simple tomato-sauce recipe is invaluable. Lightly cooked to preserve that fresh quality, this pretty version has plenty to recommend it. Wonderful hot or cold, it is superb with everything from pizza and pasta to egg dishes and seafood terrine. Since it freezes well, stock up before winter's lackluster tomatoes are your only resort.

4 pounds fresh tomatoes
¼ cup olive oil
¼ cup minced shallots
2 cups chopped onion
1¼ teaspoons salt
½ teaspoon Tabasco
2 teaspoons minced fresh basil or other herb

Saving the juice and seeds, peel, core and seed the tomatoes (see box for how to peel). Cut into ½" cubes. Heat the oil in a large saucepan. Add the shallots and onions and sauté, stirring frequently, over medium heat for 10–15 minutes until very tender but not at all brown. Strain the reserved juice and seeds and add the liquid to the cooked onions. Turn the heat to high and cook until very thick so that the mixture mounds up and juices no longer exude (about 5 minutes). Add the tomatoes, salt, and Tabasco. Keep the heat high and bring to a boil for 10–12 minutes, stirring occasionally, until all the excess liquid has evaporated. Remove from the heat. Add the basil and let cool.

SERVING SUGGESTIONS
Serve this with any of our recipes for the following:
   Deep-fried Brie, Eastern Shore Crab Cakes, Stuffed Loin of Veal, Pasta Roll, Soufflé Roll with Spinach-Mushroom Filling, Italian Scrambled Eggs, Seafood Terrine, or Deep-Dish Pizza (use 2 cups for one 14" pizza).
   And, of course, it would go well with burgers, omelets, and pasta dishes in general. A little can also be added to sauces like Béchamel to give them a beautiful rosy tint and tomato flavor.

BEURRE BLANC

Makes 1⅔ cups

So light yet so rich . . . Beurre Blanc is an ethereal creation meant to grace some of the most elegantly simple dishes such as poached fish or shellfish, seafood terrine, hot vegetable mousses, and the like. In its most classic French form, Beurre Blanc contains no cream and must be served immediately, as the butter rests in delicate suspension in a mixture of reduced wine and wine vinegar. For the needs of our restaurants where there is room for only so many last-minute things, we developed an "industrial-strength" Beurre Blanc. It contains cream as a stabilizer and can be made in advance and held on a warm shelf above our stoves for several hours without breaking. If it is cooled, however, it cannot be reheated without breaking.

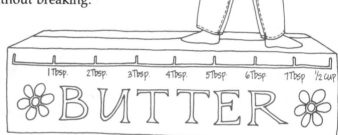

1 cup dry white wine
½ cup white wine vinegar
⅓ cup minced shallots
2 cups heavy cream
½ teaspoon salt
¼ teaspoon pepper
¼ pound butter, softened

In a 3-quart saucepan, reduce the white wine, vinegar, and shallots so that only 2 tablespoons of liquid remain. Add the cream and continue to reduce to 1½ cups (about 15 minutes). Be careful of overreducing or sauce will eventually separate into butter floating on cream. (If a perfectly smooth sauce is desired, strain to remove shallots.) Add the salt and pepper. The recipe can be made ahead to this point and held or refrigerated until serving. When ready to serve, gently reheat and whisk in the softened butter, bit by bit, while stirring constantly.

VARIATIONS
Curried: Add 1 tablespoon of good curry powder to the wine and vinegar mixture before reducing. Serve, as we have at Frog, on poached salmon scallops garnished with medallions of lobster meat and black caviar.
Herbed: Add 1 tablespoon minced fresh herbs of choice just before serving.

Here is an idea for keeping fragile sauces such as Beurre Blanc or hollandaise warm while readying the rest of the meal. Put the hot sauce into a handy thermos until ready to serve. This should help you feel less pressured timewise, and you won't have to worry about reheating the sauce and having it "break."

103

ORANGE-TARRAGON
BEURRE BLANC

Makes about 1 cup

A lovely variation on the Beurre Blanc theme that has drawn raves at Frog when served over red snapper or asparagus in puff pastry.

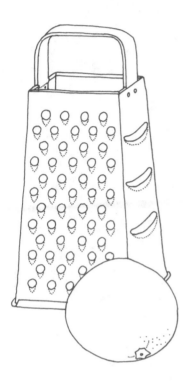

½ cup fresh orange juice
⅓ cup minced shallots
½ cup white wine vinegar
1 cup dry white wine
3 tablespoons minced fresh tarragon or 1 tablespoon
   dried
1½ teaspoons grated orange rind
2 tablespoons heavy cream
10 tablespoons butter, at room temperature, cut into bits
¼ teaspoon salt
¼ teaspoon pepper
pinch of cayenne pepper

In a small saucepan, reduce the orange juice with the shallots until almost dry. Toward the end of the reduction process, tilt the pan back and forth so that the orange juice won't burn. Add the vinegar, wine, and tarragon and reduce to ½ cup of liquid. Off the heat, add the orange rind and cream and whisk in the butter bit by bit until all is incorporated. Season with the salt, pepper, and cayenne.

Seafood Entrées

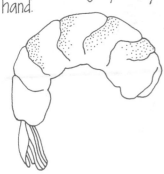

To butterfly a shrimp, first peel and devein it, leaving the tail intact. Then, with a small, sharp knife, cut the shrimp open (but NOT in half) along its inner curve. Press open and flatten slightly with your hand.

SHRIMP WITH SOY, GARLIC, GINGER, AND LEMON

Serves 2

This is one of the nicest ways we know to prepare shrimp, and the fact that it is one of Frog's most requested recipes is added testimony. The flavors are tart and refreshing, with the sparkle of lemon and fresh ginger and the peppery crunch of watercress added at the last possible moment.

MARINADE

18 shelled, butterflied shrimp with the tails left on (about ¾ pound unshelled shrimp)
1½ tablespoons soy sauce
1 tablespoon minced fresh ginger
2 tablespoons lemon juice
1 teaspoon minced garlic
¼ teaspoon pepper
2 tablespoons medium-dry sherry

SAUCE

The strained marinade
⅓ cup water
2 teaspoons cornstarch

SAUTÉ

2 tablespoons corn oil
1 teaspoon minced garlic
¾ teaspoon minced fresh ginger
½ cup cubed sweet red peppers
½ bunch watercress with 1″ of the stems cut off
Hot cooked rice or oriental noodles

MARINADE

Combine the shrimp with the marinade ingredients. Let sit 1 hour, then drain the shrimp, reserving the marinade. Strain marinade and set aside.

SAUCE

Combine the marinade with the water and cornstarch. Stir to dissolve the cornstarch. Bring the mixture to a boil stirring and cook, stirring, for 1 minute. Set aside.

SAUTÉ

Heat the corn oil in a large skillet or sauté pan. Add the shrimp, garlic, and ginger and stir-fry over high heat for 30 seconds. Add the peppers and stir-fry another 30 seconds. Add the sauce and bring the mixture to a boil while stirring. Remove the pan from the heat and immediately stir in the watercress. Serve at once over rice or oriental noodles.

LOBSTER CURRY WITH
ASPARAGUS AND SUNCHOKES

Serves 4

This was created for Steven's wedding dinner.

2 cups cooked lobster meat in bite-size pieces
½ pound asparagus, trimmed, blanched, and cut into
  bite-size pieces
¼ pound Jerusalem artichokes (Sunchokes), peeled,
  blanched, and cut into bite-size pieces
⅓ cup finely chopped shallots
1½ cups dry white wine
½ cup brandy
OPT. ⅓ cup cooking liquid from lobster
1 tablespoon curry powder
2¼ cups heavy cream
½ teaspoon salt
¼ teaspoon pepper
⅛ teaspoon cayenne pepper
Hot cooked rice

Have ready the lobster, asparagus, and Jerusalem artichokes. Combine the shallots, wine, brandy, the optional
cooking liquid, and curry powder in a 3-quart saucepan
and reduce over medium heat to ½ cup. Strain the reduction
and return it to the pan. (If necessary, add water to make
it ½ cup.) Add the cream. Reduce this to 1¾ cups over
medium heat. Season with salt, pepper, and cayenne. Add
the reserved lobster, asparagus, and Jerusalem artichokes.
Heat through and serve at once with rice.

VARIATION
Fresh water chestnuts, peeled, and sliced but not blanched,
are a delicious substitute for the Jerusalem artichokes.

SUNCHOKE

Alias Jerusalem artichoke and topinambour... that funny-looking tuber like a cross between a potato and a ginger-root. It's not even of the artichoke family (though the flavor is reminiscent of artichoke hearts), but instead is the root of a variety of sunflower. Its origins are North American, but its history is primarily European since it was in France and Italy that the sunchoke was truly cultivated and adopted into their cuisines. ☆ Crunchy, nutty, and delicately sweet, the sunchoke is enjoyed both raw and cooked in salads, soups, braised vegetable dishes, etc.

EASTERN SHORE CRAB CAKES

Serves 6

An enormously popular entrée at The Commissary, Eastern Shore Crab Cakes are easy to prepare, genuinely "crabby," and wonderfully reminiscent (thanks to the Old Bay seasoning) of Maryland's fabulous peppery steamed blue crabs.

¾ pound all-purpose potatoes, peeled and diced
¼ cup finely chopped onion
½ cup finely chopped celery
2 tablespoons butter
3 eggs, lightly beaten
3 tablespoons lemon juice
½ teaspoon pepper
¾ teaspoon salt
1 teaspoon Old Bay seasoning
½ teaspoon Tabasco
2 tablespoons minced parsley
OPT. 2 tablespoons minced fresh dill
1 pound crabmeat (lump, backfin, or claw) picked over
    for shell
¼ cup fine dry bread crumbs
Additional dry bread crumbs for coating
Vegetable oil for deep frying

In Maryland, Old Bay is the seasoning of choice when it comes to crabs. Its spiciness is best countered by beer, and we've found all sorts of other uses for it. Give tartar sauce a little pizzazz with it, add a dash to your Bloody Mary, combine with garlic butter to drizzle over fish or grilled chicken, make Old Bay butter for popcorn…

Cook the potatoes in boiling water. Meanwhile, sauté the onion and the celery in the butter until tender but not browned. Drain the potatoes and mash or rice them. Stir in the onion-celery mixture. Combine the eggs, lemon juice, seasonings, parsley, and dill and add to the potatoes. Carefully fold in the crabmeat along with the ¼ cup of bread crumbs. For easier handling, chill the mixture for ½ hour or so.

Preheat the oven to 250°. Form the crab mixture into 12 patties, each about 3" in diameter and ½" thick. Coat the patties with the additional bread crumbs. Using a mini-fryer or deep saucepan, heat at least a 2" depth of vegetable oil to 350°. Deep-fry the crab cakes, several at a time, for about 5 minutes or until they are a deep golden brown. Drain on paper toweling and keep warm in the oven while cooking the rest.

SERVING SUGGESTIONS AND VARIATIONS
Serve with lemon wedges, parsley, and your choice of cocktail, chili, or tartar sauce or with Pimento Mayonnaise.

Another good accompaniment (aside from lots of cold beer) is our Mixed Vegetable Slaw.

Instead of deep-frying the crab cakes, you can sauté them on both sides in butter and oil.

SEAFOOD STEW WITH AÏOLI

Serves 8

As one of Frog's signature dishes, this worthy descendent of the infamous bouillabaisse could hardly be more seductive in aroma and appearance. And, as if that weren't enough, each serving sports an accompanying dollop of that wonderful garlicky mayonnaise called *aïoli* to stir into the stew or spread on toasted slices of French bread. This stew can easily be made at home, especially since the stock, tomato base, and aïoli can all be made ahead of time.

FISH STOCK
2 pounds fish bones (from nonoily type fish)
3 cups dry white wine
1 cup water
2 carrots cut into chunks
2 celery stalks cut into chunks
1 small onion, coarsely chopped
1 small bunch parsley
½ teaspoon dried thyme
1 bay leaf

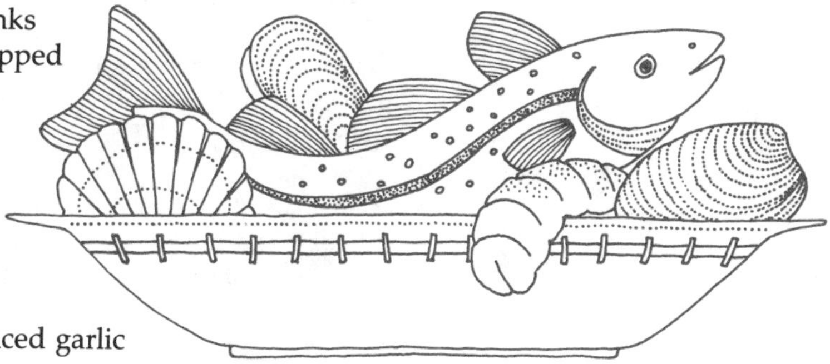

AÏOLI
1 egg yolk
¾ cup olive oil
2 teaspoons very finely minced garlic
2 tablespoons lemon juice
⅜ teaspoon salt
½ teaspoon pepper
⅛ teaspoon cayenne pepper

TOMATO BASE
⅓ cup olive oil
1½ cups chopped onions
2 tablespoons minced garlic
2 (28-ounce) cans tomatoes in heavy purée
1 (28-ounce) can tomatoes in juice
¼ cup minced parsley
1 tablespoon dried oregano
2 tablespoons fennel seed
1 tablespoon dried basil
½ teaspoon dried thyme
½ teaspoon salt
½ teaspoon pepper
2 cups fish stock (see above)
¼ teaspoon cayenne pepper
¼ cup Pernod

SEAFOOD AND ASSEMBLY
16 steamer clams, scrubbed
16 mussels, scrubbed
1 pound sea scallops
1 pound cod, rock bass, or other white, firm-fleshed fish
   cut into 8 pieces
24 medium shrimp, peeled, deveined, and butterflied
16 slices French bread, toasted

FISH STOCK
Put all ingredients in a small stockpot and bring to a boil over high heat. Reduce the heat and simmer 30 minutes. Strain through a colander lined with cheesecloth and discard the solids. Reduce the strained liquid to 2 cups.

AÏOLI
Whisk the egg yolk until light-colored. Very gradually whisk in the olive oil (almost drop by drop at first). When all the oil has been added and the mayonnaise is thick and glossy, add the garlic, lemon juice, salt, pepper, and cayenne.

TOMATO BASE
In a large saucepan, heat the olive oil. Add the onions and garlic and sauté until they soften. Add the tomatoes, parsley, herbs, pernod, and fish stock. Simmer, uncovered, for 45 minutes, stirring occasionally. Cool, cover, and refrigerate up to 2 days if not using immediately.

SEAFOOD
Twenty minutes before serving, bring the tomato base to a boil and add the clams. After 5 minutes add the mussels. Cook until the clams and mussels have fully opened. Add scallops, fish, and shrimp and cook 2–3 minutes or until the seafood is just done.

Ladle the stew at once into large soup dishes. Dust with parsley, if desired. Pass the toasted French bread and aïoli separately.

POACHED SALMON SCALLOPS WITH LEEKS, CUCUMBERS, AND SORREL BEURRE BLANC

Serves 4

This is a lovely example of a Frog reinterpretation of a now classic French dish, salmon in sorrel sauce. All pink and pale green, with a delicate freshness to match, our recipe would be a fine choice for a special dinner.

STOCK
1 cup dry white wine
½ cup water
3 tablespoons minced shallots

SORREL BEURRE BLANC
1 cup dry white wine
½ cup white wine vinegar
⅓ cup minced shallots
2 cups heavy cream
½ teaspoon salt
¼ teaspoon pepper
¼ pound soft butter
¼ cup finely chopped sorrel

SALMON
4 (6-ounce) salmon scallops
2 tablespoons butter
1 tablespoon minced shallots
1 cup peeled, seeded, and very thinly sliced cucumber
2 cups trimmed, julienned, and well-rinsed leeks
¼ teaspoon salt
¼ teaspoon pepper

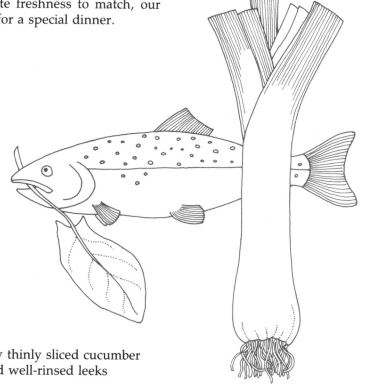

STOCK
Combine the ingredients in a small saucepan, cover, and simmer 15 minutes.

SORREL BEURRE BLANC
Following the basic method for Beurre Blanc on p. 103 up to the point *before* the butter is added using the ingredients listed here for Sorrel Beurre Blanc. Set on the back of the stove until just before serving.

SALMON
The salmon scallops should be large and thin enough so that each can be easily folded in half to form a pocket; if necessary, put each piece between wax paper and gently pound until the scallop is ⅛"–¼" thick. Set aside.
  Preheat the oven to 450°. Melt the butter in a sauté pan. Add the shallots and sauté until they have softened. Add

Perennial sorrel grows easily in most gardens when the weather isn't too hot and dry. Having it on hand is a real treat because aside from the familiar sorrel soup, sauce, purée, etc, you have it right there begging to be cut into a chiffonade for garnishing eggs, cream soups, salads and fish. Its lemony-green flavor is a sure shot of vibrancy.

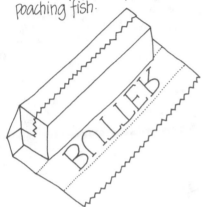

Save the waxed paper wrappers from sticks or pounds of butter, and you will have already buttered papers to put over poaching fish.

the cucumber, leeks, salt, and pepper and sauté until tender, about 4 minutes.

Put a quarter of the vegetable mixture on half of each salmon scallop and fold the other half over to enclose the filling. Arrange the packets in a buttered baking dish or individual casseroles. Pour the stock over the salmon. Cover flush with buttered parchment paper or wax paper and bake for 12–15 minutes or until just cooked through.

TO SERVE

While the fish is poaching, bring the Beurre Blanc reduction to a boil. Turn off the heat and whisk in the softened butter as described in the basic recipe. Add the sorrel. Keep warm (but don't allow to boil!) until the fish is done.

When the fish is done, remove it from the poaching liquid with a slotted spatula. Blot well with paper toweling before arranging on the dinner plates. Spoon 2 ounces of the Sorrel Beurre Blanc over each portion. Serve at once.

TURBANS OF SOLE STUFFED WITH SMOKED SALMON MOUSSE IN CURRIED BEURRE BLANC
Serves 4

SMOKED SALMON MOUSSE
½ pound scallops, rinsed
1 egg white
3 ounces smoked salmon
⅛ teaspoon pepper
Pinch of cayenne pepper
½ teaspoon salt
½ cup heavy cream

SOLE TURBANS
4 (4–5-ounce) fillets of sole (or flounder)
¼ cup dry white wine
¼ cup water
1 tablespoon minced shallots

CURRIED BEURRE BLANC
¾ cup dry white wine
⅓ cup white wine vinegar
3 tablespoons finely minced shallots
2 teaspoons curry powder
1½ cups heavy cream
¼ teaspoon salt
¼ teaspoon pepper
6 tablespoons butter, softened
1 tablespoon minced parsley

SMOKED SALMON MOUSSE

Combine all ingredients except the cream in a food processor. Whiz until smooth. Turn into a bowl and stir in the cream. Cover and refrigerate until ready to use.

SOLE TURBANS

Halve each fillet lengthwise along its seam. Roll each piece, darker side in, into a cylinder, leaving a core about 1" in diameter. Stand the cylinders, cut sides down, in a buttered baking dish. Spoon the mousse into a pastry bag (no need to use a tip) and pipe it into the center core of each fish roll. Let the mousse come a little bit above the top of each roll.

Preheat the oven to 400°. Pour the wine, water, and shallots around the turbans, cover the dish with buttered wax paper and bake for 13–15 minutes or until the mousse is firm when touched.

CURRIED BEURRE BLANC

While the fish is poaching in the oven, combine the wine, vinegar, shallots, and curry powder in a 2-quart saucepan. Bring to a boil and cook over medium heat until it has reduced to about ¼ cup. (Tilt the pan back and forth to keep the juices from burning around the edges.) Add the cream, salt, and pepper and cook until thickened over medium-high heat for about 10 minutes. Strain and return to the pan. Bring the sauce just to the boiling point. Turn off the heat. Whisk in the butter bit by bit. Put two ounces of sauce onto each of 4 plates. Blot the bottoms of the turbans with paper toweling and place two in each pool of sauce. Garnish with the minced parsley.

NOTES

The mousse can be made a day ahead and refrigerated. The turbans can be assembled and refrigerated up to 8 hours in advance. And the sauce can be made three days in advance, except for the addition of the butter. Bring the sauce to a boil and whisk in the butter just before serving. These turbans also make a lovely first course when served one to a person.

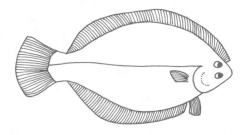

PARMESAN FRIED FLOUNDER
WITH TOMATO-BASIL BUTTER   *Serves 4–5*

TOMATO-BASIL BUTTER
1 tablespoon olive oil
1½ cups peeled, seeded, and chopped tomatoes (about 1 pound)
2 teaspoons minced garlic
½ cup butter, softened
2 teaspoons grated lemon rind
½ teaspoon salt
⅛ teaspoon pepper
¼ cup minced fresh basil

FISH
½ cup flour
¾ teaspoon salt
½ teaspoon pepper
¾ cup dry bread crumbs
¾ cup grated Parmesan cheese
2 eggs, beaten
¼ cup butter
¼ cup olive oil
1 pound flounder fillets

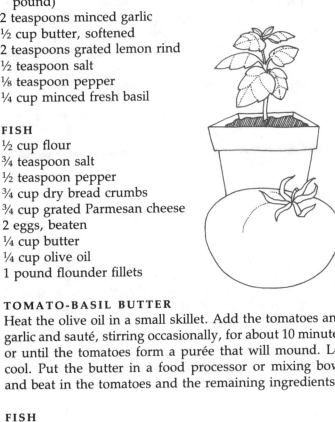

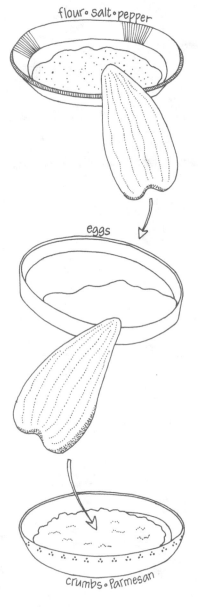

flour • salt • pepper

eggs

crumbs • Parmesan

TOMATO-BASIL BUTTER
Heat the olive oil in a small skillet. Add the tomatoes and garlic and sauté, stirring occasionally, for about 10 minutes or until the tomatoes form a purée that will mound. Let cool. Put the butter in a food processor or mixing bowl and beat in the tomatoes and the remaining ingredients.

FISH
Combine the flour, salt, and pepper in a shallow bowl or pie tin. Mix the crumbs and Parmesan cheese in another bowl. Have the eggs ready in a third shallow dish. Since the fish needs to cook in a single layer, use one very large skillet or 2 slightly smaller ones. Heat the butter and olive oil in the skillet. Dip the fish first in the seasoned flour and shake off the excess. Then dip in the egg and let the excess drip off. Finally coat completely with the Parmesan crumbs. Sauté the fillets over medium heat for 2 minutes on each side and serve at once topped with Tomato-Basil Butter.

NOTES AND VARIATIONS
The Tomato-Basil Butter can be made up to three days in advance, but it is best used at room temperature so that it will melt quickly over the fish. It is also delicious on chicken or vegetables.

114

Substitute parsley or 2 tablespoons fresh tarragon for the basil.

JAPANESE GRILLED MARINATED SWORDFISH

Serves 4

Swordfish, by nature meaty, lean, and often dry, gains both flavor and moisture from a brief bath in this sesame-oil-based marinade before hitting the grill. Steven has long been enamored of charcoal-grilled foods and devised this particular dish for an important catered party where he served the fish with grilled baby eggplants that had also been dipped in the marinade. About the same time, new Frog opened with a charcoal grill as an essential member of the kitchen *batterie*, and this recipe quickly was given its restaurant debut.

Don't be alarmed at the amount of red pepper flakes in the marinade. They really add only a little fire.

½ cup sesame oil
1 cup tamari or regular soy sauce
½ cup lime juice
¼ cup mirin (sweet cooking sake)
2 tablespoons minced garlic
2 tablespoons minced fresh ginger
3 tablespoons crushed red pepper flakes
4 (1"-thick) swordfish steaks, about 8 ounces each
Vegetable oil

Forty-five minutes before serving, light a charcoal fire. Half an hour before serving, cover the fish steaks with the sesame oil, tamari, lime juice, mirin, garlic, ginger, and pepper flakes. Let them sit 10 minutes in the marinade. Remove the fish steaks from the marinade and lightly dip in vegetable oil. Set the steaks on grill above glowing coals. Grill for 5–7 minutes on each side, depending on the thickness and the distance from coals. Brush with the marinade and serve, garnished with lime slices.

NOTE
The marinade can be kept in the refrigerator up to two weeks and used again. Try it on other fish or chicken to be grilled, broiled, or baked.

115

BLUEFISH PROVENÇALE

Serves 6

Summer brings out the bluefish in full force along our neck of the eastern seaboard. If you are one of those cooks "blessed" with a fisherman for a family member or neighbor who is forever proudly presenting you with freshly caught bluefish, here is a recipe for you. This is one of the most popular seafood *plats* at The Commissary. The Provençale sauce, consisting of a thick, aromatic tomato purée combined with a chunky tomato sauté spiked with olives, truly complements the full-flavored fish. The resulting combination is delicious—even to those who have sworn that they won't look at another blue.

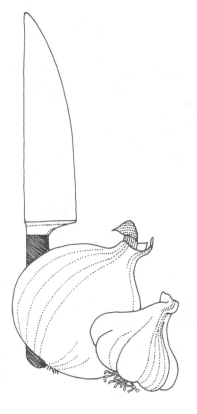

TOMATO PURÉE
2 tablespoons olive oil
2 cups chopped onions
2 teaspoons minced garlic
1 pound tomatoes, chopped (about 3 cups)
½ cup dry white wine
1 tablespoon lime juice
½ teaspoon salt
¾ teaspoon chopped fresh rosemary or ¼ teaspoon dried
¾ teaspoon chopped fresh basil or ¼ teaspoon dried
¼ teaspoon ground fennel
¼ teaspoon grated lime rind
¼ teaspoon pepper
⅜ teaspoon fresh thyme leaves or ⅛ teaspoon dried
⅛ teaspoon cayenne pepper
1 bay leaf

BLUEFISH
6 (6-ounce) skinless bluefish fillets
1 tablespoon lime juice
½ teaspoon salt

TOMATO SAUTÉ AND ASSEMBLY
2 tablespoons olive oil
1 cup finely chopped onions
1½ teaspoons minced garlic
½ teaspoon salt
½ teaspoon pepper
1 pound tomatoes, chopped (about 3 cups)
2 tablespoons chopped Greek black olives
OPT. Minced parsley

TOMATO PURÉE

In a large saucepan, heat the olive oil. Add the onions and then the garlic. Sauté until soft and translucent. Add the tomatoes, cover the pan, and let the mixture simmer 15 minutes. Add the remaining ingredients and simmer uncovered until very thick. Remove the bay leaf and purée the mixture in a food processor or through a food mill. Strain and set aside.

BLUEFISH

Preheat the oven to 400°. Arrange the fish in a single layer in a baking pan. Sprinkle with the lime juice and salt. Bake for 12–15 minutes.

TOMATO SAUTÉ AND ASSEMBLY

While the fish is baking, heat the olive oil in a large skillet. Add the onions, salt, pepper, and garlic. Sauté until the onions are wilted and translucent. Add the tomatoes, olives, and reserved purée. Keep hot. As soon as the fish is done, serve it topped with the hot sauce. Dust with minced parsley.

SERVING SUGGESTIONS

This is especially good when accompanied by Oven-Roasted Potatoes.

Use the sauce for other dishes, too, such as on eggs, chicken, eggplant, and other fish.

BAKED BLUEFISH WITH ONIONS, BACON, AND HORSERADISH SAUCE   *Serves 4*

Golden sautéed onions, crispets of smoky bacon, the bite of a creamy horseradish sauce . . . could there be a more savory combination? The mouth and mind go haywire thinking of other possible uses for this topping: burgers, grilled chicken breast, cooked broccoli, and broiled sword-fish to start the list.

HORSERADISH SAUCE
1 tablespoon minced shallots
½ cup dry white wine
1 cup heavy cream
2½ tablespoons drained horseradish
¼ teaspoon salt
¼ teaspoon pepper
2 tablespoons butter, at room temperature

FISH
¼ pound bacon in ½" dice
2 tablespoons butter
1 cup roughly chopped onions
4 (5–6-ounce) skinned bluefish fillets
Minced parsley for garnish

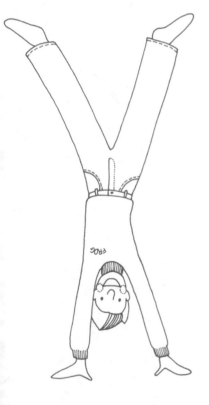

HORSERADISH SAUCE
Combine the shallots and wine in a small saucepan and reduce to 2–3 tablespoons. Add the cream, horseradish, salt, and pepper and simmer until thickened. (The butter will be added just before serving.)

FISH
Preheat the oven to 400°. Fry the bacon until crisp, drain, and set aside. Heat ⅓ of the butter in a sauté pan, add the onions, sauté until translucent, and add to the bacon. Arrange the fish in a shallow buttered baking pan and dot with the rest of the butter. Bake for 12–15 minutes. While the fish is baking, bring the sauce to a boil. Stir the softened butter into it off the heat. Gently reheat the onion-bacon mixture. When the fish is done, transfer it to dinner plates, top each portion with about 2 ounces of the sauce, and sprinkle with the bacon-onion mixture. Dust with minced parsley. Serve at once.

Poultry Entrées

What will it be today, Frog? A nice meaty duck to roast with your curry glaze? I've got some nice fat chicken breasts just right for stuffing, or maybe you're thinking of your Siamese Chicken Cu

SWENSON'S POULTRY
SINCE 1852

CHICKEN BREASTS
WITH ROQUEFORT FILLING

Serves 4

This dish lends itself well to making in quantity for a party
. . . in which case bring the filling to room temperature
and put into a pastry tube so that you can easily and
quickly fill a number of portions.

ROQUEFORT FILLING
2 ounces cream cheese
2 ounces Roquefort cheese
1 teaspoon minced shallots
¼ teaspoon minced garlic
1½ teaspoons minced parsley
1 teaspoon minced dill
¼ teaspoon pepper

chicken breast with pocket for filling

CHICKEN
¼ cup flour
½ teaspoon salt
½ teaspoon pepper
1 egg, beaten
¾ cup fine, dry bread crumbs
2 tablespoons butter, melted
4 chicken breast halves, bone in and skin on

ROQUEFORT FILLING
Cream all the ingredients and chill. Shape into four 2½"
fingers when ready to use.

CHICKEN
Preheat the oven to 375°. Combine the flour, salt, and
pepper in a shallow bowl. Put the egg in a second bowl.
Combine the crumbs and butter in a third. Roll each
chicken breast sequentially in the flour, egg, and crumbs.
Shake off excess crumbs and arrange in a greased baking
pan. Bake for 25–35 minutes.

TO SERVE
When the chicken is done, take each breast and lift away
the meat from the bone on the upper part where there is
a natural separation. Tuck 1 portion of filling into each
"pocket." Serve at once.

BRUSSELS
SPROUTS
with BACON
At The Commissary,
this is what we most often
serve with Chicken Breasts
with Roquefort Filling.

Cook until crisp, drain and
crumble 4 slices of bacon. Cut
¾ pound of brussels sprouts
in half vertically and blanche
until crisp-tender. Drain and
reheat in 3 tablespoons butter. Season with salt and
pepper, sprinkle on the bacon,
and serve.

CHICKEN FLORENTINE

Serves 8

A beautifully simple dish—perfect for easy entertaining. The spinach implied in the name "Florentine" appears in the bright green pasta and is repeated in the delicate Spinach-Flecked Mornay Sauce. Brilliant red tomato slices are a vibrant finishing touch.

SPINACH-FLECKED MORNAY SAUCE
⅓ of a 10-ounce bag fresh spinach
¼ cup butter
¼ cup flour
2¾ cups milk
¾ teaspoon salt
¾ teaspoon pepper
⅛ teaspoon nutmeg
⅛ teaspoon cayenne pepper
½ cup grated Parmesan cheese

CHICKEN AND ASSEMBLY
2 large tomatoes
1 pound fresh spinach pasta
1 tablespoon olive oil
8 boneless skinless chicken breast halves
½ cup flour seasoned with 1 teaspoon each salt and
   pepper
¼ cup clarified butter (see p. 124 for how to make)
¼ cup whole butter
½ teaspoon salt
¼ teaspoon pepper

SPINACH-FLECKED MORNAY SAUCE
Wash the spinach and cook it in the water still clinging to its leaves until wilted. Rinse under cold water and drain. Squeeze very dry and finely chop the spinach. Set aside. Melt the butter in a saucepan. Whisk in the flour and cook and stir over low heat for 2–3 minutes. Slowly whisk in the milk. Simmer and stir until thick, then add the seasonings and cheese. Simmer, whisking occasionally, until smooth, then add the spinach and set aside.

CHICKEN AND ASSEMBLY
Preheat the oven to 200°. Cut 8 thick slices from the tomatoes and set aside. Cook the pasta in a large pot of boiling salted water for several minutes until *al dente*. Drain the pasta, rinse with cold water, drain well, and toss with the olive oil. Set aside.

Coat the chicken breasts with the seasoned flour and shake off the excess. Heat the clarified butter in a large skillet. Sauté the chicken over medium heat for 5 minutes and then turn and sauté for 3–5 minutes more or until just done. Remove the chicken from the skillet to a baking pan and keep warm in the oven. Gently reheat the sauce. Melt the ¼ cup of whole butter in a saucepan, add the pasta, salt, and pepper and combine well. Cover the saucepan and gently reheat the pasta, stirring occasionally. Briefly sauté the tomato slices on both sides in the skillet, adding a little more butter if necessary.

To serve, arrange each chicken breast on a nest of the spinach pasta, spoon some of the sauce over the chicken and top with a sautéed tomato slice.

CURRIED CHICKEN BREASTS WITH TOMATOES AND FRAGRANT YOGURT SAUCE

Serves 6

YOGURT SAUCE
2 tablespoons corn oil
1 tablespoon minced fresh ginger
2 teaspoons minced garlic
¾ teaspoon curry powder
2 teaspoons ground fennel
½ teaspoon ground cumin
½ teaspoon ground coriander
2 cups plain yogurt
1¼ teaspoons salt
¼ teaspoon pepper
1 teaspoon lemon juice
1 tablespoon chopped fresh coriander

CHICKEN
¾ cup flour
4 teaspoons salt
2 teaspoons pepper
2 teaspoons curry powder
¾ teaspoon ground coriander
¼ teaspoon ground cumin
¼ teaspoon cinnamon
¼ teaspoon nutmeg
¼ teaspoon ground cardamom
3 eggs
2 teaspoons turmeric
12 tomato slices, each ¼" thick
½ cup clarified butter (see p. 124 for how to make)
6 boneless, skinless chicken breast halves (about 4–5 ounces each) pounded between sheets of wax paper to a thickness of ¼"
1 tablespoon minced fresh coriander or parsley

122

Combine all ingredients for the sauce and set aside. Serve at room temperature.

CHICKEN
Sift together the flour, salt, pepper, curry powder, and spices in a wide, shallow bowl or pie tin. Beat the eggs with the turmeric and put in another shallow container. Heat the tomato slices on a rimmed tray in a 350° oven for 5 minutes. Heat the clarified butter until hot in 2 skillets (or other pans large enough to hold the chicken in a single layer). Dip each piece of chicken first in the flour mixture, shake off the excess, and then coat with the egg, letting the excess drip off. Sauté the chicken for 2 minutes on each side over medium heat. Serve at once topped with 2 warm tomato slices, each drizzled with some of the sauce and dusted with the minced coriander. Pass the extra sauce at the table.

PISTACHIO CHICKEN BREASTS
WITH HERB-GARLIC CHEESE FILLING *Serves 8*

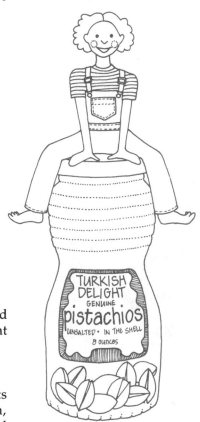

HERB-GARLIC CHEESE FILLING
8 ounces cream cheese, softened
1 teaspoon minced garlic
1 tablespoon minced parsley
½ teaspoon pepper
1–2 tablespoons minced fresh basil or ½ teaspoon dried
¼ teaspoon salt

CHICKEN
8 boneless, skinless chicken breast halves
½ cup flour combined with 1 teaspoon each salt and
    pepper
2 eggs, beaten
1½ cups finely ground pistachio nuts (about 7 ounces
    shelled)
¼ cup clarified butter (see p. 124 for how to make)

FILLING
Combine the cream cheese with the garlic, herbs, and seasonings. Chill until firm and then form into eight 2"-long cylinders. Keep refrigerated until ready to use.

CHICKEN
Preheat the oven to 350°. Gently pound chicken breasts between wax paper until each is ¼" thick. For each portion, put 1 portion of the filling along 1 edge of a pounded

CELEBRATE THE WINTER SEASON

Invite your friends for supper after the Big Game, to help trim the tree... or simply to toast the holiday season!

Hot Spiked Cider
Cheese Board
Curried Walnuts*
Chicken Breasts with Brandied
  Mustard Cream Sauce*
Brown and Wild Rice Pilaf
Steamed Carrots and Broccoli
Mixed Greens with Walnuts,
  Apples, & Cider Vinaigrette*
Warm Crusty Rolls
Pumpkin Mousse *

*See Index for recipe page number.

CLARIFYING BUTTER

Our favorite way is to put the butter in a stainless steel bowl in a 200° oven. After an hour, skim off the crust on top. Put the bowl in the refrigerator. When the butter has resolidified, turn it out of the bowl. Scrape off and discard the white layer of milk solids (this is what burns during frying). Wrap and refrigerate the yellow layer of clarified butter until needed. One pound of butter yields about 14 ounces of clarified butter.

milky solids

clarified butter

chicken breast and fold and roll the chicken over the filling to completely and securely enclose it. Repeat with each piece of chicken. Roll each piece sequentially in the seasoned flour, the beaten eggs, and finally the ground pistachios and sauté in the clarified butter over medium heat for 1–2 minutes on each side or until lightly browned. Transfer the chicken to a baking pan and put in the preheated oven for 15–20 minutes. Serve hot.

CHICKEN BREASTS WITH BRANDIED MUSTARD CREAM SAUCE

Serves 4

The piquant, mustard-tinged sauce is especially good and would be equally at home on sautéed veal, calf's liver, or fish.

4 boneless chicken breast halves, skinned
½ cup flour seasoned with 1 teaspoon each salt and
  pepper
¼ cup clarified butter (see p. 124 for how to make)
2 teaspoons minced shallots
½ cup dry vermouth
2 tablespoons brandy
5 teaspoons Dijon mustard
¼ teaspoon salt
¼ teaspoon pepper
1 cup heavy cream
2 teaspoons minced parsley

Preheat the oven to 200°. Dredge the chicken in the seasoned flour and shake off the excess. Heat the butter in a skillet. Add the chicken and sauté over medium heat for 5 minutes. Turn the chicken and sauté 3–5 minutes more or until just done. Remove from the skillet and keep warm in the oven. Discard any butter left in the pan. Add the shallots, vermouth, and brandy to the pan; turn the heat to high and reduce the liquid to 3 tablespoons while stirring to scrape up any browned bits. Whisk in the mustard. Add the salt, pepper, and cream and cook over medium-high heat for 2–3 minutes, stirring occasionally, until mixture is the consistency of a light gravy. Transfer the chicken from the oven to dinner plates, mask with the sauce, dust with parsley, and serve at once.

SWISS CHARD–STUFFED
CHICKEN BREASTS
WITH LEMON PECAN SAUCE

Serves 4

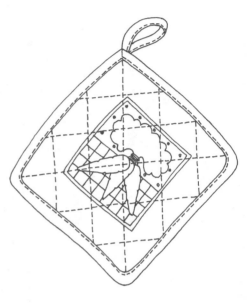

FILLING AND CHICKEN
2 pounds Swiss chard
¼ cup butter
3 tablespoons minced scallions
¼ cup coarsely chopped, lightly toasted pecans
¼ teaspoon salt
⅛ teaspoon Tabasco
⅛ teaspoon pepper
4 boneless chicken breast halves with skin (about 2
  pounds)
2 tablespoons melted butter

LEMON PECAN SAUCE
¾ cup butter
½ cup coarsely chopped, lightly toasted pecans
¼ teaspoon salt
⅛ teaspoon Tabasco
2 tablespoons lemon juice
¼ cup minced parsley

FILLING AND CHICKEN
Destem the Swiss chard and wash it well. Cook it in the water still clinging to its leaves in a large pan, stirring all the while, until it is wilted. Rinse under cold water, squeeze very dry, and finely chop. Heat the butter in a skillet and add the chard and scallions. Sauté, stirring occasionally, for 2–3 minutes over low heat. Add the pecans, salt, Tabasco, and pepper and set aside.

Put each chicken breast, skin side up, between 2 sheets of wax paper and pound against the grain with a rolling pin or meat pounder to a thickness of ¼". **Preheat the oven to 400°.** Turn each packet of chicken and wax paper upside down and remove the top piece of paper. Put ¼ of the filling, shaped into an oval, on the chicken and roll up the chicken the long way, using the bottom piece of paper as a helper. Put each piece seam side down in a buttered baking dish. Brush chicken pieces with the 2 tablespoons melted butter and bake for 20–25 minutes or until the skin begins to color.

SAUCE
While the chicken is baking, melt the butter. Add the pecans, salt, and Tabasco and heat through but do not boil. Just before serving, stir in the lemon juice and parsley. Spoon over the chicken and serve.

Try other greens in place of the chard—mustard greens, dandelion leaves, or spinach would be good. You will need 1 cup blanched, squeezed dry, and chopped greens for the filling.

CHICKEN BREASTS WITH APPLES AND CIDER CREAM SAUCE

Serves 6

The first whiff of autumn makes us think of this dish. (So does the Art Museum, where we turned out eight hundred portions in twelve minutes for a catered party there.) Try the sauce, too, with roast chicken, Cornish hens, or pork.

CIDER CREAM SAUCE
2 cups filtered cider
2 tablespoons Dijon mustard
2½ cups heavy cream
⅛ teaspoon cayenne pepper
¼ teaspoon salt
¼ teaspoon pepper

CHICKEN
6 boneless chicken breast halves, skinned
¾ cup flour seasoned with 1½ teaspoons each salt and
  pepper
½ cup clarified butter (see p. 124 for how to make)
2 large tart apples, cored and cut into ¼"-thick circles

SAUCE
In a 2-quart saucepan, reduce the cider to ½ cup. Whisk in the mustard and cream and reduce to about 2 cups over medium-high heat or until thickened like a sauce. Add the seasonings and set aside.

CHICKEN AND ASSEMBLY
Preheat the oven to 200°. Dredge the chicken in the seasoned flour and shake off the excess. Heat 6 tablespoons of the butter in a large skillet. Add the chicken and sauté on one side over medium heat for 5 minutes. Turn the chicken and sauté for 3–5 minutes more or until just done. Remove the chicken from the skillet and keep warm in the oven.

Add the remaining 2 tablespoons of butter to the pan. Add the apple slices and sauté for 3–5 minutes or until just tender. Remove the apples and keep them warm. Pour off any excess butter from the pan. Add the cider cream

sauce to the pan and heat through while scraping up any little browned bits from the bottom of the pan. When hot, serve over the chicken breasts and garnish with the apple rings.

SMOKED CHICKEN IN BUCKWHEAT CRÊPES WITH HORSERADISH CREAM SAUCE

Serves 6

These wonderful crêpes were devised for the opening menu of the Commissary's Piano Bar, and helped inspire the Piano Bar's tag line then: "Cocktails, Calla Lilies, Crêpes and Cole Porter." While today the menu there features hearty sandwiches, this particular dish is much too good to be forgotten.

CRÊPES
¾ cup milk
¾ cup water
1 egg
1 egg yolk
¼ cup melted butter
⅔ cup white flour
⅓ cup buckwheat flour
½ teaspoon salt

FILLING
2 cups diced smoked chicken breast (½" dice) (cooked unsmoked chicken may also be used)
2 cups coarsely chopped broccoli, blanched
6 tablespoons butter
⅔ cup finely chopped onions
6 tablespoons flour
2 cups chicken stock
2 tablespoons drained horseradish
½ teaspoon pepper
¼–½ teaspoon salt

HORSERADISH CREAM SAUCE
2 tablespoons minced shallots
1 cup dry white wine
2 cups heavy cream
⅓ cup drained horseradish
½ teaspoon salt
½ teaspoon pepper
4 tablespoons butter at room temperature

CRÊPES

Combine the milk, water, eggs, and butter. Blend the flours and salt in a bowl and whisk in the wet ingredients until smooth. Brush a 6″ crêpe pan lightly with corn oil and heat it until very hot. Pour about 1 ounce of the batter into the pan and quickly swirl to cover the bottom. Cook until the bottom is set, then turn the crêpe and lightly brown the other side. (The first crêpe often sticks. Throw it out and continue with the others.) Repeat until you have at least 12 crêpes.

FILLING

Have ready the chicken and broccoli. Melt the butter in a saucepan. Add the onions and sauté over medium heat until transparent. Whisk in the flour and cook 2 minutes. Whisk in the chicken stock, horseradish, pepper, and salt. Bring to a boil. Stir and cook 2 to 3 minutes. Chill. Add the chicken and broccoli. Set aside.

ASSEMBLY AND HORSERADISH CREAM SAUCE

Preheat the oven to 325°. Roll each of the 12 crêpes with about ⅓ cup of the filling. Arrange the crêpes in a buttered baking pan and cover with foil. Put in the oven for 20–30 minutes or until heated through. While the crêpes are heating, make the sauce.

Combine the shallots and wine in a saucepan and reduce to 5–6 tablespoons. Add the cream, horseradish, salt, and pepper and simmer until thickened. Stir in the softened butter in bits and serve at once over crêpes.

NOTES AND SUBSTITUTIONS

The crêpes and sauce, without the butter, can be made up to 2 days ahead. The filling is best made early in the day and refrigerated. This way the filling firms up, making it easier to roll the crêpes.

By all means, feel free to substitute smoked turkey, ham, or regular cooked chicken or turkey for the smoked chicken.

SIAMESE CHICKEN CURRY
WITH BROCCOLI AND PEANUTS

Serves 2

With this dish, Frog made its first excursion into the style of cooking that would become known as a "quixotic blend of French, Asian, and American cuisines." Frog was still quite young at the time. The Thai members of the kitchen staff often brought to work with them packets of curry paste which they used to flavor the stir-fries, soups, and cold meat salads that they made for staff meals. Steven was intrigued by these curry pastes, and one day, while experimenting in the kitchen, he stirred some basic French Béchamel sauce into a bit of curry paste that he had sautéed in oil. The larder yielded the rest of the ingredients: chicken, broccoli, and some all-American salted peanuts. The dish has been a staple at Frog ever since; its occasional vacations from the menu have always been cut short by cries of distress from long-time customers. So indigenous is Siamese Chicken Curry to Frog that it was chosen to star at a luncheon for James Beard at the restaurant in the spring of 1980.

Both smooth and crunchy, spicy with a touch of fire and hint of sweetness, intriguing in its mysterious tangle of flavors and at the same time very soothing, Siamese Chicken Curry is absolutely delicious! It translates beautifully to the home kitchen, too, as it is quick and easy to prepare, and relatively inexpensive.

BÉCHAMEL
2 tablespoons butter
2 tablespoons flour
¼ teaspoon salt
Dash of pepper
1 cup half-and-half

CURRY
1½ cups broccoli flowerets
2 tablespoons corn oil
1 packet (½ ounce) green Thai curry paste
12 ounces boneless skinless chicken breast, cut into
  strips 1½" long by ½" wide
¼ teaspoon salt
2 tablespoons sugar
½ teaspoon minced garlic
2 tablespoons soy sauce
OPT. ½ teaspoon sriraja (Thai hot sauce) or Tabasco
¼ cup roasted peanuts
Hot cooked rice or lo mein noodles

THAI CURRY PASTES

Curry pastes are a key ingredient in much of Thai cooking and are, as we discovered, an excitingly different taste experience and lend themselves well to the kind of culinary experimentation we so enjoy. Totally unlike the more familiar Indian curry powder, these pastes are concocted from an exotic lineup of pungent spices, chilies and aromatic leaves. The more adventurous cook might try one from scratch by grinding together some combination of chilies, ginger, garlic, lemongrass, basil, lime, peppercorns, coriander, dried shrimp, shallots, and the like. For the rest of us, commercially prepared ½-ounce packets available in many Oriental food markets. The color of the label denotes the type and degree of hotness. "Krung gaeng" means curry paste, and the 4 basic types are:

Krung Gaeng Ped (red) • searingly hot from dried red chilies and used mainly for meat dishes

Krung Gaeng Keo Wan (green) • made from the hottest green chilies and dark green herbs and used mainly with poultry

Krung Gaeng Som (orange) • "som" means "sour" and refers to the rice vinegar used in this paste which is often used for seafood curries

Krung Gaeng Karee (yellow) • similar to the red but has lots of turmeric in it and is used for poultry as well as beef

129

BÉCHAMEL

Melt the butter in a small saucepan and stir in the flour, salt, and pepper. Cook and stir over low heat for several minutes. Add the half-and-half all at once and stir over medium heat until the sauce thickens and bubbles. Set aside. If not using immediately, cover flush with plastic wrap to prevent a skin from forming.

CURRY

Blanch the broccoli for 1 minute in boiling salted water. Drain and set aside. Have assembled the rest of the ingredients for the curry.

In a large skillet, heat the corn oil. Stir in the curry paste and cook for 1 minute over low heat to blend. Turn the heat to medium high and add the chicken, salt, sugar, and garlic. Stir-fry the chicken until the sugar begins to caramelize, increasing the heat if necessary.

Immediately add the soy sauce and continue to stir-fry until the liquid has almost all evaporated and the chicken is cooked through. Blend in the reserved Béchamel sauce. If the resulting mixture seems too thick, add some additional milk, beginning with 2 tablespoons. When the sauce is smooth, add the broccoli and quickly heat through. Taste and add the optional sriraja or Tabasco if desired. Stir in the peanuts and serve at once over rice or noodles.

SERVING SUGGESTIONS AND NOTES

A vinegary sweet-and-sour cucumber salad would provide a good contrast to the richness of the curry. For a beverage, ice cold beer or a spicy, slightly sweet Gewurztraminer would fill the bill nicely.

This recipe can be easily doubled to serve 4. To serve more than 4, multiply the recipe accordingly, but you will need to use 2 skillets.

Although this recipe is best cooked just before serving, all the ingredients can be readied earlier in the day, including the making of the Béchamel. (If the béchamel is cold when you are ready to use it, heat and whisk it before adding to the sauté.)

SWEET-SOUR CUCUMBER SALAD

An appropriately refreshing accompaniment to any dish using Thai curry paste.

° ° ° ° ° ° ° ° ° ° ° ° ° ° ° ° °

Halve lengthwise 2 medium-size cucumbers (peeled or unpeeled according to your preference) and slice thin. Combine with 1/4 cup white wine vinegar, 1 tablespoon sugar, 1/2 teaspoon salt and 1/2 teaspoon pepper. Let marinate for several hours in the refrigerator. Before serving, sprinkle with chopped roasted peanuts. Serves 6.

BASIC ORIENTAL STIR-FRY
WITH CHICKEN

Serves 2

When Eden was in the works, the menu blueprints called for a daily stir-fry dish to be served with or without meat. Anne, then in her role as testing chef, came up with a repertoire of four different stir-fry sauces that could be used interchangeably. Just as the stir-fry concept fits ideally into Eden's scheme of gourmet fast food, it is perfectly suited for home meals when time is of the essence. The dish is a wonderful standby—it takes minutes to prepare, makes a filling, well-rounded meal when teamed with rice or noodles (Eden always serves it with brown rice), and lends itself to countless variations of vegetables and meats. The sauce can be made in quantity and kept on hand in the refrigerator.

SAUCE
1½ teaspoons sesame oil
½ teaspoon minced ginger
½ teaspoon minced garlic
½ cup chicken stock
1 tablespoon soy sauce
1 tablespoon brown sugar
⅛ teaspoon Tabasco
½ teaspoon salt
¼ teaspoon pepper
1½ teaspoons lemon or lime juice
1½ teaspoons cornstarch
1 tablespoon rice wine or dry sherry

STIR-FRY
2 tablespoons corn oil
6 ounces boneless, skinless chicken breast cut into
   2" × ½" strips
½ cup sliced mushrooms
½ cup julienned red or green pepper
20 snow peas, stemmed (about 2¼ ounces)
½ cup bean sprouts
¼ cup toasted slivered almonds
Cooked brown rice or noodles

SAUCE
Heat the sesame oil in a small saucepan. Add the ginger and garlic and stir-fry 15–30 seconds over medium heat to bring out the flavor. Add the chicken stock, soy sauce, brown sugar, Tabasco, salt, pepper, and lemon juice. Bring just to a boil, stirring. Dissolve the cornstarch in the rice wine and whisk into the sauce. Heat until sauce thickens and reaches a full boil. Simmer for 30 seconds. Remove from the heat and set aside.

STIR-FRY

Have all the ingredients ready. Heat the corn oil in a large skillet over high heat until very hot. Add the chicken and stir-fry 1–2 minutes. Add the vegetables except for the bean sprouts, and sauté until they are crisp-tender—about 1–2 minutes. Add the sauce, bean sprouts, and the almonds. Heat through briefly and serve at once over brown rice or noodles.

NOTES AND VARIATIONS

The recipe can be doubled to serve 4, but be sure to use a very large skillet so that the chicken and vegetables sauté quickly in the proper amount of time, otherwise the dish may be overcooked or soupy.

Substitute beef, pork, lamb, or shrimp for the chicken— and feel free to try other vegetables and nuts.

Substitute either of the following two stir-fry sauces.

It really does pay to have good knives. Where a cook could manage without a food processor, he'd have a rough time of it without sharp, high quality knives. Buy the best you can afford. Don't hesitate to splurge. The knives will last for years. Keep a sharpening steel handy and use it regularly. Dull knives are the bane of any good cook.

GARLIC SESAME STIR-FRY SAUCE   *Serves 2*

This is the most popular of Eden's stir-fry sauces. It is especially good with a stir-fry mixture that includes lamb and broccoli.

½ teaspoon pepper
2 tablespoons soy sauce
3 tablespoons chicken stock
1 tablespoon sugar
2¼ teaspoons lemon juice
⅓ cup sesame oil
2¼ teaspoons minced garlic
1 teaspoon cornstarch mixed with 1½ teaspoons water

Combine the pepper, soy sauce, chicken stock, sugar, and lemon juice. In a small saucepan heat the sesame oil. Add the garlic and sauté 1 minute until soft but not browned. Add the soy-sauce mixture and bring just to boil. Whisk in the cornstarch mixture and let boil 20 seconds. Remove from the heat. Use in a stir-fry as described in the preceding Basic recipe.

SZECHUAN STIR-FRY SAUCE

Serves 2

True to its name—hot and intriguingly spicy.

1½ teaspoons sesame oil
½ teaspoon minced fresh ginger
½ teaspoon minced garlic
½ cup chicken stock
2 whole anise "stars"
1½ teaspoons red wine vinegar
1 tablespoon soy sauce
½ teaspoon salt
1 teaspoon hoisin sauce
⅛ teaspoon siraja (Thai hot sauce) or Tabasco
⅛ teaspoon crushed red pepper flakes
¼ teaspoon pepper
⅛ teaspoon 5 spice powder
¼ teaspoon finely chopped Szechuan peppercorns
2 teaspoons cornstarch dissolved in 1 tablespoon water

Heat the oil in a small saucepan. Add the ginger and garlic and sauté 1 minute until softened but not browned. In a bowl combine the remaining ingredients *excluding* the cornstarch mixture. Add them to the saucepan and bring to a simmer, covered, for 10 minutes. Remove star anise. Whisk in the cornstarch mixture and let boil 1–2 minutes. Taste and add more siraja if desired.

FIVE SPICE POWDER

This mixed-breed Chinese seasoning blends equal parts of ground star anise, ginger, cinnamon, cloves, and fennel seed. It is very fragrant and pungent. Used sparingly, it adds some most interesting undertones to roast meats and poultry (try rubbing on steak before grilling), toasted nuts, salad dressing with sesame oil and sweets such as gingerbread, applesauce, and spice cookies.

1 STAR ANISE 2 GINGER 3 CINNAMON 4 CLOVES 5 FENNEL SEED

MEXICAN "LASAGNA" WITH CHICKEN, PORK, AND TOSTADOS

Serves 8

No pasta here. In its place, though, are crispy fried tortillas layering wonderfully spicy fillings of chicken, pork, and onions counterbalanced by milder, soothing layers of Crème Fraîche, tomatoes, and Chedder cheese. Plan to make your Crème Fraîche a day or so in advance. The onion, tomato, chicken, and pork mixtures can also be prepared a day or two ahead. Leave the final assembly, however, until just before baking so that the tostados don't become soggy.

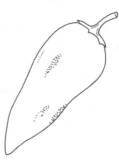

CHICKEN LAYER
1½ cups chicken stock
2 teaspoons crushed coriander seeds
6 bay leaves
1 pound boneless, skinless chicken breasts cut into
   1" strips
¼ teaspoon salt
½ teaspoon pepper

PORK LAYER
¾ pound ground pork
1½ teaspoons ground coriander
⅛ teaspoon ground cloves
¼ teaspoon pepper
½ teaspoon dried oregano
½ teaspoon ground cumin
1 teaspoon minced garlic
¾ teaspoon salt
2 tablespoons minced roasted jalapeño peppers or
   ¼ teaspoon crushed red pepper flakes
2 tablespoons white vinegar

ONION MIXTURE
2 tablespoons olive oil
3 cups thinly sliced onions
½ teaspoon salt
2 (4-ounce) cans mild green chilies, chopped

TOMATO SAUCE
4 pounds ripe tomatoes
2 tablespoons olive oil
1 tablespoon minced garlic
2 tablespoons sugar
1¾ teaspoons salt
½ teaspoon pepper

ASSEMBLY
18 5" tostados (corn tortillas fried until crisp in ½" corn
   oil and then drained well)

tostados

onions

pork

chicken

tomatoes

134

3 cups Crème Fraîche (see recipe on p. 101) or 3 cups
   sour cream mixed with 3 tablespoons lemon juice
2 eggs
1 pound Cheddar cheese, grated
1 tablespoon minced fresh coriander or parsley

CHICKEN LAYER
Combine the stock, coriander seeds, and bay leaves in a
deep skillet and bring to a boil. Simmer 5 minutes. Add
the chicken, cover, and again bring to a boil. Reduce the
heat to very low and cook 7–10 minutes more or until the
chicken is just done. Pour the contents of the skillet into
a sieve set over a bowl to catch the broth. Let the chicken
cool. Return the broth to the pan and reduce the liquid
over medium heat to ½ cup. Set aside. Remove any bay
leaves and seeds from the chicken and cut the meat into
½" dice. Combine the chicken with the reduced broth, the
salt, and the pepper.

PORK LAYER
Combine all the ingredients in a skillet and cook over a
medium heat until the pork loses its pink color and the
vinegar has evaporated. Set aside.

ONION MIXTURE
Heat the olive oil in a 9" skillet. Add the onions, salt, and
chilies and cook over medium heat for about 10 minutes,
stirring frequently. Set aside.

TOMATO SAUCE
Preheat the oven to 475°. Put the tomatoes stem side down
in a single layer on a rimmed baking sheet lined with
aluminum foil. Bake for 25–30 minutes or until the skins
are lightly charred. Purée tomatoes, skins, stems and all,
in a food processor and then put them through a sieve.
Heat the olive oil in a skillet. Add the garlic and sauté for
about 15 seconds. Add the puréed tomatoes, sugar, salt
and pepper. Cook, while stirring occasionally, over medium heat for 10–15 minutes until the mixture has thickened
(like canned tomato sauce). Set aside.

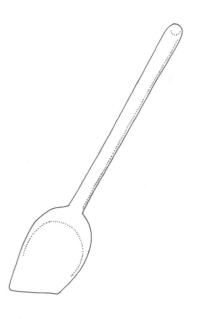

ASSEMBLY
Lightly oil a 9" × 13" × 2" baking dish. **Preheat the oven
to 350°.** Combine the Crème Fraîche with the eggs and set
aside. Put down a layer of 6 tostados. Mix the chicken
with half the onion mixture, and 1 cup of the tomato sauce
and spread over the tostados. Drizzle on 1 cup of Crème
Fraîche. Scatter on 1 cup of the cheese. Put down 6 more
tostados, pressing down to level and compact the fillings
below. Combine the pork with the remaining onions and
1 cup of tomato sauce. Spread this over the tostados and

top with 1 cup of Crème Fraîche and 1 cup of the cheese. Put down the last 6 tostados. Spoon the remaining Crème Fraîche over the top. Put down the remaining cheese. The dish will be quite full. Set the pan on a rimmed baking sheet and bake for 35–45 minutes or until golden and bubbly. Let rest 15 minutes before serving. Garnish with the minced coriander or parsley.

STIR-FRIED DUCK WITH CHINESE SAUSAGE
Serves 4–5

Bits of savory, sweet Chinese cured pork sausage add an exotic note to this duck stir-fry. It is one of our most popular catering dishes. All the components of the dish can be readied in advance so that you need to allow only a few minutes just before serving for the final assembly.

Chinese sausages are stiff little links of cured ground pork and are sweeter and fattier, but no less delicious, than other sausages we are more familiar with. Chinese sausage must always first be blanched for at least 5 minutes, then you can slice it and serve as is for hors d'oeuvres, add it to scrambled eggs or pasta, scatter it on a pizza with Chinese mushrooms, toss it into a stir-fry, roll and bake it in brioche dough, or pop it on the grill alongside the hamburgers.

Double recipe of Basic Stir-fry Sauce (see p. 131)
1 (4½-pound) duck
½ cup corn oil
½ cup roasted unsalted cashews
2 tablespoons soy sauce
⅛ teaspoon pepper
2 cups broccoli flowerets, blanched
2 cups julienned red peppers (about 2 peppers)
1 cup thinly sliced Chinese sausage (5 ounces)
¼ cup water
Cooked rice

Have ready the double recipe of Basic Stir-fry Sauce.
Preheat the oven to 425°. Prick the skin of the duck all over without piercing the meat. Set the duck in a roasting pan and roast for 45 minutes. Let cool a bit, then remove the skin. Lower the oven heat to 325° and return the skin, skin side up, to the oven until it is crisp like bacon. Remove to paper toweling to drain, then cut into ½" dice. Remove the meat from the duck and cut into bite-size pieces.

In a small skillet heat 2 tablespoons of the corn oil. Add the cashews and stir 30 seconds over medium-low heat. Add the soy sauce and pepper and continue to stir and toast the nuts for 2–3 minutes until well-coated with the soy sauce. Remove with a slotted spoon and cool in a single layer on paper toweling.

Combine the Chinese sausage and water in a small saucepan, cover, and simmer for 5 minutes. Drain and set aside. Heat the basic stir-fry sauce.

Just before serving, have ready all the ingredients. Heat the remaining corn oil in a large skillet or wok. When the oil is very hot, add the julienned peppers and stir-fry 30

136

seconds. Add the sausage and broccoli and stir 10 seconds. Add the duck, cashews, crisped duck skin, and stir-fry sauce. Bring just to a boil over high heat while stirring. Serve immediately with rice.

ROAST DUCK WITH THAI CURRY GLAZE AND BAKED GARLIC

Serves 4

During his apprentice days in old Frog's basement kitchen, Mitchell Eisen absorbed much from his Thai colleagues there. Later, when on his own as chef of The Commissary's second-floor restaurant, he applied some of those Thai techniques to come up with this duck recipe. Crisp, spicy roast duck is caramelized with honey—and then there's all that garlic . . . baked, glazed, and baked again until it is just as sweet as can be.

2 (4½-pound) ducks
2 heads of garlic
1 packet (½ ounce) red Thai curry paste
2 teaspoons sesame oil
½ teaspoon minced fresh ginger
½ teaspoon minced garlic
¼ teaspoon dried thyme
½ cup honey

PREROASTING DUCKS
(Can be done a day in advance)
Preheat the oven to 425°. Trim excess flaps of fat from around the opening cavity of the ducks and cut off the wing tips. Separate the heads of garlic into cloves and remove the papery coverings but leave the skin. Stuff the ducks with the garlic cloves and set them in a large, deep roasting pan (ducks give off lots of grease).

Prick the skin of the ducks all over without piercing the meat. Roast for 1 hour, pricking several times during the cooking period. Remove the ducks from the oven and remove and set aside the garlic cloves. If there is time, cool the ducks completely, since that will make it easier to remove the bones as next described. With a sharp knife, split the ducks in half and (optional) remove the backbone, rib cage, breastplate, and all but the leg bones and first wing joints with your fingers. This will facilitate the eating of the duck.

GLAZING
One hour before serving, **preheat the oven to 350°.** Combine the curry paste, sesame oil, ginger, minced garlic, thyme, and honey until smooth. Put the reserved garlic cloves

Anne loves garlic, and to assure herself a ready supply, she peels 10 heads of garlic and whizzes them in her food processor. The minced garlic is then shaped into a log, rolled up in plastic wrap, given a second wrapping in foil, and tucked in the freezer. When she needs a little garlic, Anne just lops a slice off the frozen log and returns the rest to the freezer.

onto a 12″ square of aluminum foil in a single layer and drizzle 2 tablespoons of the curry mixture over them. Crimp the four corners of the foil together tightly and place the package on a baking sheet. Bake the garlic for ½ hour or until very soft.

Twenty minutes before serving, turn the oven to 500°. Put the ducks cut side down on foil-lined rimmed baking sheets and put ¼ of the garlic cloves under each piece. Bake for 15 minutes in the upper half of the oven. Remove from the oven and blot the ducks' skin with paper toweling to remove excess oil. Brush the skin well with the curry glaze. Return to the oven for an additional 5–7 minutes to caramelize the glaze. (Watch carefully, as it burns easily at this point.)

VARIATIONS
Recipe can be halved to serve 2.

The glaze is so good; try it on chicken, ribs, or even soft-shelled crabs.

ROAST DUCK BREASTS WITH RASPBERRY VINEGAR SAUCE AND MANGO

Serves 4

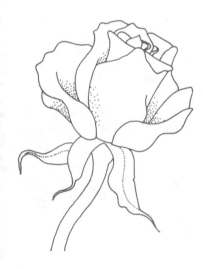

This is one of our more elegant dishes and owes its conception to a day when Steven was faced with creating a menu for a very lavish catered dinner party for 120 guests. Having decided to do something with duck and keeping in mind that the hosts of the dinner had requested a dinner with oriental overtones, Steven stepped into the kitchen for inspiration. What resulted was another example of the spontaneous "East meets West" culinary reaction that has been a hallmark of our kitchens. Roast duck (in this case, just the elegant, more easily managed breast meat) came to be sauced with a rich combination of reduced duck stock, caramelized sugar and raspberry vinegar, soy, garlic, ginger, and sherry and was then stunningly presented with bright sliced mango, an accent of julienned red Japanese pickled ginger, and for dramatic effect . . . a deep red rose.

But lest you be intimidated, this is not a terribly difficult dish to prepare. Cooking a duck is really no different from cooking a chicken, except that the duck has on it a great deal more fat which melts off while the bird is roasting. Nor is the Raspberry Vinegar Sauce at all complicated, except that it requires a bit of time for making and reducing the stock. The results will be well worth the extra time involved.

This is also a particularly fine dish for entertaining, since not only is it delicious and quite striking in appearance, but most of the work can be done in advance so that you need only reheat the sauce and the duck briefly before serving.

DUCKS
2 ducks, approximately 4½ pounds each

STOCK
1 tablespoon rendered duck fat
Uncooked wings, necks, and gizzards from 2 ducks
½ cup chopped onions
1½ tablespoons sliced unpeeled fresh ginger
1½ teaspoons chopped garlic
1 chopped carrot
1 chopped celery rib
¼ bunch washed parsley, chopped
Roasted duck carcasses
Water to cover

RASPBERRY VINEGAR SAUCE
½ cup plus 1 tablespoon raspberry vinegar
2 tablespoons sugar
1½ tablespoons soy sauce
1 teaspoon finely minced garlic
¼ teaspoon sriraja (Thai hot sauce) or Tabasco
¼ teaspoon pepper
1 tablespoon medium-dry sherry
1 teaspoon cornstarch
1½ teaspoons water or fruit juice
The reduced duck stock

ASSEMBLY
1 ripe mango
4 teaspoons julienned red Japanese pickled ginger
OPT. 4 deep red roses

ROASTING THE DUCKS
(Do 1–3 days ahead)
Preheat the oven to 425°. Prepare the ducks by chopping off the wings at the elbows, removing and setting aside the giblets and necks, cutting off the excess neck skin, and discarding any loose interior fat. Prick the skins all over with a fork, being careful not to pierce the meat. Put the ducks in a large roasting pan and roast for 1 hour, pricking the skins every 15 minutes or so to release the fat. Cool the ducks to room temperature. Reserve 1 tablespoon of

RASPBERRY VINEGAR
Boil 3 cups of white or red wine vinegar in a non-aluminum saucepan. Add 1 cup of raspberries and boil 5 minutes. Pour into another non-aluminum container to cool. When cool, cover and let sit undisturbed for 2 weeks or so. Strain into a glass bottle and cap or cork.

raspberry vinegar summer '85

139

the fat for the stock and discard the rest (or save for another use such as sautéing potatoes).

Using your fingers and a small sharp knife to cut where necessary, remove the breast meat from the ducks in 4 neat pieces. Leave the skin attached but remove any excess fat globules. Wrap the pieces in plastic wrap and refrigerate. Remove the legs (twist to find the joint, then cut) and the rest of the meat from the ducks and reserve for another use (see suggestions under Notes). Remove and discard any excess fat and skin remaining on the carcasses.

STOCK
(Make 1–3 days ahead)

Heat the duck fat in a large 8-quart stockpot. Add and brown the reserved wings, necks, and giblets over medium heat. Add the onions, ginger, garlic, carrot, celery, and parsley. Stir and sauté until the vegetables begin to brown. Break up the duck carcasses so that they take up as little room as possible and add them to the pot. Add water just to cover and simmer uncovered for 2–3 hours, adding water as necessary to keep bones covered. Strain off all the solids, let the stock cool, and then refrigerate overnight or at least until the fat solidifies on top.

Remove and discard the solidified fat from the top of the stock and bring the stock to a boil over high heat. Boil the stock until it has been reduced to about 1 cup. (To speed this process, you can put it into 2 large, wide skillets, which would allow the liquid to evaporate more quickly.) Proceed directly to make the sauce or cool the reduced stock and store in the refrigerator up to a day in advance.

RASPBERRY VINEGAR SAUCE
*(Make the day before, the morning of
or just before serving)*

Remove the reduced stock from the refrigerator and peel off and discard the fat that accumulated on top. Bring the stock to a boil.

In a 1-quart copper or other heavy saucepan, stir the ½ cup of raspberry vinegar and the sugar over medium heat until the sugar dissolves. Watching carefully so that the mixture doesn't burn, turn the heat to high and cook, swirling the pan occasionally but not stirring, until much of the liquid has evaporated and the sugar-vinegar mixture begins to caramelize and turn a deep amber color. Remove immediately from the heat. Immediately add the hot stock in a thin stream, stirring all the while. Add the soy sauce, garlic, sriraja, pepper, sherry, and the additional 1 tablespoon of raspberry vinegar. Bring to a boil. Combine the cornstarch and water and whisk into the boiling sauce. Let simmer, stirring occasionally, for 2–3 minutes over low

Sriraja, the Thai hot sauce, makes anything better. It is as hot as Tabasco but also a touch sweeter and less sour.

heat. Taste for seasoning and adjust if necessary. If not using immediately, cool the sauce and chill until ready to serve.

ASSEMBLY
Have the mango at room temperature. Peel it with a paring knife and slice down the 2 flat sides so that you have 2 nice ovals. Cut each oval into 4 long pieces. Set aside. Also have ready the julienned pickled ginger.

Heat the sauce in a small saucepan. Preheat the broiler. Set the 4 portions of duck breast skin side up in a roasting pan 3"–4" under the broiler and broil until the skin is crisp and bubbly and the meat is heated through. Blot the skin well with paper toweling and arrange each piece in the center of a dinner plate. Divide the hot sauce over the meat, tilting each plate so that the sauce forms a pool around the meat. Arrange 1 slice of mango on either side of each duck breast and top each with 1 teaspoon of the pickled ginger. Then, if desired, garnish each plate with a rose.

NOTES AND VARIATIONS
Accompany the duck with side plates of lightly sautéed bright green snow peas. A fairly rich, medium-bodied Zinfandel would be a good wine to serve here.

Use the leftover duck meat in other recipes such as Duck Lasagna, Spinach Spaetzle with Duck and Wild Mushroom Sauce, and Duck and Asparagus Salad with Curried Vinaigrette.

Try substituting other vinegars, such as sherry or cider, in the sauce.

If mangoes are unavailable, you could substitute slices of ripe peaches or warmed ripe pear wedges.

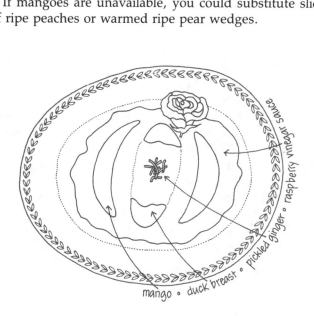

mango ○ duck breast ○ pickled ginger ○ raspberry vinegar sauce

TURKEY SCALLOPS
WITH LEMON-CAPER BUTTER   *Serves 6*

Precut turkey scallops are becoming increasingly available these days; otherwise, you can cut your own from a whole turkey breast or even substitute chicken or veal scallops.

LEMON-CAPER BUTTER
2½ cups dry white wine
3 tablespoons minced shallots
¼ teaspoon pepper
½ pound butter, at room temperature
2–3 tablespoons lemon juice
¼ teaspoon salt
3 tablespoons capers

TURKEY
1½ pounds turkey scallops cut from the breast
1 cup fine dry bread crumbs
½ cup ground toasted almonds
½ teaspoon salt
½ teaspoon pepper
2 eggs
6 tablespoons clarified butter (see p. 124 for how to make)

LEMON-CAPER BUTTER
In a small skillet, combine the wine, shallots, and pepper. Reduce to ½ cup. Lower the heat and whisk in the soft butter bit by bit. Do not boil. Add the lemon juice, salt, and capers. Whisk until well blended and set aside off the heat.

TURKEY
Pound the slices of turkey breast between wax paper until ¼" thick. Combine the bread crumbs, almonds, salt and pepper in a pie pan. In a separate bowl, beat the eggs. **Preheat the oven to 200°.**

Plan to cook the scallops in 3 batches, as they should be done in a single layer in the frying pan. Heat 2 tablespoons of the butter in a large skillet. Dip the first batch of scallops in the beaten eggs and then in the crumb mixture. Fry until crisp and golden on both sides. Remove the scallops to an oven dish and keep warm in a low oven as you cook the other 2 batches. Wipe out the pan between batches and add 2 tablespoons of the butter for each batch.

Reheat without boiling the Lemon-Caper Butter and spoon about 4 tablespoons of it over each portion of turkey.

Meat Entrées

"Mmm...I had to come back for a second helping. Is that mesquite you're burning there? It reminds me of the way the campfires smelled at summer camp. What's the secret"

"You give the best parties, Frog! This is so good..."

THAI BEEF CURRY

Picking up the Thai-French-American theme first established in Frog's classic Siamese Chicken Curry, this delectable dish was introduced in The Commissary's second-floor restaurant. Tender strips of beef meet snow peas, orange segments, and cashews with seeming naturalness in a Béchamel sauce enlivened by spicy hot Thai curry paste. Like its chicken and lamb siblings, the dish may be assembled in advance and then quickly cooked just before serving.

BÉCHAMEL
2 tablespoons butter
3 tablespoons flour
1 cup half-and-half

CURRY
1 packet (½ ounce) red or green Thai curry paste
2 tablespoons sesame oil
2 teaspoons minced ginger
2 teaspoons minced garlic
2 tablespoons sugar
1 pound trimmed sirloin or fillet of beef, cut into
   1" × 2½" pieces
¼ cup soy sauce
½ cup orange juice
¾ teaspoon salt
1 cup peeled and seeded orange segments (about 3
   oranges)
½ pound snow peas, trimmed and halved on the
   diagonal
½ cup whole roasted cashews
Hot cooked somen or buckwheat noodles
Watercress for garnish

BÉCHAMEL
Heat the butter in a small saucepan. Add the flour. Stir and cook 2 minutes. Add the half-and-half. Stir and cook over low heat for several minutes until the sauce thickens and bubbles. Remove from the heat. (If making in advance, cover the surface flush with plastic wrap to prevent a skin from forming.)

CURRY
Have all the curry ingredients ready. In a 10" skillet over low heat, sauté the curry paste in the sesame oil for 2 minutes. Add the ginger, garlic, and sugar and stir ½ minute over high heat. Add the beef and quickly stir-fry about 1 minute until browned on the outside and still pink inside. Add the soy sauce, orange juice, and salt. Cook 1

THAI POPCORN

Have ready 3 quarts of unseasoned, freshly made popcorn. Heat 2 tablespoons of corn oil. Add 1 packet (½ ounce) of red or green Thai curry paste, 2 teaspoons minced garlic, 1 teaspoon minced fresh ginger, and 1 tablespoon sugar. Sauté for 2 minutes over medium heat while stirring to break up the curry paste. Remove from the heat and blend in ⅓ cup butter. Add salt to suit your taste. Stir until the butter is melted, toss with the popcorn, and serve.

minute. Whisk the Béchamel well and add to the stir-fry mixture. Add the orange segments with their juice and the snow peas. Heat through and add the nuts. Serve over noodles and garnish with watercress.

GRILLED MARINATED
FLANK STEAK

Serves 6–8

Get out that grill and treat yourself to one of the best and easiest summer meals we know: grilled marinated flank steak redolent of fresh herbs; sliced giant Jersey tomatoes; sweet, tender corn on the cob, dripping butter; a garden-greens salad; garlic bread toasted on the grill; and perhaps a bottle of fruity Zinfandel. Invite in a few fireflies for atmosphere and you're all set.

The garlic bread is actually a lovely dividend from this recipe. When you drain the marinade from the meat, strain off the solids and combine them with a stick of soft butter. Slather this now very tasty butter on a loaf of French or Italian bread and either toast on the grill or wrap the loaf in foil and heat on the back of the grill.

¼ cup red wine vinegar
¾ cup olive oil
2 tablespoons minced garlic
1 teaspoon pepper
2 bay leaves, crumbled
1–2 tablespoons minced fresh herbs (rosemary, thyme, basil, oregano . . .)
1 (2½-pound) flank steak

Six to 24 hours before serving, whisk together the vinegar and oil. Add the garlic, pepper, bay leaves, and herbs. Combine with the flank steak in a deep bowl and refrigerate to marinate. Turn once during this time.

To grill the meat, prepare your fire to the glowing coal stage or preheat the broiler. Remove meat from marinade and grill to your liking. Sprinkle with salt to taste. Let sit several minutes before serving, then slice very thinly on a slant against the grain.

NOTES
Simplicity is the key here, as our proposed menu above suggests. And, if you are lucky, you'll have leftovers and be able to make yourself a wonderful sandwich with greens and homemade mayonnaise on the best fresh bread you can find.

FIREFLY FEAST
After a sun-filled summer's day of leisure, nothing seems quite as appropriate for dinner as dining outdoors. Ideally, we'd gather round good company, clothe ourselves in cool white linen, set the table with checkered cotton, giant napkins, fresh cut flowers... then, while the grill gets going, we'd sit back for a bit, G & T's in hand, and watch the day wind down into a firefly-flecked evening.

Gin and Tonics • Salted Almonds •
  Skewered Melon and Prosciutto
  with Mint
Grilled Marinated Flank Steak *
Corn on the Cob • Chili Butter
Sliced Tomatoes with Dill Mayonnaise
Garden Greens with Herb Vinaigrette*
Garlic Bread
Beer and/or Zinfandel
Blueberry Sour Cream Streusel Pie*

*see Index for recipe page number

145

BRAISED BEEF
WITH STAR ANISE

Serves 6–8

Pot roast with a sweet oriental kick. Mother never made it this way—but we did, for a giant catered affair (featuring an oriental buffet) in honor of Liza Minnelli. Plan to start the recipe a day ahead to give the meat plenty of time to marinate and be transformed by all the wonderful flavorings.

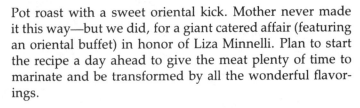

Star anise is the pungent, licorice-flavored dried fruit of a tree in the magnolia family and is a favored seasoning in Chinese cooking. You can add the whole "stars" to any spiced, braised dishes, to a hot fruit or wine punch, to a creamed soup (for the last 15 minutes of cooking), to the liquid used for cooking rice, or use them as you would cloves to stud a ham about to be roasted.

3–3 ½ pound rump roast (or any braising roast of your
   choice)
1 cup soy sauce
¼ cup hoisin sauce
½ cup brown sugar
1 tablespoon molasses
¼ cup sherry
1½ tablespoons minced fresh ginger
1 tablespoon minced garlic
5 star anise "stars"
2 cups water
2 tablespoons corn oil
2 tablespoons cornstarch mixed with ¼ cup water
2–3 scallions, julienned

The night before you cook the roast, combine the soy sauce, hoisin sauce, brown sugar, molasses, sherry, ginger, garlic, star anise, and water. Pour over the meat in a large bowl and refrigerate overnight.

Remove the meat from the marinade and pat dry. Reserve the marinade. Heat the oil in a Dutch oven or other heavy pot with a lid and, when hot, add the meat, fat side down. Brown the meat well on all sides over medium heat—about 15–20 minutes. Remove the meat to a platter. Discard the grease in the pan. Add 2 tablespoons of water to the pan and stir to loosen any browned bits. Return the meat to the pan and add the marinade. Bring to a boil. Lower heat, cover the pan tightly, and simmer for 3–4 hours, turning the meat occasionally. Remove the meat from the pan and degrease the remaining liquid as much as possible. Measure off 3½ cups of this liquid and strain into a saucepan. Whisk in the combined cornstarch and water and bring to a boil. Stir and cook 2 minutes until thickened.

Slice the meat as thinly as possible, spoon some of the sauce over each portion, and garnish with the minced scallions.

SERVING SUGGESTIONS
Arrange thin slices of the meat on a bed of rice or oriental noodles, top with the sauce, and serve snow peas sautéed with baby corn ears on the side.

146

Leftovers are good in an oriental-style salad or turned into a sandwich with lettuce and some of our Oriental Dressing.

LOIN OF VEAL STUFFED WITH SPINACH, PROSCIUTTO, AND FUNGHI PORCINI

Serves 10

After an autumn vacation in northern Italy several years ago, Becky and her husband, Paul, who was our executive chef, returned to work at The Commissary greatly inspired by and addicted to the simplicity of cooking they had encountered in their travels. Memories of such superlative ingredients as extra virgin olive oil, Reggiano Parmigiana, prosciutto and funghi porcini filled their heads. While still in the wake of that trip to gustatory heaven, Paul devised this elegant entrée in the northern Italian tradition to offer as part of our catering repertoire. The pale pink juicy meat with its heart of deep green makes for a beautiful presentation. This luxury entrée is even lovely served at room temperature and thus would be quite suitable for a buffet.

You can be flexible with this dish, especially considering the cost and size of a loin of veal. The filling is such that it would also be memorable as a stuffing for veal chops, rolled veal scallops, flank steak, omelets, or chicken breasts.

1 ounce dried funghi porcini or cèpes
2 (10-ounce) bags fresh spinach
4 tablespoons butter
1 tablespoon minced shallots
¼ pound thinly sliced prosciutto, julienned
¼ teaspoon salt
½ teaspoon pepper
⅛ teaspoon red pepper flakes
1 (4-pound) loin of veal, boned and butterflied

Soak the funghi porcini in 2 cups warm water for about 15 minutes or until "reconstituted." Drain, chop them, and rinse to remove any residual grit.

Wash the spinach well and remove any large stems. Blanch, refresh under cold running water, squeeze very dry, and coarsely chop. Heat the butter in a sauté pan. Add the shallots and sauté 1 minute to soften. Add the prosciutto and cook it a minute to frizzle slightly. Add the mushrooms, sauté briefly, and follow with the spinach. Season with the salt, pepper, and red pepper flakes. Let cool.

FUNGHI PORCINI

are wondrous large Italian mushrooms that are said to grow best under Tuscan chestnut trees. (Cèpes are their French counterparts.) They are sometimes so big that Italians will grill and serve a single cap as an entrée. We, however, see them mostly in their dried state. Drying intensifies their complex, woodsy flavor. The mushrooms are easily reconstituted in warm water. ☆ Use reconstituted funghi porcini or other dried mushrooms to give new flavor to a mess of sautéed cultivated mushrooms. Consider, too, what they would do for mashed potatoes, beef stew, potato gratin, pasta, omelets... just remember that the flavor is potent and that a few will go far.

147

Preheat the oven to 375°. Spread the filling over the interior of the loin. Roll up as you would a jelly roll, starting from the long side, and tie securely with string. Set on a rack in a baking pan. Roast for 45 minutes or until the internal temperature reaches 130° to 135°F. This will produce a moist pink meat. Let rest 5 minutes before removing strings and then carefully cut into ½"-thick slices. Skim the grease off the juices, reheat them, and check for seasoning. Pour the juices over the sliced meat.

VEAL SCALLOPS WITH LILLET CREAM SAUCE AND VIOLETS

Serves 6

Back when The Commissary first opened, we were asked to participate in a cooking demonstration at a nearby housewares store. The theme was "Cooking with Flowers," and Gary Bachman, our head chef at the time, contributed the following—one of the most gorgeously colored, simply elegant dishes we've ever encountered. The violets (as long as they are not the African houseplant variety) are edible and add the brilliant final touch to an already exquisite presentation. Although bunches of fresh violets are sadly an almost extinct commodity at the florist's these days, many of us are fortunate enough come springtime, to be able to scavenge some from the woods or backyard.

¼ cup plus 2 tablespoons butter
6 (5-ounce) veal scallops, pounded thin
1 cup blond Lillet
2 cups heavy cream
½ teaspoon salt
½ teaspoon pepper
1½ cups finely julienned carrots
1½ cups finely julienned zucchini
¾ cup finely julienned red bell pepper
OPT. 1 bunch fresh violets (*not* African!), stems and
   leaves removed

Preheat the oven to 200°. Melt ½ cup of the butter in a large skillet. When hot, add the veal scallops and sauté briefly on both sides, about 30 seconds a side. Remove to an ovenproof platter and keep warm in the oven. Add the Lillet to the skillet and deglaze the pan, scraping the bottom and letting the juices reduce to ⅓ cup. Add the cream, salt, and pepper and reduce over high heat until the sauce has the consistency of a thin gravy.

Don't forget your flower garden when you're looking for something to accent your plates. Marigolds, gladiolas, violets (not African?), roses, and nasturtiums, for instance, are all decorative and edible (providing they haven't been sprayed).

nasturtium

Meanwhile, heat the remaining 2 tablespoons of butter in a second skillet. Add the vegetables and stir-fry several minutes until crisp-tender. Remove the veal from the oven, transfer to warm plates, distribute the vegetables over each portion, and mask with the sauce. Decorate with the violet blossoms.

SAUTÉED SWEETBREADS
WITH LEMON-HAZELNUT BUTTER   *Serves 6*

This dish has drawn connoisseurs of sweetbreads to Frog for many years. Sweetbreads themselves are not at all difficult to prepare, but you should plan on beginning the process the day before so that there is enough time to soak, poach, and weight the sweetbreads. This particular method of preparing sweetbreads leaves them firm yet tender, with a crispy golden exterior. The sauce, made shortly before serving, beautifully highlights this dish without overwhelming the delicacy of the sweetbreads.

SWEETBREADS
3 pairs of sweetbreads (about 2½ pounds)
¼ cup vinegar

LEMON BUTTER SAUCE
2½ cups dry white wine
3 tablespoons minced shallots
¼ teaspoon pepper
OPT. 1½ teaspoons minced fresh lemon thyme
3 tablespoons lemon juice
½ pound butter, softened and in bits
¼ teaspoon salt
⅛ teaspoon cayenne pepper

These are a "pair of sweetbreads"...

according to one eleven-year-old who was enormously disappointed when the sweetbreads her father ordered one evening did not turn out to be a plate of cinnamon buns.

TO SERVE
½ cup flour
¼ teaspoon salt
¼ teaspoon pepper
3 ounces clarified butter (see how to make, on p. 124)
⅓ cup chopped toasted hazelnuts

SWEETBREADS
Soak the sweetbreads in 3 quarts of water with the vinegar overnight. The next morning, bring 2 quarts of fresh water to a boil, add the sweetbreads, and return to a boil. Reduce the heat and let simmer for 5 minutes. Drain and rinse with cold water. When cool, put in a large bowl of ice

149

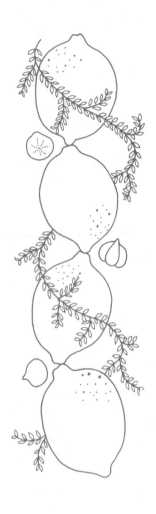

water to chill. Peel off and discard only the outer membrane and any fat lumps. Butterfly the sweetbreads by slicing each piece horizontally but not quite all the way through. Open each piece and push flat. Arrange the sweetbreads in a single layer on a plastic-wrap-covered baking sheet. Cover with more plastic wrap and top with a second baking sheet. Put 10 pounds of weight on top (two 5-pound sugar bags work well) and refrigerate for 3–24 hours. This will firm the sweetbreads so that they aren't mushy when sautéed.

LEMON BUTTER SAUCE

Shortly before serving, combine the wine, shallots, pepper, and thyme in a saucepan and reduce to ⅓ cup. Off the heat, add the lemon juice and whisk in the bits of butter. Season with the salt and cayenne pepper. Set on the back of the stove.

TO SERVE

Combine the flour, salt, and pepper. Heat the clarified butter in 1 very large skillet or in 2 smaller ones until quite hot. Coat the pieces of sweetbreads in it, shaking off any excess. Add the sweetbreads in 1 layer. Lower the heat to medium and sauté 7 minutes or until crisp and golden. Turn and sauté for 5–7 minutes more. While the second side is cooking, *very gently rewarm* the lemon butter. Add the hazelnuts. Arrange the sweetbreads on plates and distribute the sauce over them. Serve at once.

VARIATION

SWEETBREADS WITH ROASTED CHESTNUTS AND SHERRY VINEGAR BUTTER

3 pairs of sweetbreads, prepared as described above
1 cup sweet sherry
1 cup dry white wine
¼ cup white wine vinegar
¼ teaspoon salt
¼ teaspoon pepper
8 ounces butter, softened and in bits
2 tablespoons lemon juice
⅔ cup chopped fresh or canned roasted chestnuts

In a small saucepan, reduce the sherry, wine, vinegar, salt, and pepper to ¼ cup. Off the heat, whisk in the butter, bit by bit. Add lemon juice. Stir in the chestnuts and serve hot over the sautéed sweetbreads.

SAUTÉED CALF'S LIVER WITH MUSTARD, SHALLOTS, AND WHITE WINE

Serves 4

We've seen even the most ardent liver haters ooh and aah over this dish at Frog. This divinely palatable rendition demands only that the liver be sliced ever so thinly and sautéed very, very briefly before being bathed in the pungent, buttery sauce. And, as is typical of restaurant sauté dishes, it all just takes minutes to prepare.

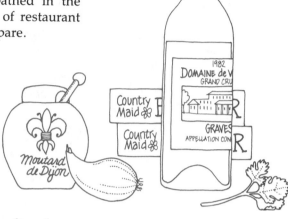

SAUCE
2 cups dry white wine
3 tablespoons minced shallots
2 tablespoons Dijon mustard
¾ cup butter
¼ teaspoon pepper
1 tablespoon minced parsley

LIVER
1 pound calf's liver, sliced ¼"–⅛" thick
½ cup flour seasoned with ½ teaspoon each salt and
   pepper
2 tablespoons clarified butter (see p. 124 for how to
   make)

SAUCE
In a saucepan, reduce the wine with the shallots until 2 tablespoons of wine remain. Tilt the pan back and forth toward the end of the reduction period so the mixture doesn't burn. Whisk in the mustard. Take off the heat and whisk in the butter in bits. Stir in the pepper and parsley. Set the pan in a warm but not hot place while preparing the liver.

LIVER
Just before cooking, dredge the pieces of liver in the seasoned flour and shake off the excess. Heat the butter in a wide sauté pan and sauté the liver in a single layer over high heat for 30–45 seconds a side. Serve immediately topped with the sauce.

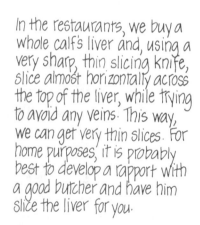

In the restaurants, we buy a whole calf's liver and, using a very sharp, thin slicing knife, slice almost horizontally across the top of the liver, while trying to avoid any veins. This way, we can get very thin slices. For home purposes, it is probably best to develop a rapport with a good butcher and have him slice the liver for you.

BACON, CORN, AND CHEESE STUFFED PORK CHOPS IN SAGE CREAM SAUCE *Serves 4*

4 strips of bacon cut into ½"-wide pieces
½ cup chopped onions
1 cup cooked corn
½ cup diced fresh bread (½" dice)
¼ teaspoon salt
¼ teaspoon pepper
¾ cup grated Cheddar cheese or Monterey Jack cheese
4 (1½"-thick) loin pork chops, with bone
Corn oil
1 cup chicken stock
1 teaspoon rubbed sage
¼ teaspoon thyme
1½ cups heavy cream
¼ teaspoon pepper
Salt, if needed
1 tablespoon minced parsley

Cook the bacon until crisp and drain well. Set aside 2 tablespoons of the bacon fat. In the fat remaining in the pan, sauté the onions over medium heat until tender. Combine the bacon with the onions, corn, bread cubes, salt, pepper, and cheese. Cut a pocket through to the bone in each of the chops. Compact the stuffing and push as much of it as possible into each pocket while still being able to close the chop. Secure the opening with toothpicks inserted horizontally.

Preheat the oven to 350°. Heat the reserved 2 tablespoons of bacon fat in a skillet large enough to hold the chops in a single layer. If necessary, add corn oil so that the bottom of the pan is covered. Heat the pan until very hot and then add the chops and cook for 5 minutes on each side. Pour on the chicken stock, cover the pan tightly, and put in the oven for 1 hour or until very tender. Remove from the oven, turn off the heat, leave the door ajar and let the oven cool to 200°. Transfer the chops to a baking pan, cover tightly with foil, and keep warm in the 200° oven. Strain the chicken stock into a saucepan. Add the sage and thyme and reduce the liquid until syrupy—about ⅓ cup. Stir in the cream and pepper and cook to the consistency of a light gravy. Check for seasoning. Spoon some of the sauce over each chop and dust with the parsley.

NOTES AND VARIATIONS
The filling is enough for 6 small, 5 medium, or 4 large chops. It will also fill a 3-pound boneless pork loin, butterflied, stuffed, and tied. Roast the whole loin at 350° for 1 hour and 15 minutes or to an internal temperature of 160°.

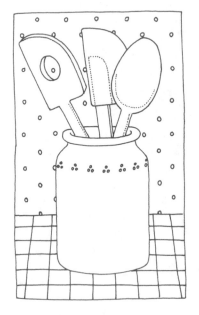

Substitute Monterey Jack cheese with jalapeño pepper bits in it for a spicy alternative.

PORK WITH GARLIC AND NAM PLA   *Serves 2*

An extremely simple dish that is tasty either hot or at room temperature.

½ pound boneless pork loin sliced ¼" thick
2 tablespoons corn oil
½ teaspoon minced garlic
¼ teaspoon pepper
1 tablespoon nam pla (Thai fish sauce)

In a skillet large enough to hold all the meat in a single layer, heat the corn oil until very hot. Add the pork slices in a single layer and cook over medium heat for 3–4 minutes. Turn the meat and sprinkle with the garlic, pepper, and nam pla. Cook for 3–4 minutes more while shaking the pan to keep the garlic from burning. Flip the meat over and cook 30 seconds more. Serve the pork with the pan juices.

Nam pla is the liquid extract from salted and fermented fish. Thais use it in much the same way that the Japanese and Chinese use soy sauce.

RACK OF LAMB WITH MUSTARD   *Serves 4*

Rack of lamb is certainly one of the most patrician of entrées, irresistible to those stalwart meat eaters among us—especially when a fine bottle of red wine is the possible accompaniment. Frog's treatment of the rack is elegantly simple. The meat is roasted at a high temperature until the outside is crusty but the inside is still rare. A savory blanket of mustard, crumbs, and herbs is then spread on, and the meat is returned to the oven for a brief moment before serving.

2 racks of lamb of 6–8 chops each, the fat scraped from
   between the bones to within 1" of the meat, each rack
   cut in half so that there are 4 portions
¼ cup corn oil
¾ cup Dijon mustard
2 tablespoons minced parsley
3 teaspoons minced garlic
1 tablespoon minced shallots
1 tablespoon crumbled dried rosemary
1 teaspoon dried marjoram
2 teaspoons dried oregano
½ teaspoon dried thyme
3 tablespoons dry white wine
¼ cup fine dry bread crumbs

Preheat the oven to 475°. Rub each portion of rack with some of the corn oil and set with the fat side down in a roasting pan. Wrap aluminum foil around the rib bones. Roast the racks for 12–14 minutes for medium-rare meat. Meanwhile, combine the remaining ingredients except for the crumbs. Remove the racks from the oven and turn them over. Spread a thick layer of the mustard mixture over the fat side of the racks. Sprinkle each with 1 tablespoon of the crumbs. Baste with some of the grease from the roasting pan. Return the racks to the oven for 3–5 minutes more or until the crumbs are golden. For medium-rare meat the internal temperature will be about 145°.

ORIENTAL LAMB CURRY
WITH EGGPLANT AND PECANS

Serves 3–4

So enthusiastic was the reception to Steven's Siamese Chicken Curry back in Frog's early days that he was encouraged to apply to other ingredients the same technique of blending a curry-paste-flavored stir-fry with Béchamel. (See notes at end of Siamese Chicken Curry.)

This particular curry happens to be somewhat drab in appearance. Other more colorful vegetables could be substituted for the eggplant, but it just wouldn't be the same. So, we suggest that you serve the curry on colorful plates, garnish it with lots of watercress, and/or serve a bright vegetable such as peas, carrots, green beans, or snow peas as an accompaniment.

EGGPLANT
¼ cup corn oil
3 cups peeled and cubed eggplant (¾ pound in 1″ cubes)
¼ teaspoon salt

BÉCHAMEL
4 tablespoons butter
¼ cup flour
2 cups half-and-half
¼ teaspoon salt

CURRY
2 tablespoons corn oil
1 packet (½ ounce) red or green Thai curry paste
2 tablespoons sugar
2 tablespoons plus 1 teaspoon soy sauce
2½ teaspoons minced ginger
2½ teaspoons minced garlic
2½ teaspoons ground coriander
12 ounces well-trimmed boneless lamb from leg or loin, sliced ¼″ thick, in bite-size pieces
¼ teaspoon salt
OPT. ½ teaspoon sriraja (Thai hot sauce) or Tabasco
½ cup lightly roasted pecan halves
Hot cooked rice

EGGPLANT
Heat the corn oil in a large skillet or wok. Add the eggplant and salt and stir-fry for 4–5 minutes or until just cooked through. Transfer eggplant to a bowl and set aside.

THAI COOKING
The food is sweet, sour, spicy, hot, bitter, salty and/or mild. Think of sugar, fish sauce, tear-inducing curry pastes, coconut milk, and basil all flavoring the same dish. A unique cuisine, Thai cooking, like the country itself, has known many foreign influences but has never been ruled by any particular one. The Chinese, Indians, Portuguese (who introduced chili peppers), and others all left their marks, but the Thai style of cooking and seasoning (especially) has maintained its individuality. Theirs is a sort of free-form cooking which relies heavily on experience and taste rather than on strict recipes. One of the most distinctive elements in the Thai kitchen is the curry pastes (see page 129) made from ground chilies, herbs, and/or fragrant leaves. For balance, though, there are many gently aromatic dishes, light salads and soothing fruits.

BÉCHAMEL

Melt the butter in a small saucepan. Blend in the flour and cook 1 minute. Whisk in the half-and-half and salt. Cook and stir over low heat until the sauce thickens and bubbles. Set aside. (If not using immediately, set aside and cover surface flush with plastic wrap.)

CURRY

Heat the corn oil. Blend in the curry paste. Add the sugar and soy and cook, while stirring, for 1–2 minutes. Add the ginger, garlic, and coriander and sauté 1 minute. Turn up the heat and add the lamb and salt. Quickly stir-fry for 1–2 minutes until the meat is cooked. Lower heat, add the Béchamel and eggplant, and heat through. If the resulting mixture seems too thick, add some additional half-and-half, beginning with 2 tablespoons. Stir until smooth, taste, and add the sriraja or Tabasco if desired. Stir in the pecans and serve immediately over rice.

Pasta Entrées

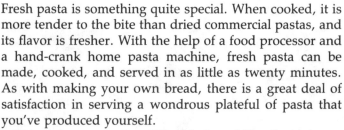

FRESH PASTA

Makes approximately one pound
Serves 4–6 as an entrée

Fresh pasta is something quite special. When cooked, it is more tender to the bite than dried commercial pastas, and its flavor is fresher. With the help of a food processor and a hand-crank home pasta machine, fresh pasta can be made, cooked, and served in as little as twenty minutes. As with making your own bread, there is a great deal of satisfaction in serving a wondrous plateful of pasta that you've produced yourself.

This recipe comes from The Market of The Commissary where we produce about five hundred pounds of pasta a week, some of which is sold in The Market and the rest used in our restaurants. Because we use durum flour, the pasta is more yellow in color and firmer in texture than that made with all-purpose flour.

2½ cups durum flour
¼ teaspoon salt
3 eggs
1–2 tablespoons water
Cornmeal or semolina

Put the flour and salt in the bowl of a food processor. Add the eggs and 1 tablespoon of the water. Whiz for 10 seconds. The dough should be crumbly and form a ball when squeezed together. If too dry, add more water, a teaspoon at a time. Form the dough into a ball with your hands and knead briefly on a lightly floured surface until smooth. If not using immediately, dough can be wrapped in plastic wrap and left at room temperature for several hours. Before rolling, cut the dough into quarters.

To roll the dough using a hand-crank home-size pasta machine, set the machine at its widest setting and feed the dough through. Begin rolling the dough through the thinner settings on the machine, one step at a time. When the desired thickness is reached with each length, spread it out on a lightly floured surface and dust lightly with more flour. When all the dough has been rolled, run it through the cutters on the machine for fettuccine or cut by hand for cannelloni, lasagna, ravioli, tortellini, etc. If not using immediately, toss the pasta with a little semolina or cornmeal and store in the refrigerator if using the same day (or in the freezer if using the next day or later).

To cook the pasta, add it to a large pot (about 5 quarts) of boiling water and stir for about 10 seconds to keep the pasta pieces separated. Cook for just 2–4 minutes, depending on the thickness of the pasta and your personal taste. Drain and rinse well and proceed with however you are going to serve it.

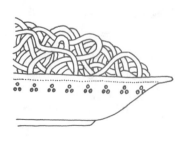

To make fresh pasta with all-purpose flour, simply use 2½ cups of regular flour in place of the durum and *only* 1–3 teaspoons of water rather than 1–2 tablespoons.

To roll pasta by hand, let the dough rest for 15–30 minutes in order for the gluten to relax before you begin to roll. Then roll the dough to a thickness of ¹⁄₁₆″ on a lightly floured surface and cut to desired shapes with a knife.

To cook pasta that has been frozen, take it from the freezer and drop directly into boiling water. Stir it to separate. It will cook in the same amount of time as fresh.

WHOLE WHEAT PASTA WITH GOAT CHEESE AND FRESH HERBS

Serves 6 as entrée or 10 as a first course

A dinner invitation to Steven's home is always cause for great anticipation as the meal is sure to be magnificent. The atmosphere will be gracious and comfortable, the food gloriously simple and vibrant, the wine fabulous and generously offered . . . in short, a most convivial evening that will linger long in one's memory. One summer dinner party for a small group of staff began with this luscious pasta creation devised to take advantage of Steven's prolific herb garden.

1 pound fresh whole wheat fettuccine or ⅔ pound dried
¾ cup olive oil, extra virgin if possible
1 tablespoon minced garlic
7 ounces creamy goat cheese such as Montrachet or
  Vacherin, at room temperature
⅓ loosely packed cup of finely chopped mixed fresh
  herbs (mint, oregano, lemon thyme, basil, marjoram,
  etc.), all stems removed before chopping
1 teaspoon salt
1 teaspoon pepper
¾ cup grated Parmesan cheese

Cook the pasta until *al dente* in a large pot of boiling salted water. Drain well. Heat the olive oil in a skillet. Add the garlic and sauté 1 minute over very low heat. Add the pasta and toss with the oil. Add most of the goat cheese (reserving a little to crumble on top), herbs, salt, and pepper. Stir well to blend and serve immediately topped with the reserved goat cheese, the grated Parmesan, and, if desired, some additional minced herbs.

It's great to have goat cheeses so readily available these days. We even have a superb local source for fresh goat cheese in Doug Newbold, who was one of The Commissary's first chefs and now has her own flock of Nubian goats and a thriving business. ☆ If we had a pound of Doug's cheese in our refrigerator, we might crumble some over a green salad, toss some with pasta and black olives, spread some on garlic toast and dust with fresh herbs, fold some into an omelet with sun-dried tomatoes, stir some into scrambled eggs with smoked salmon and scallions, top a "lamburger" with some and serve with sautéed eggplant, tomatoes and rosemary ... get the idea?

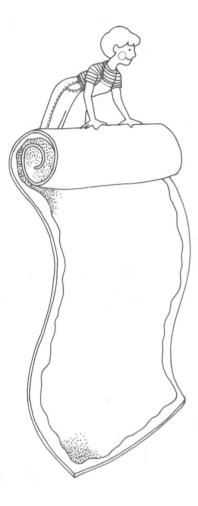

PASTA ROLL WITH SPINACH
AND RICOTTA FILLING
AND TWO SAUCES
Serves 8–10

Here is pasta in yet another guise—that of a long log spiraled with a gloriously green filling of spinach, ricotta, and prosciutto, to be sliced and smothered with a twin saucing of Béchamel and tomato cream. This is a very pretty dish, all white, green, and red. In the Downstairs restaurant at The Commissary, we further accent each serving with a grilled tomato half, topped with crumbs.

If there are any tricks to this dish, they consist of obtaining such a large sheet of fresh pasta and then cooking it without tearing or sticking. Neither, though, should be a problem. If you have access to a shop which sells fresh pasta, you could ask them to roll you a 12″ × 16″ sheet as we do at The Market. But, on the other hand, fresh pasta is really quite easily made at home (see recipe and directions for rolling on p. 158), and you could roll the pasta out by hand.

TOMATO COULIS
1 tablespoon olive oil
½ cup minced onions
1 pound fresh tomatoes
¼ teaspoon salt
⅛ teaspoon Tabasco
2 teaspoons minced fresh basil, tarragon or other herb

BÉCHAMEL SAUCE
4 tablespoons butter
¼ cup flour
2½ cups half-and-half
¾ teaspoon salt
¾ teaspoon pepper
⅛ teaspoon nutmeg

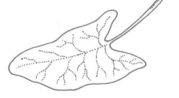

FILLED PASTA ROLL
12″ × 16″ sheet of fresh pasta
2 tablespoons butter
3 (10-ounce) bags fresh spinach, well washed
½ cup finely chopped onion
15 ounces ricotta cheese
2 egg yolks
1½ cups grated Parmesan cheese
1 teaspoon salt
1 teaspoon pepper
⅛ teaspoon cayenne pepper
¼ pound thinly sliced and slivered prosciutto
Minced parsley and additional Parmesan cheese for
   sprinkling

TOMATO COULIS

Using a small saucepan and the ingredients above, follow the procedure for making Tomato Coulis (see p. 102). Set aside.

BÉCHAMEL SAUCE

Melt the butter in a saucepan over low heat. Whisk in the flour. Whisk well to get rid of any lumps. Cook over a low flame for several minutes, stirring frequently. Steadily add the half-and-half to the flour mixture while whisking constantly. Simmer several minutes, then add the seasonings. Cover the surface flush with a piece of buttered plastic wrap. Set aside.

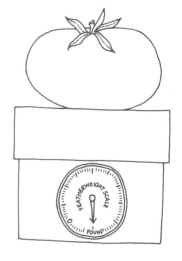

PASTA ROLL

Have ready a large pot of gently boiling salted water. Carefully lower the sheet of pasta (so that it doesn't clump) into the water. Cook for 3–7 minutes or until done (taste a corner). Trying to keep it from tearing, carefully pour the pasta into a colander. Rinse with cold water, drain well, lay it flat, and blot between dish towels.

Preheat the oven to 350°. Butter well a baking sheet or large dish. Blanch the spinach to wilt it, squeeze it very dry, and finely chop. Sauté the onion in the butter until golden. Add the chopped spinach and sauté until there is no moisture left in the pan. In a bowl, combine the spinach with the ricotta, egg yolks, Parmesan, and seasonings. Sauté the prosciutto until lightly frizzled and add to the filling. Spread the filling evenly over the sheet of pasta and roll it up lengthwise as you would a jelly roll. Using a towel to help you, transfer the roll, seam side down, to the baking sheet. Place the roll diagonally across the sheet, if necessary, to make it fit. Brush with butter, cover with foil, and bake for 30–45 minutes until filling is set. Let sit 8–10 minutes before slicing and serving.

While the pasta roll is sitting, gently reheat the Béchamel and tomato sauces. Stir half of the Béchamel into the tomato sauce for a tomato-cream sauce. To serve, cut the pasta roll into ¾" slices, and top each serving with some of the Béchamel and tomato sauces. Dust with additional Parmesan and sprinkle with parsley.

NOTE

The pasta roll can be frozen (unbaked) and then defrosted and cooked at a later date. If you simply wish to bake it earlier in the day, do so and then arrange slices of the roll in individual buttered gratin dishes. Cover and heat. Just before serving, top with the Béchamel and tomato sauces (and perhaps even some grated mozzarella or Parmesan cheese) and heat in the oven until bubbling.

TORTELLINI WITH HERBED
BLUE CHEESE FILLING

Serves 6 as an appetizer

Tortellini are surprisingly easy and fun to make and a great way to involve your dinner guests in the meal's preparation. Everyone likes to get into the act of filling and shaping the little packets. This particular filling is creamy and pungent but not overpowering, and if you've never made your own tortellini, you'll be amazed at how much better these are than most any you might purchase.

These little morsels make great hors d'oeuvres, too, passed on trays while still hot. They were the hit of a Zinfandel wine tasting we held one spring, and Steven specially requested to have them served at his wedding reception.

BLUE CHEESE FILLING
3 tablespoons grated Parmesan cheese
3 ounces softened blue cheese such as Gorgonzola or
  Danablu
3 ounces softened cream cheese
1½ teaspoons finely chopped parsley
¼ teaspoon grated nutmeg
¾ teaspoon minced fresh marjoram or ¼ teaspoon dried
¼ teaspoon salt
¼ teaspoon pepper

ASSEMBLY AND SERVING
1 pound Fresh Pasta thinly rolled but not cut (see recipe
  on p. 158)
½ cup hot melted butter
¼ cup grated Parmesan cheese
2 tablespoons minced parsley
Freshly ground black pepper to taste

BLUE CHEESE FILLING
Combine all the ingredients and set aside.

ASSEMBLY
Spread out the sheet(s) of pasta on a lightly floured surface and cut circles with a 2½" cookie cutter or empty soup can. Dust circles lightly with flour to prevent sticking. You should have about 50 circles. Keep them covered with plastic wrap to prevent their drying out. Put ¼ teaspoon of the filling in the center of each circle. Dip your finger in water and moisten the edges of the circle lightly to help form a seal. Fold the circle nearly in half so that the upper edge doesn't quite meet the lower edge. Press the edges together firmly and gently stretch the 2 points of the half circle around to meet each other and firmly press together to form a little concave ring. Set the tortellini in a single

HOW TO FOLD...

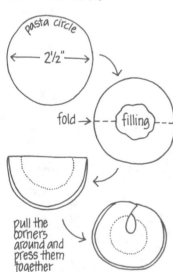

fold →

pull the
corners
around and
press them
together

layer without touching on a plastic-wrap-lined or lightly floured tray. (You will most likely have extra filling. Save it to use as an omelet filling or as a spread.)

TO SERVE
Have ready in a flame-proof mixing bowl the melted butter and the Parmesan cheese. Bring a large pot of salted water to a boil. Drop in the tortellini. They cook very quickly (about 2 minutes) and are done when they float to the top of the pot. Remove them with a slotted spoon, draining off as much water as possible. Gently toss the tortellini with the butter and the Parmesan cheese in the mixing bowl set over medium heat. Turn out onto warm plates, dust with the parsley and pepper, and serve immediately.

VARIATIONS AND NOTES
Once you have the technique down, experiment with other fillings. Just be sure to have the ingredients finely chopped or creamed. Goat cheese would be a good substitution for the blue cheese.

Once assembled, the tortellini should either be cooked and served immediately or frozen, uncooked. To freeze, spread on a baking tray and freeze until stiff, then gather into plastic bags and wrap tightly. To cook frozen tortellini, simply transfer from freezer directly to boiling water; they should take only a few minutes more to cook. Test the first one up.

PARMESAN CHEESE
Reggiano-Parmigiano is the name to look for... stamped on the rind. That is the real thing, strictly made only in the region around Parma. Your piece will be cut from a 50 to 80 pound round. It should be crumbly and have a buttery, mellow taste that also pairs beautifully on its own with a glass of fine Italian red wine. ☆ By all means don't buy your Parmesan pre-grated; it will have dried out and lost its delicacy. Grating it yourself using the smallest holes on the grater, also produces a soft, incredibly fine dusting of cheese that is aesthetically much more pleasing.

PASTA WITH CRAB, TOMATOES, CREAM, AND TARRAGON

Serves 3 as an entrée or 6 as a first course

This luscious dish took first place in a staff recipe contest held for our First Annual Pasta and Zinfandel Festival in 1982. It is divinely rich, yet the tomato and lemon contribute a sprightly accent.

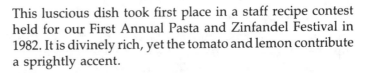

To chase away the February blues one winter, we threw a Pasta and Zinfandel Festival for 2 weeks at The Commissary. To share our enthusiasm for these 2 products with our customers, we made lots and lots of different noodle dishes, of course, held a staff pasta recipe contest, offered a host of Zinfandels by the glass, organized an exhaustive Zinfandel tasting, strung pasta all around, and generally managed to forget how gloomy February can be.

PASTA AND SAUCE
½ pound fresh cappellini pasta or ⅓ pound dried
3 tablespoons minced shallots
¼ cup Madeira
½ cup dry white wine
2 teaspoons minced fresh tarragon or ¾ teaspoon dried
½ teaspoon pepper
1⅔ cups heavy cream
¼ teaspoon grated lemon peel
1 teaspoon salt
1 cup peeled, seeded, chopped tomatoes (see how to peel on p. 102)
1 tablespoon lemon juice

CRAB SAUTÉ
¼ cup butter
3 tablespoons minced scallions
1 teaspoon minced fresh tarragon or ¼ teaspoon dried
½ cup peeled, seeded, chopped tomatoes (see p. 102 for how to peel)
½ teaspoon salt
⅛ teaspoon pepper
2 tablespoons lemon juice
½ pound lump or backfin crabmeat, picked over for shell
1 tablespoon minced parsley

PASTA AND SAUCE
Cook the pasta in a large pot of boiling water until *al dente*, rinse under running water, drain well, and set aside.

In a wide saucepan, combine the shallots, Madeira, wine, tarragon, and pepper. Reduce the mixture to ¼ cup. Toward the end of the reduction, tilt the pan back and forth so that the mixture doesn't burn around the edges. Add the cream, lemon peel, and salt. Bring it to a hard boil for 5 minutes, stirring occasionally. Stir in the tomatoes and lemon juice and set aside.

CRAB SAUTÉ
Heat the butter in a sauté pan. Add the scallions, tarragon, tomatoes, salt, pepper, and lemon juice. Heat until very hot. Add the crabmeat and shake the pan gently so as to heat the crab without breaking up the lumps. Cover and keep hot.

To serve, reheat the pasta in the cream sauce, bringing it just to a boil. Divide among individual plates; top each portion with some of the crab sauté and sprinkle with parsley.

"Al dente" means "to the tooth," or, in other words, the cooked pasta should not be mushy but have a touch of resistance to the teeth. So, watch your pot closely. Fresh pasta, especially, cooks very, very quickly.

CAPPELLINI WITH BAY SCALLOPS AND CHAMPAGNE CREAM SAUCE

Serves 6 as first course or 3–4 as entrée

1 bottle inexpensive dry *(brut)* champagne
¼ cup white wine vinegar
¼ cup minced shallots
1 quart heavy cream
½ pound fresh cappellini or ⅓ pound dried
1 tablespoon lemon juice
1 teaspoon salt
1½ teaspoons pepper
½ pound bay scallops
GARNISH: Chopped parsley

In a 6-quart saucepan over high heat, reduce the champagne, vinegar, and shallots to 2 cups. Add the cream and reduce to 3½ cups or until thickened to the consistency of light gravy. Be careful not to reduce too far or the butter will separate from the cream. Cook the cappellini in boiling salted water until *al dente*. Drain and rinse well. Add the lemon juice, salt, pepper, and scallops to the sauce and heat until the scallops are cooked—about 2–3 minutes. Add the pasta and heat through. Turn out onto warm plates and sprinkle with chopped parsley.

VARIATIONS
Substitute shrimp and blanched asparagus tips for the bay scallops, or you might like to add tiny slivers of sautéed julienned carrots and leeks. Then, you could go all the way and garnish each portion with a spoonful of red or black caviar.

LINGUINI WITH BROCCOLI AND BAY SCALLOPS
Serves 4

This recipe was featured on our first Commissary recipe calendar in 1979, and judging from the feedback we received, it was the most frequently tried and enjoyed recipe on the calendar that year.

4 cups broccoli flowerets and stems (sliced ¼" thick)
¾ pound fresh linguini or ½ pound dried
¾ cup butter
2 teaspoons minced garlic
1 pound bay scallops
2 teaspoons salt
1 teaspoon pepper
⅔ cup grated Parmesan cheese or more, to taste

Peel broccoli stems and cut into ¼"-thick slices. Blanch broccoli in boiling salted water, drain, refresh under cold water, drain and set aside. Cook the linguini until *al dente* in a large pot of boiling salted water. Drain well and toss with ¼ cup of the butter. Heat remaining ½ cup of butter in a large skillet. Add the garlic and sauté until softened. Add the scallops, salt, and pepper. Sauté 3 minutes or until scallops are just opaque. Add the broccoli and heat 1 minute. Add the pasta and heat through. Add the cheese and serve at once.

WALNUT BUTTER SAUCE   *Makes 4 cups or 8 servings*

A squirrel would be in seventh heaven with this sauce. We found it pretty tantalizing ourselves, and it has been a staple in the Downstairs restaurant's Pasta Bar for ages.

1 pound butter
3 tablespoons heavy cream
3 egg yolks
1 cup grated Parmesan cheese
1 cup lightly toasted ground walnuts
2 teaspoons salt
2 teaspoons pepper
1½ tablespoons minced garlic

In a food processor or blender, or by hand, cream the butter. Add the cream and egg yolks and blend until smooth. Add the remaining ingredients. Refrigerate, well covered, if not using immediately.

For one entrée or 2 appetizer servings, have ½ cup of the butter at room temperature, cook ¼ pound fresh pasta and toss with the butter over low heat. Dust with minced parsley and additional Parmesan, if desired.

VARIATIONS
Toasted almonds or hazelnuts are a delicious substitute for the walnuts.

Try the butter, too, on baked potatoes, rice, grilled chicken, or fish.

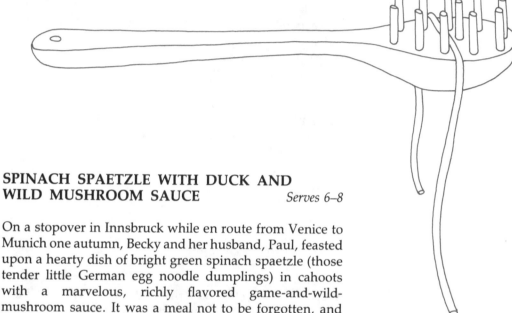

SPINACH SPAETZLE WITH DUCK AND WILD MUSHROOM SAUCE
Serves 6–8

On a stopover in Innsbruck while en route from Venice to Munich one autumn, Becky and her husband, Paul, feasted upon a hearty dish of bright green spinach spaetzle (those tender little German egg noodle dumplings) in cahoots with a marvelous, richly flavored game-and-wild-mushroom sauce. It was a meal not to be forgotten, and upon their return from vacation, a new *plat du jour* (this particular recipe) was hatched at The Commissary.

The sauce lends itself well to advance preparation. Make the stock and assemble the sauce (note the Commissary-esque touch of soy sauce) 2–3 days ahead (it even freezes well). The spaetzle, too, can be made a day ahead and reheated in butter just before serving.

DUCKS
2 (4½-pound) ducks

STOCK
⅓ cup butter
Duck carcasses (broken up), giblets, and necks
1 cup chopped onions
1 cup chopped carrots
1 cup chopped celery
1 cup dry sherry
5 quarts water

SAUCE

1 ounce dried imported mushrooms (cèpes, funghi
  porcini, morels, etc.)
6 tablespoons butter
1 pound small mushrooms, quartered
3 tablespoons flour
2½ cups reduced duck stock
¼ cup soy sauce
3 tablespoons dry sherry
¼ teaspoon salt
½ teaspoon pepper
1 bay leaf
⅛ teaspoon dried thyme
¼ teaspoon dried tarragon
¼ teaspoon Tabasco
Reserved roast duck meat

SPAETZLE AND ASSEMBLY

1 (10-ounce) bag spinach
1 tablespoon corn oil
2 cups flour
¾ teaspoon salt
⅛ teaspoon nutmeg
3 eggs
¾ cup milk
2 tablespoons butter

DUCKS

Preheat the oven to 425°. Remove the livers from the ducks
and reserve the necks and giblets for the stock. Cut off
excess neck skin and remove any loose interior fat. Prick
the skin all over without piercing the meat. Set the ducks
in a roasting pan and roast for 1 hour. Let cool until the
ducks can be easily handled, then remove the meat, wrap
it, and refrigerate it until shortly before serving.

STOCK

Melt the butter in a stock pot and heat until very hot. Add
duck necks, giblets and vegetables. Sauté over medium-
high heat until the vegetables are lightly browned—about
10 minutes. Add the sherry, water, and duck carcasses.
Bring to a boil and then let simmer 2–3 hours. If necessary
add more water to keep the carcasses covered. Strain off
and discard the solids. Cool the stock. Skim off and reserve
the fat. Bring the stock to a boil and reduce it to 2½ cups.
Cool and refrigerate the stock if not proceeding with the
sauce immediately.

168

SAUCE
Soak the dried mushrooms in warm water to cover until soft and "reconstituted." Strain and rinse the mushrooms well several times. Coarsely chop them and rinse again.

In a saucepan, melt half the butter. Add the 1 pound of quartered mushrooms and sauté until most of the liquid has evaporated. Transfer the mushrooms to a bowl. Add the remaining butter to the saucepan. Add the flour and cook 2–3 minutes to make a roux. Whisk in the reserved duck stock, the soy sauce, sherry, and seasonings. Simmer 5–10 minutes, stirring occasionally, until the sauce thickens.

Remove and discard the skin from the reserved duck meat. Cut the meat into ½" pieces and add to the sauce along with the sautéed mushrooms and wild mushrooms. Simmer 10 minutes.

SPINACH SPAETZLE AND ASSEMBLY
Wash the spinach well. With the water still clinging to the leaves, put the spinach in a large skillet or pot and steam until thoroughly wilted. Drain and rinse with cold water. Squeeze the spinach very dry and purée with the corn oil in a food processor or blender until very smooth. Combine the flour, salt, and nutmeg. Add the eggs, milk, and spinach purée. Combine well to make a thick batter.

Heat the sauce. Have ready 3 quarts of boiling salted water. Force the spaetzle dough through a spaetzle press into the boiling water. The spaetzle are cooked as soon as they rise to the top. Drain well. (At this point they can be tossed with a tablespoon of butter and held for several hours.) Heat the 2 tablespoons butter in a skillet. Add the spaetzle and toss to coat them with butter and heat them. Serve at once topped with the hot duck sauce.

NOTES AND VARIATIONS
Substitute spinach noodles for the spaetzle.

Serve spaetzle by themselves instead of rice, noodles, or potatoes. Fry them a little longer in the butter so that they become slightly crispy.

Steamed baby carrots would be our first choice for an accompaniment, and a good crisp salad on the side would help cut the richness. Serve with a German beer or perhaps a German or Austrian white wine. (A light Zinfandel would also be quite nice.)

A spaetzle press is definitely very handy when you're making spaetzle. For some reason, neither a potato ricer nor a colander does the job properly. The press isn't always easy to find, though. (Check specialty kitchenware shops, especially around German neighborhoods.) Lacking a press, your best bet is to put the dough in a pastry bag fitted with a tip with a ⅛" opening. Squeeze long noodles of dough in the boiling water. Drain and cool the cooked noodles. Before serving, coarsely chop them and sauté in butter.

PESTO POSSIBILITIES

- toss with orzo for a hot side dish
- toss with boiled new potatoes
- spread on a pizza shell
- mix into butter and serve with corn on the cob, grilled steak or veal chops
- make pesto bread instead of garlic bread
- add a little to the filling for Crab and Brie in Phyllo Dough
- add to a simple vinaigrette to serve with sliced tomatoes or mixed vegetable salad
- smear on hamburgers and top with mozzarella and tomato slices
- try different nuts and greens in pesto... such as pistachios and mint
- swirl into mayonnaise and use for crudités, potato salad or cold roast chicken, beef or fish
- dab onto scrambled eggs, or drizzle onto an omelet, add grated fontina, and roll.

SPINACH-WALNUT PESTO

Makes 2 cups
Enough for 2 pounds of fresh pasta

The minute summer's fresh basil appears, we run about like mad making huge batches of pesto for the restaurants. With a little foresight, we make enough to freeze some for the winter months, but should we fail to do so or should we run out come mid-January, we don't hesitate to resort to this fine variation that makes good use of the constant year-round abundance of spinach. Use and enjoy Spinach-Walnut Pesto just as you would the traditional pesto.

¾ cup chopped walnuts
1 (10-ounce) bag fresh spinach, washed and stemmed
¼ cup olive oil
1 tablespoon chopped garlic
½ teaspoon salt
½ teaspoon pepper
¾ cup grated Parmesan cheese

Preheat the oven to 300° and lightly toast the walnuts on a baking sheet for 7 minutes. Let cool. Whiz the nuts until fine in a food processor. Remove to a bowl. Put the spinach, oil, garlic, salt, and pepper in the food processor and whiz until just smooth. Add the cheese and nuts and whiz just to combine. To serve, toss with hot cooked pasta over low heat. Add a little stock or water if the sauce is too thick to combine evenly with the pasta. The pesto can be covered with a thin layer of olive oil and stored in the refrigerator or freezer.

25 QUICK PASTA IDEAS

Hot Dishes: Cook and drain fresh pasta, then toss immediately with . . .

Crumbled goat cheese, slivered sun-dried tomatoes, freshly ground pepper, and minced garlic that has been briefly sautéed in virgin olive oil

Melted butter, sour cream, cottage cheese, poppy seeds, sliced scallions, and bits of crisp bacon

Melted butter, ricotta cheese, Parmesan cheese, sautéed garlic, minced basil, and toasted pine nuts

Fresh and wild (if possible) mushrooms sautéed in butter with minced shallots, hot reduced heavy cream, Parmesan cheese, and minced parsley

Slivered black olives, cubed feta cheese and tomatoes, sliced scallions, olive oil, and freshly ground pepper

Chopped blanched spinach sautéed in lots of olive oil with minced garlic, freshly ground pepper, slivers of roasted red peppers, and Parmesan cheese

Briefly sautéed bay scallops, pesto, and Parmesan cheese

American golden caviar, melted butter, and Crème Fraîche

Blanched asparagus, sautéed slivered prosciutto, hot reduced heavy cream, melted butter, and Parmesan cheese

Crumbled crisp bacon, chopped roasted red peppers, melted butter, cooked peas, a little reduced heavy cream, and Parmesan cheese

Ricotta cheese, melted butter, Parmesan cheese, cooked peas, and small sautéed cubes of salami

Lump crabmeat sautéed in butter with a little curry powder, cooked peas, and melted butter

Slivered smoked salmon, warmed sour cream or Crème Fraîche, snipped fresh dill, or a garnish of caviar

Pieces of peeled shrimp sautéed briefly in butter with lots of minced garlic, crushed red pepper flakes, melted butter, reduced white wine, and minced parsley

Pieces of shrimp sautéed in butter, flamed with Pernod, and heated with cream with the addition of chopped blanched spinach that has also been sautéed in butter

Olive oil heated with crushed rosemary, minced onion and garlic sautéed in olive oil, sautéed slivered prosciutto, and blanched green beans

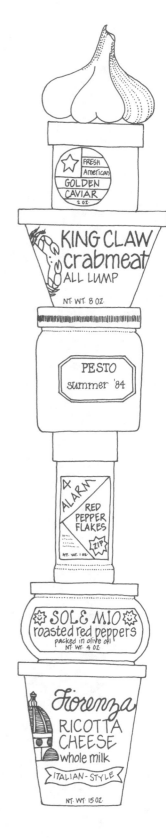

171

Chopped summer tomatoes, minced basil, freshly ground pepper, small cubes of mozzarella or goat cheese, and olive oil that has been heated with garlic cloves.

Butter melted with minced sage, seared cubes of sirloin or fillet of beef, and Parmesan cheese

Cold Dishes: Cook and drain fresh or dried pasta (be especially careful not to overcook), rinse under cold water, drain again, toss with corn oil, and let cool. Combine with:

Blanched broccoli flowerets, Oriental Dressing, and chopped roasted peanuts

Cubed fresh tomato and avocado, virgin olive oil, balsamic vinegar, salt, and freshly ground pepper

Pesto, olive oil, and cubed fresh tomato

Blanched carrots and broccoli flowerets, zucchini slices, cubed tomato, and Herb Vinaigrette or dressing of choice

Canned white meat tuna, chopped red pepper, slivered black olives, blanched green beans, and Caesar Dressing or dressing of choice

Buckwheat pasta, Curried Vinaigrette, chopped roasted cashews, and assorted oriental vegetables (blanched if necessary)

Chicken, Garlic Vinaigrette, chopped fresh basil, cherry tomatoes, and chopped red onion

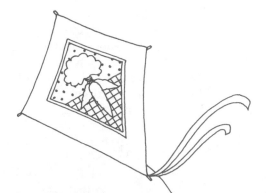

Pizzas and Sandwiches

16TH STREET DEEP-DISH PIZZA

Makes one 14" deep-dish pizza or two 10" deep-dish pizzas. Serves 4–6

Pâtés, fancy salads, poached fish, rack of lamb, etc. are all perfectly divine, but deep down inside, we all crave PIZZA! Few recipes have received as much of our attention as this one did when we decided to make Chicago's famous deep-dish pizza the hallmark item on the menu at 16th Street Bar & Grill, when it opened in September 1981. The recipe testing began at Steven's house with a giant pizza tasting which featured two "authentic" deep-dish pizzas (partially baked) that Steven had carried with him from Chicago the day before. For comparison we rounded up a number of pizzas from Philadelphia's best parlors, plus several pizzas that Anne had whipped up that afternoon. We sampled, rated, and, when we couldn't face another bite, drew up a list of criteria for our "ideal" pizza. Anne went back to work. The crust alone went through seven or eight permutations before we arrived at what we think is the ultimate in pizza crust—a crisp, crusty, nutty, rich yellow casing that doesn't play second fiddle to the topping as so many crusts do.

Thick, filling, oozing with gooey cheese and other treats, this pizza wins our vote. Better yet, it takes relatively little time to make, is ripe for all sorts of imaginative interpretations, and even freezes and reheats with the greatest of ease—and results.

Durum flour and semolina are both made from durum wheat, an exceptionally high-gluten strain. (Gluten is what gives a dough its elasticity and expansion capabilities.) Semolina is a more granular form of the flour and is prized for the making of commercial dried pasta because of its strength. Durum wheat flours are actually too tough to be good for breadmaking on their own.

CRUST
¼-ounce package dry yeast
1⅓ cups warm water
3 cups durum flour
¾ cup semolina
1 teaspoon salt
1 teaspoon sugar
⅓ cup olive or corn oil

TOMATO SAUCE
2 cups diced onions (½" dice)
2 tablespoons olive oil
1 tablespoon minced garlic
1 (28-ounce) can whole tomatoes, chopped, or 1¾ pounds chopped fresh tomatoes
1 teaspoon basil
½ teaspoon oregano
1 teaspoon salt
½ teaspoon pepper
¼ teaspoon Tabasco
¼ teaspoon fennel seed
¼ teaspoon thyme

ASSEMBLY
3 tablespoons semolina
1¼ pounds mozzarella or Icelandic Lapi cheese, grated
Toppings of choice

CRUST

Combine the yeast with the warm water. Let sit several minutes to soften, then stir to dissolve. Whiz the dry ingredients in a food processor. Add the dissolved yeast and oil. Whiz until the dough begins to ball up. The dough will be soft. Transfer it to a greased bowl, cover, and leave to double (about ½–1 hour) in a warm spot. The dough can be punched down at this point and used at once or refrigerated and used within 24 hours (in which case you may need to punch it down occasionally).

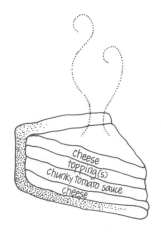

TOMATO SAUCE

Slowly sauté the onions in the oil until brown (about 20 minutes). Add the garlic and sauté 2–3 minutes. Add the remaining ingredients, including the juice from the canned tomatoes, and simmer, uncovered, until very thick.

ASSEMBLY

Preheat the oven to 400°. Lightly oil a 14″ × 2″ deep-dish pizza pan and dust with the semolina. Put the dough in the pan and press and stretch it so it fills the pan and is slightly thicker around the edges. Sprinkle ⅔ of the cheese on the crust, follow with the sauce and then any toppings you have chosen. Bake for 20 minutes. Sprinkle with the rest of the cheese and bake an additional 5 minutes more. Let cool several minutes and serve hot from the pan.

VARIATIONS

The dough can also be mixed by hand or with an electric mixer fitted with a dough hook or paddle.

Make two 10″ flat pizzas (or one 14″ flat pizza). Press the dough flat into two 12″ circles and roll under a 1″ rim on each or fit into two greased shallow 10″ tart pans. Use half the sauce and half the cheese for each pizza.

GOAT CHEESE PIZZA

Makes one 10" pizza

After our success with Deep-Dish Pizza at 16th Street Bar & Grill, we started experimenting with other kinds of pizza. This sophisticated variation is a real winner, too. It uses the same delicious crust we devised for the Deep-Dish Pizza—but instead it's done in a "free form" shape and topped with golden sweet sautéed onions, tangy goat cheese, and tiny bits of intensely flavored sun-dried tomatoes.

SUN-DRIED TOMATOES

Of all the "new" food products we've seen in recent years, these are definitely a favorite. The taste reminds us of eating simple olive oil-and-tomato-topped pizzas in Italy. It's as if the Italian sun has been captured in a jar. (Beware of some brands that are shriveled and salty. They should be red, soft, covered with olive oil and irresistible.) Chop up sun-dried tomatoes and use them as an accent. They're especially good in egg and pasta dishes, broiled with mozzarella and pesto on Italian bread, added to spinach sautéed in olive oil, or accenting a demi-glace sauce for a roast fillet of beef.

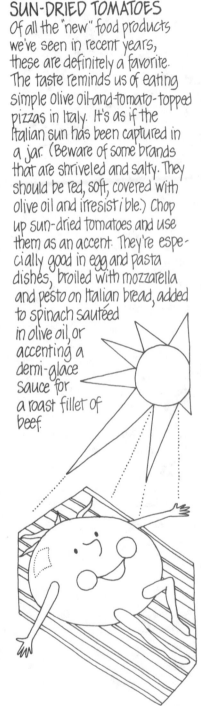

CRUST

1¼ teaspoons dry yeast
⅔ cup warm water
1½ cups durum flour
6 tablespoons semolina
½ teaspoon salt
½ teaspoon sugar
3 tablespoons olive oil or corn oil

TOPPING

¼ cup olive oil
3 cups diced onions
2 teaspoons minced garlic
¼ teaspoon dried oregano
¼ teaspoon red pepper flakes
2 tablespoons grated Parmesan cheese
OPT. 2 tablespoons chopped fresh basil or rosemary
6 ounces goat cheese, crumbled
¼ cup julienned sun-dried tomatoes or slivered red
    peppers (fresh or roasted)
8 quartered imported black olives
½ teaspoon minced parsley

CRUST

Combine the yeast with the warm water and let rest several minutes to soften. Stir to dissolve. Whiz dry ingredients in a food processor. Add the dissolved yeast and oil. Whiz until the dough begins to ball up. The dough will be soft. Transfer it to a greased bowl. Cover and leave to double (about ½ hour) in a warm spot.

TOPPING AND ASSEMBLY

While the dough is rising, heat the olive oil in a skillet. Add the onions, garlic, oregano, and pepper flakes, and sauté over medium-low heat until the onions are soft and golden.

Preheat the oven to 375°. Set the dough on a baking sheet that has been lightly oiled and dusted with semolina. With your hands, pat the dough evenly into a 12" circle. Roll under 1" of the dough around the edge to make a slight rim. Spread the onion mixture over the dough. Sprinkle on the Parmesan cheese. Bake 15 minutes. Remove from the oven. Distribute the basil and crumble the goat cheese over the onions. Arrange the sun-dried tomatoes and olives on top. Bake 5 to 10 minutes more. Dust with minced parsley and serve at once.

CLAM PIZZA WITH FRESH HERBS

Makes one 10" pizza

Often during the year, Don Falconio finds good reason to entertain staff members at his home. Not only does he have a lovely home, but the food is always wonderful, too. This pizza, which Don made up for one of his annual catering staff parties, was particularly memorable.

CRUST
1¼ teaspoons dry yeast
⅔ cup warm water
1½ cups durum flour
6 tablespoons semolina
½ teaspoon salt
½ teaspoon sugar
3 tablespoons olive oil or corn oil

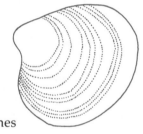

TOPPING
18 littleneck clams or 12 cherrystones
¼ cup olive oil
3 cups diced onions
¼ teaspoon salt
½ teaspoon crushed red pepper flakes
1 tablespoon minced garlic
3 tablespoons minced fresh herbs (sage, rosemary, thyme, basil)
½ cup grated Parmesan cheese
10 ounces mozzarella cheese, grated
OPT. 2 tablespoons wine vinegar

CRUST
Combine the yeast with the warm water and let sit several minutes to soften. Stir to dissolve. Whiz the dry ingredients in a food processor. Add the dissolved yeast and oil. Whiz until the dough begins to ball up. The dough will be soft. Transfer the dough to a greased bowl, cover and leave to double (about ½ hour) in a warm spot.

TOPPING AND ASSEMBLY
While the dough is rising, scrub the clams and put them

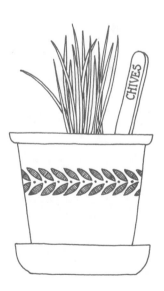

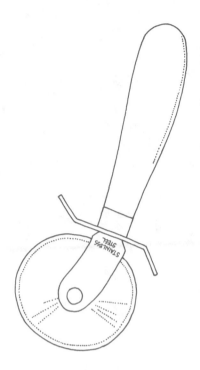

in a pot filled with boiling water an inch deep. Cover the pot and cook the clams over medium-high heat for about 5 minutes or until the clams have just opened. Turn the clams into a colander and rinse with cold water. Remove the clams from their shells and pull off the 2 tough muscles from the end of each clam. Cut each clam into quarters and set aside.

Heat the olive oil in a skillet. Add the onions, salt, and red pepper flakes and sauté until the onions are soft and golden, about 10 minutes. Remove from the heat and stir in the garlic and 2 tablespoons of the herbs.

Preheat the oven to 375°. Set the dough on a baking sheet that has been lightly oiled and dusted with semolina. With your hands, pat and push the dough evenly into a 12″ circle. Roll under an inch of the dough all around the edge to make a rim. Spread the onion mixture over the dough. Scatter on the Parmesan cheese and 1 cup of the mozzarella. Bake the pizza for 15 minutes. Arrange the clams on the pizza and top with the remaining mozzarella. Bake 10 minutes more. Sprinkle with the vinegar, dust with the remaining herbs, and serve at once.

VARIATION
Cook ½ pound of diced bacon until crisp. Drain well and add to the onion mixture before spreading on the dough.

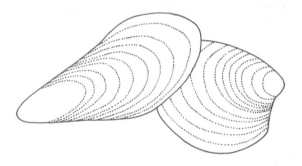

PIZZA WITH MUSSELS, SAFFRON, SUN-DRIED TOMATOES, AND THREE ITALIAN CHEESES   *Makes one 10″ pizza*

CRUST
1¼ teaspoons dry yeast
⅔ cup warm water
1½ cups durum flour
6 tablespoons semolina
½ teaspoon salt
½ teaspoon sugar
3 tablespoons olive oil or corn oil

TOPPING

18 mussels
¼ cup olive oil
3 cups diced onions
¼ teaspoon salt
¼ teaspoon crushed red pepper flakes
¼ teaspoon powdered saffron or 1 teaspoon saffron
    threads (¹⁄₂₈ ounce)
1 tablespoon minced garlic
¼ pound provolone, grated
6 ounces fontina cheese, grated
¾ cup chopped tomato in ½" cubes
3 tablespoons chopped sun-dried tomatoes
2 tablespoons grated Parmesan cheese
1 tablespoon minced fresh basil or oregano

CRUST

Combine the yeast with the warm water and let sit several
minutes to soften. Stir to dissolve. Whiz the dry ingredients
in a food processor. Add the dissolved yeast and oil. Whiz
until the dough begins to ball up. It will be soft. Transfer
to a greased bowl, cover, and leave to double (about ½
hour) in a warm spot.

TOPPING AND ASSEMBLY

While the dough is rising, scrub the mussels and put in a
pot with 1" of boiling water. Cover the pot and cook over
medium-high heat for about 2 minutes or until the mussels
have just opened. Turn the mussels into a colander and
rinse with cold water. Remove the mussels from their
shells and pull away the hairy "beard" and the 2 tough
muscles from the ends of each mussel. Set aside.

   Heat the olive oil in a skillet. Add the onions, salt,
pepper flakes, and saffron and sauté over medium heat
until the onions are soft and golden, about 10 minutes.
Remove from the heat and stir in the garlic.

   Preheat the oven to 375°. Set the dough on a baking
sheet that has been lightly oiled and dusted with semolina.
With your hands, pat and push the dough evenly into a
12" circle. Roll under an inch of the dough all around the
edge to make a rim. Spread the onion mixture over the
dough and sprinkle on the provolone. Bake the pizza for
15 minutes. Sprinkle on 1 cup of the grated fontina. Arrange
the mussels, fresh tomatoes and sun-dried tomatoes on
top. Scatter on the remaining fontina along with the
Parmesan. Bake 5 to 10 minutes more. Dust with the basil
or oregano and serve at once.

EGGPLANT PEPPERONI TART

Serves 8

For those who live for spicy food and always order extra cheese on their pizza, this is your recipe. A thin, crisp pastry crust barely contains its burden of garlicky sautéed eggplant, spicy pepperoni, and a thick layer of molten mozzarella . . . need we say more?

CRUST
1¾ cups flour
¾ teaspoon salt
½ teaspoon sugar
6 tablespoons cold unsalted butter
3 tablespoons cold vegetable shortening
¼ cup ice water

FILLING
⅓ cup olive oil
10 cups peeled, diced eggplant (⅜" dice) (about 2½ pounds)
1 tablespoon minced garlic
¾ teaspoon crumbled dried rosemary
1 teaspoon dried thyme
1 teaspoon salt
¼ teaspoon pepper
6 ounces pepperoni, very thinly sliced
1½ pounds mozzarella, or Muenster cheese grated

CRUST
Whiz the flour, salt, sugar, butter, and shortening in a food processor. Start and stop the machine until the mixture is crumbly. Add the ice water and whiz briefly until the mixture begins to pull away from the sides and form a ball. Let the dough rest ½ hour at room temperature.

Preheat the oven to 375°. On a lightly floured surface, roll the dough out to fit an 11" tart shell. Ease it into the pan and trim the edges. Prick the dough all over with a fork, then line with parchment or foil and fill with dried beans or rice. Bake for 8 minutes, then remove liner with its filling and bake the shell for 7 minutes more or until lightly browned. Cool to room temperature.

FILLING
Heat the olive oil in a large skillet. Add the eggplant, garlic, and herbs. Sauté the eggplant over medium-low heat about 15 minutes or until tender. Season with the salt and pepper. Drain the mixture if necessary.

Preheat the oven to 375°. Spread the sautéed eggplant in the prebaked tart shell. Arrange the pepperoni slices on top. Bake for 15 minutes. Sprinkle on the mozzarella. Bake 10–15 minutes more until the cheese is bubbly. Let sit 5 minutes before slicing.

EDEN BURGERS

Makes nine 5-ounce burgers

The carnivores among us were really surprised at how delicious these vegetarian burgers are. Nutty, crunchy, spicy, wholesome and not at all dry or boring, they are served at Eden II on toasted, garlic-buttered buns with tomato and sprouts—just as the real hamburgers are. Eden II, located just off the University of Pennsylvania campus, caters to a health-conscious student crowd, and these burgers have been a big hit there.

¼ cup corn oil
½ pound mushrooms, finely chopped (about 1¼ cups)
1½ cups finely chopped carrots
2 cups finely chopped onions
2 tablespoons minced garlic
¾ cup walnuts
½ cup sunflower seeds
½ cup sesame seeds, toasted
2 ounces bulgur wheat (7 tablespoons) soaked 10
    minutes or until tender in hot water and drained well
⅔ cup wheat germ
⅓ cup chopped parsley
2 tablespoons chopped dill
3 tablespoons tahini
1¼ cups cooked chickpeas, drained
3 tablespoons tamari or soy sauce
3 tablespoons lemon juice
¼ teaspoon cayenne pepper
½ teaspoon salt
¾ teaspoon pepper
¾ teaspoon ground cumin

Heat the corn oil in a skillet and sauté the mushrooms, carrots, onions, and garlic for about 15 minutes or until golden. Cool. Whiz the walnuts and sunflower seeds in a food processor for 3 seconds. Turn into a bowl and add the sesame seeds, bulgur, and wheat germ. In the food processor, whiz the sautéed vegetables with the remaining ingredients until just blended. Add to the bulgur mixture and mix well. The texture will be coarse and somewhat soft. Chill thoroughly so the mixture will firm up. Shape into 3″ patties. Sauté for 4 minutes on each side in a little corn oil over medium-low heat. Flip with a wide spatula for support.

25 SANDWICH SUGGESTIONS

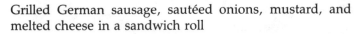

Grilled German sausage, sautéed onions, mustard, and melted cheese in a sandwich roll

Commissary Hoagie: baked ham, smoked turkey, goat cheese, Greek black olives, roasted peppers, and Clear Garlic Vinaigrette in a roll

Baked ham and Cheddar cheese with honey mustard and tomatoes on whole grain bread

Roast beef, Dill-Horseradish Mayonnaise, and watercress on French bread

Roast beef, Herb and Garlic Cheese, and sliced green pepper on black bread

Smoked turkey, mayonnaise, and cranberry-orange relish

Roast turkey, roasted peppers, and Tapenade Mayonnaise

Baked ham, cream cheese mixed with fruit chutney, and watercress

Goat cheese, spinach, roasted peppers and Olive Oil–Anise Seed Dressing in pita bread

Salami, sliced green peppers, and cream cheese on black bread

Grated carrots, Cheddar cheese and green pepper mixed with Basic Creamy Vinaigrette with chives on whole grain bread

Curried egg salad with cashews, raisins, and grated carrots on whole grain bread

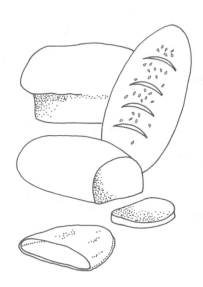

Hot open-faced sandwich of tomato, roasted chili peppers, and Monterey Jack cheese on an English muffin topped with Guacamole

Mozzarella and sautéed spinach and mushrooms in a soft roll, wrapped in foil and heated until the cheese melts

Roast pork, apple slices, and Cheddar cheese served open face on whole grain bread and broiled

Broccoli frittata (cooked in olive oil and sprinkled with Parmesan cheese) on French bread

Roast chicken, Gruyère cheese, bacon, and Avocado Mayonnaise

Herbed egg salad, cucumbers, and Westphalian ham

Baked ham, sliced mushrooms, toasted walnuts, and Basic Mayonnaise flavored with mustard in pita bread

Shrimp, pieces of blanched asparagus, and Basic Mayonnaise flavored with tarragon in pita bread

Bacon, roasted peppers, and mayonnaise on whole grain bread

Fresh spinach, sprouts, tomato, red onion, Swiss cheese, and Basil Garlic Mayonnaise on pumpernickel

Cubes of Gruyère cheese, tomato, and mushrooms mixed with Pimento Mayonnaise in pita bread

Soft Armenian lavash spread with Anchovy-Feta Dressing, topped with thinly sliced cucumbers, tomatoes, and black olives, then rolled up and cut into 3" pieces

Sautéed soft-shell crab with Dill Mayonnaise (made with lemon juice) on a soft roll

Breakfast Entrées

A small stack of oatmeal sunflower seed pancakes, a few sausage links, a touch of freshly squeezed orange juice, a mug or two of my Commissary blend coffee... that should get me going

ITALIAN SCRAMBLED EGGS WITH
ASPARAGUS AND PROSCIUTTO   *Serves 6*

This is a wonderful dish for asparagus lovers . . . and is also very popular with those who aren't normally fond of eggs.

6 tablespoons butter
1¼ cups sliced mushrooms
¼ pound prosciutto or ham, diced or slivered
¾ teaspoon minced garlic
½ medium green pepper, cut into ¼" dice
½ pound asparagus, trimmed and cut into 1" lengths
10 eggs
1½ tablespoons minced fresh basil or 1 teaspoon dried
1 teaspoon dried oregano
¼ teaspoon salt
¾ teaspoon pepper
¾ teaspoon crushed red pepper flakes
6 ounces cream cheese at room temperature
6 ounces mozzarella, shredded (about 1½ cups)
⅓ cup grated Parmesan cheese

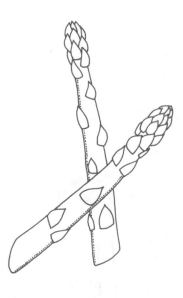

In a large skillet, heat 2 tablespoons of the butter. Add the mushrooms, prosciutto, garlic, and green pepper. Sauté over medium heat until the vegetables are tender. Remove with a slotted spoon and set aside. Blanch the asparagus in boiling salted water for 1–2 minutes until crisp-tender. Drain well and set aside. Whisk together the eggs, herbs, and seasonings. Cut the cream cheese in bits into the eggs.

Just before serving heat the remaining 4 tablespoons of butter in the skillet. Add the egg mixture. Cook over medium heat while folding the mixture with a spatula to blend in the cream cheese. When the eggs are half set, add the warm vegetable-prosciutto mixture, the mozzarella, Parmesan, and warm asparagus. Continue to cook while gently folding in the cheeses with the spatula. When the eggs are just done, serve at once.

VARIATIONS AND SERVING SUGGESTIONS
If asparagus is not available, broccoli would be a good substitute.

Try salami or capocollo instead of the prosciutto.

Slivered black olives and diced red peppers would be good additions.

For a good accompaniment, try toasted Basil Parmesan Bread or Oven-Roasted Potatoes made with olive oil.

INDIAN SCRAMBLED EGGS WITH FRAGRANT RICE AND MINTED TOMATO SAUCE

Serves 8

A beautiful dish . . . rich, fragrant, gently spicy, a medley of textures and seasonings . . . in itself a reason to invite friends in for brunch. On Sundays at The Commissary, we often serve the dish arranged in a long casserole to resemble a brilliant striped flag with the vibrantly red sauce separating the golden eggs from the lentil-dotted rice. If you prefer, make the sauce and rice ahead of time and reheat them before serving.

MINTED TOMATO SAUCE
2 tablespoons butter
4 cups coarsely chopped onions
4 teaspoons curry powder
2 teaspoons minced garlic
2 teaspoons minced fresh ginger
2 teaspoons ground coriander
1½ teaspoons ground cumin
1½ teaspoons turmeric
1¼ teaspoons salt
¼ teaspoon pepper
1 (20-ounce) can crushed tomatoes (2⅓ cups)
¼ cup chopped fresh mint (omit mint if fresh is
   unavailable)

FRAGRANT RICE
½ cup red lentils
¼ cup butter
1½ cups chopped onions
1½ teaspoons curry powder
2¼ teaspoons salt
½ teaspoon pepper
1½ cups white rice
2 tablespoons lemon juice
2¼ cups water

SCRAMBLED EGGS
16 eggs, lightly beaten
1 teaspoon salt
½ teaspoon pepper
⅛ teaspoon cayenne
⅛ teaspoon nutmeg
1½ teaspoons sugar
8 ounces cream cheese
½ pound butter
2¼ teaspoons minced fresh ginger
½ cup sliced scallions

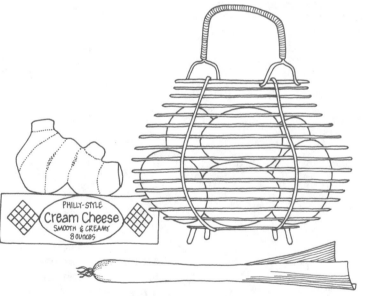

PHILLY-STYLE
Cream Cheese
SMOOTH & CREAMY
8 OUNCES

MINTED TOMATO SAUCE

Heat the butter in a large saucepan. Add the onions and curry powder and sauté until the onions are tender. Add the garlic, ginger, coriander, cumin, turmeric, and salt and cook 2 minutes. Add the pepper, crushed tomatoes, and mint. Bring to a boil, reduce the heat, and simmer 20 minutes, stirring occasionally, until very thick. Set aside.

FRAGRANT RICE

Pour boiling water over the lentils to cover by an inch and let soak 15–30 minutes or until tender. Drain and set aside. **Preheat the oven to 250°.** Melt the butter in a large saucepan. Add the onions and sauté until tender. Stir in the curry powder, salt, and pepper. Add the rice and sauté 2–3 minutes. Add the lemon juice and water, cover, and cook about 15 minutes or until the liquid is absorbed. Add the reserved lentils, stir, and cover tightly. Keep warm in the oven until ready to serve (or cool and reheat later).

SCRAMBLED EGGS

Have the tomato sauce hot. Combine the eggs with the seasonings. Cut the cream cheese in bits into the eggs. Melt the butter in a 12″ skillet (or use two 9″ skillets). Add the ginger and sauté 1 minute. Add the eggs and cook until barely set. At the last minute, stir in the scallions. Serve at once accompanied by the sauce and rice.

If you don't make up your own curry blend, the trick for good curry flavor is to find the freshest brand possible, since spices, once ground, begin to lose their potency and will become "musty". We personally like the Sun Brand Madras Curry Powder. ☆ If you have the inclination, though, do try making your own. (Indian cookbooks by Madhur Jaffrey and Julie Sahni are good sources for directions.) You can vary the spices to suit your taste, and the results should be superior to anything you can buy.

WESTERN SCRAMBLED TOFU   *Serves 6*

Inspired by a dish he had breakfasted on one sunny spring morning in Carmel during a trip to California, Steven devised this vegetable-laden tofu scramble for Eden II's Sunday brunch menu. Remarkably like scrambled eggs in appearance, it has a good spicy flavor and teams up well with home fries or brown rice.

¾ cup butter
2½ cups diced onions
2½ cups diced red peppers
2½ cups diced green peppers
2½ cups diced carrots
2 tablespoons minced garlic
1¾ teaspoons curry powder
1½ pounds firm-style tofu, coarsely chopped
1¾ teaspoons tamari or soy sauce
1 cup crushed canned tomatoes
1 teaspoon Tabasco
2¼ teaspoons salt

1½ teaspoons pepper
1 teaspoon turmeric
OPT. 1 tablespoon minced dill or chives
2½ tablespoons minced parsley

In a large sauté pan, heat the butter. Add the onions, red peppers, green peppers, carrots, garlic, and curry powder. Sauté about 15 minutes until the vegetables have softened. Turn the heat to high and add the tofu, tamari, tomatoes, Tabasco, salt, pepper, and turmeric. Continue to cook, while stirring, until mixture looks like scrambled eggs. Add the dill and parsley. Serve at once.

POACHED EGGS WITH TOMATOES AND SAUSAGE ON TOASTED BRIOCHE

Serves 6

FRENCH-TOASTED BRIOCHE
½ recipe Brioche dough (see p. 217) baked in a greased 8" × 4" × 3" loaf pan for 20–25 minutes, turned out and cooled
2 tablespoons melted butter
4 eggs, beaten

SAUSAGE-TOMATO FILLING
6 ounces bulk pork breakfast sausage
1 tablespoon olive oil
1 tablespoon minced shallots
2 cups chopped fresh tomatoes
2 tablespoons finely chopped sun-dried tomatoes in oil (1 ounce)
¼ teaspoon nutmeg
Salt, pepper, sage to taste

ASSEMBLY
¼ cup vinegar
6 eggs
6 tablespoons grated Parmesan cheese
2 tablespoons melted butter
Minced parsley for garnish

FRENCH-TOASTED BRIOCHE
Cut 6 slices of brioche, each 1" thick. Melt the butter in a skillet over medium-low heat. Dip the brioche slices in the beaten eggs and "pan toast" in the butter on both sides until golden, watching carefully, as they brown very quickly. Set aside on a foil-covered baking sheet.

see p. 217

SUNDAY BRUNCH
Was there ever a better way to wind down the weekend and fortify your spirits for the week to come? Anytime between 11 and 3 will do. Open a little wine... champagne even. Grind and brew an endless pot of coffee. Set out bright dishes, linens, and flowers. And··· don't let Monday even cross your mind.

Honeydew Melon Splashed with Sambuca
Freshly Squeezed Orange Juice
Poached Eggs with Tomato and Sausage on Toasted Brioche *
Coffee Walnut Chocolate Chip Muffins *
Coffee · Decaffeinated Coffee · Tea

*see index for location of recipe

189

SAUSAGE-TOMATO FILLING

Cook the sausage, breaking it up as finely as possible. Remove from the pan and drain well. Heat the olive oil. Add the shallots and briefly sauté to soften. Add the fresh tomatoes and cook 3 minutes. Add the sun-dried tomatoes and cook another minute. Add the sausage with the nutmeg. Add salt, pepper, and sage to taste. Cook 2 minutes more. Keep warm.

ASSEMBLY

Preheat the broiler. Have ready a large pot filled with 4″ of simmering water and the vinegar.

Crack the eggs into the simmering water and poach them to taste (2–4 minutes). Remove with a slotted spoon to paper toweling to drain. Put 3 tablespoons of the hot filling on each brioche toast, leaving a slight depression in the center. Using the toweling to help, lift and roll each egg into its nest of sausage-tomato filling. Combine the Parmesan and melted butter and distribute over the eggs. Broil 6″ from the flame for 30 seconds to one minute. Garnish with the parsley and serve immediately.

VARIATIONS

Substitute scrambled eggs for the poached eggs.

If you don't have time to make brioche, see if you can purchase an unsliced loaf of egg bread or simply serve on toasted English muffins.

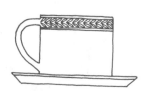

POACHED EGGS AND SMOKED SALMON IN DILL CRÊPES WITH BEURRE BLANC
Serves 6

Frog's Sunday brunch has become one of the most popular and deliciously indulgent ways to start off a Sunday in Philadelphia. This recipe is from that Sunday morning repertoire. Because we as a restaurant have to be very conscious of timing, this dish allows for the advance preparation of all the elements except for the actual poaching of the eggs and finishing of the sauce which is done just a few minutes before serving.

190

DILL CRÊPES
¾ cup flour
½ teaspoon salt
¼ teaspoon pepper
1 egg
1 egg yolk
½ cup milk
½ cup water
½ teaspoon grated lemon rind
2 tablespoons minced dill
Corn oil

BEURRE BLANC
1 cup dry white wine
½ cup white vinegar
⅓ cup minced shallots
2 cups heavy cream
½ teaspoon salt
¼ teaspoon pepper
¼ pound butter, softened

ASSEMBLY
¼ cup vinegar
3 ounces very thinly sliced smoked salmon
6 eggs
Sprigs of dill for garnish

DILL CRÊPES
Combine the flour with the salt and pepper. Beat together the egg, egg yolk, milk, water, lemon rind, and dill. Make a well in the dry ingredients and pour in the wet ingredients. Whisk to combine well. Batter will have consistency of heavy cream. Brush a crêpe pan (7" across the bottom) lightly with corn oil. Heat until quite hot but not smoking. Pour in about 3 tablespoons of batter and quickly swirl to coat the bottom evenly. Cook until surface bubbles and bottom is lightly browned and can be easily lifted from the pan. Turn the crêpe with a spatula and brown on the other side. Continue with the rest of the batter.

BEURRE BLANC
Follow procedure for basic Beurre Blanc on p. 103. Keep warm or make up to a day ahead without adding the butter. Bring to a boil just before serving, adding the butter off the heat at the end.

ASSEMBLY
Preheat the oven to 375°. Warm the sauce and have ready a large pot filled with 4" of simmering water and the ¼ cup of vinegar. Put the crêpes, lighter sides up, on a baking sheet. Top each with ½ ounce of smoked salmon.

We confess. We love good coffee... especially first thing in morning. Some of us have 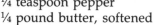 switched over to the Swiss water process decaffeinated beans, and others debate the best brewing method... some preferring the deep, rich results of the Melior plunger to the clear, oil-free brew that has dripped through a Melitta filter. We all agree, though, that you have to begin with good, fresh beans. That means finding a shop that sells a lot of coffee and doesn't let any bean sit around for long. At The Commissary, we've always brewed a blend that is 60% Mocha Java (for smooth flavor) and 40% French Roast (for richness and body). This "Commissary Blend" is also the biggest seller in our Market. ☆ At The Commissary's first-floor bar in addition to all the alcoholic offerings, 6 varieties of coffee are available... ground to order and brewed in individual-size Melior pots. If a certain variety particularly strikes you, you can hop around the corner to The Market afterward and pick up a pound of the beans.

Crack the eggs into the simmering water and poach to taste (2–4 minutes). Transfer the eggs with a slotted spoon to paper toweling to drain and then set each egg in the center of a crêpe. Fold opposite sides of the crêpe over so that they meet in the middle. Reheat in the oven for 3–4 minutes. Transfer to warm individual plates. Pour 2 ounces of the beurre blanc over each portion and garnish with a sprig of fresh dill. Serve at once.

VARIATIONS

For an extra-special touch, garnish each portion with a dab of caviar.

Instead of wrapping the eggs in crêpes, serve them on a bed of cappellini (use ½ pound dried or ¾ pound fresh for 5 servings) tossed with a little butter, pepper, minced dill, and slivers of smoked salmon. Top with Beurre Blanc.

Substitute scrambled eggs for the poached eggs.

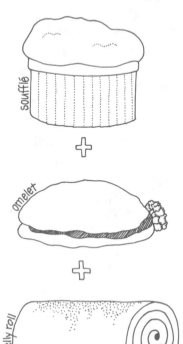

SOUFFLÉ ROLL WITH
SPINACH-MUSHROOM FILLING   *Serves 10*

Imagine a dish that combines the delicate rich texture of a soufflé, the comforting goodness of a plump stuffed omelet and the visual excitement of a spiral-patterned jelly roll. Add to that the convenience of advance preparation and, for a final fillip, a quickly made fresh tomato sauce, and you have for your repertoire one of the most delightful brunch dishes going.

SOUFFLÉ ROLL
2½ cups milk
¼ pound butter
1 cup flour
1 teaspoon salt
¼ teaspoon pepper
⅛ teaspoon cayenne pepper
10 egg yolks
10 egg w.

192

SPINACH FILLING

1 (10-ounce) bag of fresh spinach
3 tablespoons butter
¼ cup minced shallots
½ pound mushrooms, sliced
1 teaspoon dry mustard
¾ teaspoon salt
¾ teaspoon pepper
⅛ teaspoon cayenne pepper
12 ounces cream cheese, softened
1 tablespoon lemon juice

TOMATO COULIS

4 pounds fresh tomatoes
¼ cup olive oil
¼ cup finely minced shallots
2 cups minced onion
1¼ teaspoons salt
½ teaspoon Tabasco
2 teaspoons minced fresh basil or tarragon or ¾
   teaspoon dried

SOUFFLÉ ROLL

Preheat the oven to 325°. Grease a 15½″ × 10½″ × 1″ jelly-roll pan, line it with wax paper, and thoroughly grease the paper.

Heat the milk. Melt the butter in a saucepan. Stir in the flour, salt, pepper, and cayenne and cook over low heat, stirring occasionally, for 2–3 minutes. Whisk in the hot milk. Bring to a boil, stirring, and simmer 1 minute. Beat the egg yolks in a bowl and whisk some of the hot mixture into them. Stir the yolks back into the sauce and cook and stir 1 minute without letting the mixture boil. Cool to room temperature.

Beat the egg whites until stiff but not dry. Whisk ¼ of the whites into the yolk mixture to lighten it, then gently fold in the remaining whites with a spatula. Turn out immediately into the prepared pan and bake about 25 minutes. Immediately invert the soufflé roll onto a dish towel topped with wax paper and peel off the paper lining. Roll up the long way in the towel and wax paper. Let cool.

SPINACH FILLING

Wash the spinach well and cook it in the water still clinging to its leaves until just wilted. Drain and squeeze it dry. Coarsely chop the spinach and set aside. In a saucepan, heat the butter. Add the shallots and sauté 1 minute. Add the mushrooms and cook until they are tender and their liquid has evaporated. Add the spinach, dry mustard, salt, pepper, and cayenne. Cook 1 minute more and then

SPIRITED HOT CHOCOLATE

In a mug, make a paste of 1 teaspoon cocoa, 1-2 teaspoons sugar, and a little milk. Stir in hot milk to within ½″ of the rim. Add a splash each of Grand Marnier and Kahlua. Top with sweetened whipped cream.

remove from the heat. Blend in the cream cheese and lemon juice. Let cool to room temperature.

TOMATO COULIS
Follow procedure for making Tomato Coulis on page 102.

ASSEMBLY AND SERVING
Preheat the oven to 325°. Gently unroll the soufflé roll and spread with the filling. Roll back up (without the dish towel and wax paper). Set the roll in a lightly buttered baking pan and cover tightly with foil. Put in the oven for 15–20 minutes. Meanwhile, reheat the Tomato Coulis. To serve, cut into 1″ slices and top with the hot Tomato Coulis.

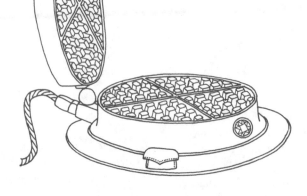

PUMPKIN WAFFLES WITH HOT CIDER SYRUP

Serves 3–4

At one time, we tried serving waffles for breakfast on the line at The Commissary. It didn't work out very well; they took too long to cook for the type of quick breakfast our customers came in for. So, we ditched that idea—but not the recipes. This was a favorite from that short-lived episode.

CIDER SYRUP
1½ cups clear apple cider
1 cup brown sugar
1 cup corn syrup
4 tablespoons butter
2 tablespoons lemon juice
⅛ teaspoon cinnamon
⅛ teaspoon nutmeg
Grated rind from 1 lemon
2 tart apples, peeled, cored, and thinly sliced

WAFFLES

2 cups flour
2 tablespoons sugar
4 teaspoons baking powder
¾ teaspoon salt
½ teaspoon ground coriander
1 tablespoon cinnamon
½ teaspoon nutmeg or mace
1½ cups milk
1 cup canned unsweetened pumpkin purée
4 egg yolks
¾ cup butter, melted
1 tablespoon vanilla extract
4 egg whites

CIDER SYRUP

In a saucepan, bring to a boil all the ingredients except the apple slices. Reduce the heat and simmer, uncovered, for 15 minutes or until mixture is the consistency of maple syrup. Just before serving, add the apple slices and heat several minutes.

WAFFLES

Have your waffle iron hot. **Preheat the oven to 200°.** Sift together the dry ingredients. In a separate bowl, combine the milk, pumpkin purée, egg yolks, butter, and vanilla. Pour this mixture into the dry ingredients and stir just to blend. Beat the egg whites stiff but not dry and fold into the batter. Cook the batter on the hot, lightly oiled waffle iron until the waffles are crisp, browned, and come away easily from the iron. Keep finished waffles warm in the oven while the rest cook. Serve with butter and the hot syrup.

VARIATIONS AND NOTES

For pancakes, reduce butter to ½ cup and cook on a lightly oiled griddle.

Syrup is also delicious on other kinds of waffles and pancakes; you might even try it over ice cream.

These waffles also freeze very well. To reheat, warm in a 350° oven for 3–5 minutes, uncovered.

CORNMEAL WAFFLES
WITH WESTPHALIAN HAM

Serves 3–4

1 cup flour
1½ teaspoons baking powder
1 teaspoon baking soda
1 tablespoon sugar
¼ teaspoon salt
1 cup cornmeal
2 eggs
2 cups buttermilk
¼ cup melted butter or bacon drippings
¼ pound Westphalian ham, thinly sliced and slivered

Preheat the oven to 200° and let your waffle iron get hot. Sift together the flour, baking powder, baking soda, sugar, and salt. Add the cornmeal. Beat the eggs slightly and add the buttermilk. Stir in the butter or bacon drippings and the slivered ham. Combine the dry ingredients with the wet using a few quick strokes. Pour enough batter for 1 waffle onto the hot waffle iron. Cook the waffle until browned and crisp. Keep finished waffles warm, uncovered, in the preheated oven while cooking the rest of the waffles. Serve with butter and maple syrup or preserves.

VARIATIONS
Prosciutto, baked ham, or cooked, crumbled bacon can be substituted for the Westphalian ham.

If you happen to be in "maple syrup land" (that's Vermont or New Hampshire for us), keep an eye out for the B or Dark Amber A grade of maple syrup. It is darker and not as clear and refined as the generally available A grade, but it does have a deeper and more pronounced maple flavor.

BUCKWHEAT PECAN WAFFLES
WITH STRAWBERRY BUTTER

Serves 4–6

What could be more comforting on a cold, blustery winter's morning than a hearty warming breakfast to get you going? With that in mind, we put these savory waffles on the menu when Frog opened for breakfast in February of 1981. In our opinion, these waffles are a darn good reason to crawl out from under the blankets and face the day. And, if you don't have time for a leisurely breakfast, reward yourself later with a cozy dinner of the following teamed with sausages and sautéed apples.

STRAWBERRY BUTTER
1 cup sliced fresh strawberries
½ cup powdered sugar
½ pound very soft unsalted butter

WAFFLES
1 cup buckwheat flour
1 cup white flour
¾ teaspoon salt
2½ teaspoons baking powder
2 eggs
1¾ cups milk
½ cup melted butter
1½ cups finely chopped pecans

STRAWBERRY BUTTER
Purée the berries in a food processor. Add the sugar. With the machine on, gradually add the butter in bits. Whiz until well blended—about 30 seconds.

The mixture looks curdled at first but will pull together. Pack the butter into small crocks, or for a fancy presentation, put it into a pastry bag fitted with a star tip and pipe rosettes onto a large plate covered with plastic wrap. Chill until ready to serve.

BUCKWHEAT WAFFLES
Sift together the flours, salt, and baking powder. Beat the eggs until foamy and add the milk. Mix the liquid ingredients into the dry with a few quick strokes. Stir in the melted butter. Meanwhile, heat a waffle iron and **preheat the oven to 200°**. Stir the pecans into the batter and cook the waffles until browned and crisp. As they finish cooking, put them into the oven, uncovered, to keep warm until all are ready. Serve the waffles hot with the strawberry butter or with butter and maple syrup.

NOTES AND VARIATIONS
Make other fruit butters by substituting raspberries, bananas, peaches or the like for the strawberries. Fruit butters are also delicious to serve with Brioches.

Try the waffles as a base for creamed dried beef.

So that the butter doesn't pick up any surrounding odors, cover crocks tightly with plastic wrap and do the same with the rosettes after they have first chilled enough to harden. Refrigerate until ready to serve. The butter does not keep well for more than a few days in the refrigerator. It does, however, freeze very well if wrapped tightly.

To make the Strawberry Butter without a food processor, mash the strawberries and sugar together with a fork. Transfer to an electric mixer and blend in the butter gradually until homogeneous.

Buckwheat's nutty, wholesome flavor is appropriate for such a sturdy plant. It thrives in colder, inhospitable climates (it's native to Siberia), grows very rapidly, and is one of the few commercial crops that don't need chemicals. It is very low in gluten and so fails at breadmaking. It is, however, "de rigueur" for Breton crêpes, Japanese soba, and Russian blini. The whole grains or groats are called "kasha." American settlers first used buckwheat for livestock feed and later added it to their own diets. As a child growing up on a Maryland dairy farm, Becky's mother recalls having buckwheat pancakes every morning for breakfast during the winter. ☆ Buckwheat can be substituted for ¼ to ⅓ of the regular flour in recipes for pancakes, pasta, crêpes, and muffins.

197

OATMEAL SUNFLOWER SEED
PANCAKES WITH HONEY BUTTER   *Serves 4*

When you need a substantial breakfast to get you going, it is hard to beat these pancakes chock-full of good things. Steven developed the recipe as a Sunday brunch item for Eden II with its health-conscious, neighborhood university clientele.

HONEY BUTTER
6 ounces softened butter
½ cup honey

PANCAKES
½ cup shredded, sweetened coconut
1 cup whole wheat flour or 1¼ cups white flour
1 cup old fashioned oats
1 tablespoon baking powder
1 teaspoon salt
¾ cup raw sunflower seeds
⅓ cup brown sugar
1 tablespoon corn oil
2 cups milk
1 egg

HONEY BUTTER
Whip the ingredients together until smooth.

PANCAKES
Preheat the oven to 300°. Spread the coconut on a baking sheet and bake for about 5–7 minutes, tossing occasionally so that it colors evenly, until golden. Cool and combine with the other dry ingredients. Beat together the oil, milk, and egg. Add the wet ingredients to the dry ones and stir just to combine. Cook the pancakes on a greased griddle until browned and golden on both sides. Serve hot with the Honey Butter.

VARIATIONS AND NOTES
Serve with warm sautéed peaches or apples or with maple syrup.

Substitute chopped pecans or walnuts for the sunflower seeds.

Leftover pancakes can be frozen as soon as they are cool. To reheat, wrap in foil in a single layer and warm in 350° oven.

This batter (increase corn oil to ¼ cup) makes great waffles, too.

Vegetables and Side Dishes

If you want my advice, you'll take a few of these Jersey tomatoes. They're the last of the season, and there's nothing like them for ten more months. Those potatoes there are fresh dug. I'll give you a great easy recipe fo

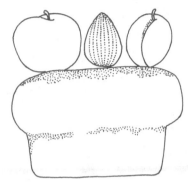

FROG'S APRICOT, ALMOND, AND APPLE BREAD STUFFING

Serves 10–12 to accompany roast chicken or turkey

At Frog in the early days, this was a beloved menu item served with half a roast chicken and Madeira sauce.

1 pound loaf of firm white bread cut into ¾" cubes
¾ cup butter
2 cups chopped onions
2 cups finely chopped celery
2½ cups coarsely chopped Winesap apples
½ cup chopped dried apricots
¼ cup sliced almonds, lightly toasted
1½ teaspoons dried sage
1½ teaspoons dried thyme
1 teaspoon dried rosemary
1 teaspoon salt
1 teaspoon pepper
1 cup chicken stock

Preheat the oven to 325° and toast the bread cubes in a single layer on baking trays for 10 minutes or until lightly browned. Set aside.

In ¼ cup of the butter, sauté the onions and celery until translucent, about 2–4 minutes. Add the apples, apricots, and almonds and sauté briefly. Season with the herbs, salt, and pepper and cook 2 minutes. Combine with the bread cubes. Heat together the chicken stock and ½ cup of the remaining butter. When the butter is melted, pour it over the stuffing mixture while tossing.

Preheat the oven to 350°. Twenty minutes before serving, put the stuffing into a 9" × 13" buttered baking pan or casserole and bake for 20–25 minutes, or until heated through.

BASIC ROAST CHICKEN

The most simple, unadorned way is to… Preheat the oven to 400°. Tie together the feet of a 3-pound chicken. Rub the bird all over with butter and set it breast side down on a rack in a roasting pan. Roast for 15 minutes then turn it on one side and roast 10 minutes. Turn it to the other side for 10 minutes and finish it breast side up 20 to 25 minutes (longer if stuffed). For a really gorgeous glaze, brush the bird with heavy cream about 15 minutes before it is done. ☆ To jazz it up just a little bit, rub the chicken before roasting with garlic, olive oil and fresh herbs… inside, outside, and under the skin. The aromas while it is roasting will be unbelievable.

CORN BREAD AND WILD MUSHROOM STUFFING

Makes 7 cups

CORN BREAD
1 cup flour
1 cup cornmeal
2 tablespoons sugar
1 tablespoon baking powder
¾ teaspoon salt
1 egg

1 cup milk
⅓ cup melted butter

STUFFING
1 cup butter
3 cups sliced fresh shiitake mushrooms (½ pound)
1 teaspoon salt
1½ cups chopped onions
1 cup chopped celery
2 tablespoons minced shallots
1 teaspoon pepper
1½ teaspoons ground or pulverized rosemary
1½ teaspoons dried thyme
½ teaspoon dried marjoram
2 teaspoons rubbed sage
½ cup minced parsley
2 cups chicken stock

CORN BREAD
Preheat the oven to 350°. Sift together the dry ingredients. Combine the egg, milk, and butter and pour over the dry ingredients. Mix to combine. Spread the batter in a greased 10½" × 15½" baking pan. (The batter will be about ¼" deep.) Bake for 20 minutes. Invert the bread onto the counter and tear into 1" pieces with 2 forks. Pile the pieces back into the pan and return to the oven for 10 minutes more. Turn off the oven, stir the cornbread, and leave it in the oven to cool and dry out some more.

STUFFING
Heat half (3 ounces) of the butter. Add the mushrooms and the salt and sauté for 5 minutes over medium heat, stirring occasionally. Turn into bowl and set aside. Add the remaining butter to the pan and add the onions, celery, shallots, pepper, rosemary, thyme, marjoram, and sage. Sauté over medium low heat, stirring occasionally, for 10 minutes. Add the onion mixture, mushrooms, and chicken stock to the crumbled corn bread and mix well. Use to stuff bird of choice.

VARIATIONS
To serve as a separate side dish with roast fowl or pork, bake in a buttered 9" square pan, covered with foil, for 30–35 minutes at 350°. Uncover and bake 15 minutes more.

Any other fresh mushroom may be substituted for shiitake.

POTATO-RUTABAGA GRATIN

Serves 5–6

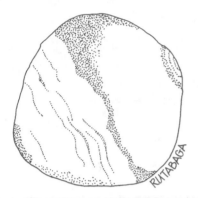

RUTABAGA

Rich with cream and gooey with cheese, this goes well with the likes of grilled meat or fish, steak and eggs, and sausages.

1 tablespoon butter
½ cup chopped onions
½ teaspoon minced garlic
2 cups heavy cream
1 teaspoon salt
½ teaspoon pepper
⅛ teaspoon grated nutmeg
1 pound all-purpose or baking potatoes, peeled and sliced (⅛" thick)
2 cups grated Gruyère cheese
1 pound rutabaga, peeled and sliced (⅛" thick)

Preheat the oven to 375°. Heat the butter in a small pan. Add the onions and garlic and sauté briefly to soften. Combine the mixture with the cream, salt, pepper, and nutmeg. Spread half the potatoes in a 11" × 7" baking pan. Sprinkle with ½ cup of the cheese. Spread on half the rutabaga followed by another ½ cup of cheese. Top with the remaining potatoes, then ½ cup of cheese and finish with the rest of the rutabaga. Pour the cream mixture over all. Bake for 35 minutes. Sprinkle on the remaining ½ cup of cheese and bake 10 minutes more, or until most of the cream is absorbed and the vegetables are tender.

VARIATIONS
Try adding fresh herbs (tarragon would be especially good) or perhaps bits of sautéed ham for additional flavor. The recipe is also just fine made entirely with potatoes.

PEPERONATA WITH POTATOES   *Serves 8*

Red and green peppers together are so pretty that we're always pleased to find a new way to use them. In this case, peperonata (*peperoni* is Italian for peppers), a classic Italian dish of stewed peppers and tomatoes, is given new heartiness by the addition of potatoes, black olives, basil, and vinegar. Letting it sit a few hours or even a day helps all the flavors to develop, and the dish, whether served hot or at room temperature, makes a fine accompaniment to grilled meat, sausages, or fish.

6 tablespoons butter
2 tablespoons olive oil
1½ pounds small red-skinned new potatoes, sliced ½"
  thick and boiled until just tender
1¼ cups very thinly sliced onions
1½ teaspoons minced garlic
1½ cups cubed red peppers (1" dice)
1½ cups cubed green peppers (1" dice)
4 cups diced tomatoes (about 1¾ pounds)
2 tablespoons minced parsley
1¾ teaspoons salt
1 teaspoon pepper
⅓ cup pitted and slivered Greek black olives
3 tablespoons balsamic vinegar or red wine vinegar
¼ cup finely sliced scallions
2 tablespoons fresh, chopped basil

Aceto balsamico or balsamic vinegar, from the area around Modèna, Italy, is unlike any other vinegar. It is rich and syrupy, sweet and piquant, and complex from years of aging in a succession of barrels of different woods. The production of aceto balsamico is primarily a cottage industry in Italy where families hoard their oldest specimens and often serve them as a liqueur. Larger companies make the vinegar on a commercial scale, but it is often thin with only a hint of the real balsamico richness. One good quality example we've found is that made by Fini and available by mail order from Williams-Sonoma in San Francisco.

ACETO BALSAMICO FINI

In a large sauté pan over medium heat, heat half the butter with half the olive oil. Add the potatoes and sauté until crisp and browned. Transfer to a bowl. Add the remaining butter and olive oil to the pan and heat. Add the onions and garlic and sauté until softened. Add the peppers and tomatoes and cook until just tender. Combine with the potatoes, parsley, salt, pepper, olives, and vinegar. Let sit several hours. When ready to serve, garnish with the scallions and basil. Serve at room temperature.

OVEN-ROASTED POTATOES

Serves 6–8

These are wonderful potatoes, simple to prepare and very tasty. They can even be made a day in advance and reheated just before serving. We serve them with many of our entrées in The Commissary's Downstairs restaurant and especially love them with Bluefish Provençale or any of our scrambled egg dishes.

2½ pounds unpeeled all-purpose potatoes
1½ teaspoons salt
½ teaspoon pepper
⅔ cup corn oil
2½ cups finely chopped onions

Preheat the oven to 450°. Cut the potatoes into ½"–¾" dice and toss them with the salt, pepper, and corn oil. Spread them in a single layer on a rimmed baking sheet or pan for 20 minutes. Remove the pan from the oven and combine the potatoes with the onions. Return to the oven and continue to roast for 25 minutes more or until browned and crisp. Stir occasionally.

VARIATIONS
Instead of cubing the potatoes, quarter or halve them and slice ⅛" thick.

Substitute olive oil for the corn oil, particularly if the potatoes are to accompany a Mediterranean-style dish.

SWEET POTATO FRITTERS WITH APPLES AND RAISINS

Makes about 30 small fritters

Try these instead of your usual sweet potato dish. Served with slices of grilled ham or the like, they would also be great for brunch.

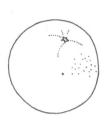
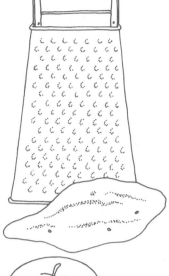

1 pound sweet potatoes
1 Granny Smith apple
1 egg
2 tablespoons brown sugar
½ teaspoon grated fresh ginger root
1 teaspoon orange zest
¾ teaspoon salt
scant ¼ teaspoon pepper
¼ cup raisins
¼ to ½ cup flour
Vegetable oil for deep frying
OPT. maple syrup

Peel and coarsely grate the sweet potatoes. Cover them with boiling water for 15 minutes. Meanwhile, peel and grate the apple and set it aside. In a mixing bowl, whisk the egg and add the brown sugar, ginger root, orange zest, salt, pepper, and raisins. **Shortly before frying, heat the oil to 275°.**

Drain the potatoes well and turn out onto a double layer of paper toweling. Cover with paper towels and blot firmly. Add the potatoes to the bowl along with the grated apple. Stir in the ¼ cup of flour. Test a fritter. If it doesn't hold together, add the additional flour.

Form the mixture into large walnut-sized balls and flatten slightly. Gently slide them into the oil. Turn them over once they float to the top. Cook, turning occasionally, until lightly browned, about 7 minutes. Drain on paper towels and salt lightly. Keep warm in a slow oven or reheat in a 350° oven for 5 minutes at serving time. Serve, if desired, with maple syrup.

NOTES

Add ¼ cup chopped walnuts or pecans.

The sweet potato mixture should not be made more than 2 hours in advance of frying because the apple will exude liquid and make the mixture watery.

CAPONATA

Serves 8–10 as a side dish

Caponata is an Italian eggplant salad of Sicilian origin. We're particularly fond of it because it is quick to prepare, versatile, keeps well, and, most important, is very tasty.

½ cup olive oil
3 cups diced eggplant (⅜" dice) (about 1 medium)
1½ cups coarsely chopped onions
1 cup celery in ¼" slices
2 cups chopped tomatoes
3 tablespoons minced garlic
2 tablespoons tomato paste
¼ cup wine vinegar
24 small stuffed green olives, sliced into thirds
½ cup small capers, drained
2 ounces anchovies, drained and chopped
1 tablespoon sugar
½ teaspoon crushed red pepper flakes
½ cup lightly packed minced parsley
½ teaspoon salt
½ teaspoon pepper

In a large skillet, heat the olive oil. Add the eggplant and sauté several minutes until partially soft. Add the onions, celery, tomatoes, and garlic and cook for about 10 minutes, stirring occasionally. Remove from the heat, add the remaining ingredients and toss lightly. Chill until ready to serve. Serve chilled or at room temperature.

SERVING SUGGESTIONS

As an appetizer, serve on a bed of greens accompanied by black bread or crisp pita toasts.

As an hors d'oeuvre, pass with toasted Italian bread slices or pita triangles.

Try as an omelet filling; as an accompaniment to cold roast meats; tossed with pasta for a cold salad; or even mounded hot on black bread, topped with mozzarella, and broiled for a quick snack.

KITCHEN EQUIPMENT FAVORITES

We particularly value...
- good knives and a steel
- a gas range
- heavy pans...copper ones especially and Silverstone ones for their no-stick finish
- multiples of cutting boards, wooden spoons, whisks, and strainers
- chopsticks for stirring small amounts
- a good big trash can
- a grill or hibachi that lets you adjust the distance between the food and the coals
- a long, strong fork for grilling
- tongs
- a food processor and Kitchenaid mixer

AND... Steven loves his Japanese knives, which, once he got used to them (their balance is different from that of western knives), he found exceptionally pleasing to use.

206

TOMATOES STUFFED WITH SPINACH, RICE, AND PINE NUTS

Serves 6–8

A little "pizzazz" on the dinner plate never hurts, especially when that "pizzazz" is as delicious as these colorful stuffed tomatoes are. For just that reason, we have often included these tomatoes on catering menus to give a little life to such elegantly restrained entrées as stuffed loin of veal, rack of lamb, or roast fillet of beef. In fact, they're nice enough that you might even like to let them star as a first course.

1 cup water
OPT. ⅛ teaspoon powdered saffron
½ cup Carolina long-grain rice
½ teaspoon salt
2 teaspoons olive oil
2 teaspoons minced shallots
5 ounces spinach, stemmed, washed, blanched, squeezed dry, and chopped
¼ teaspoon pepper
¼ cup toasted pine nuts
6–8 small tomatoes

Bring the water to a boil in a 1 quart saucepan. Stir in the saffron, the rice, and ¼ teaspoon of the salt. Cover and cook over medium-low heat until water is absorbed and rice is tender. Remove to a bowl and let cool. Heat the oil in a small skillet. Add the shallots and spinach and sauté a minute or so. Add the remaining ¼ teaspoon of salt, the pepper, and the pine nuts and sauté 1 minute. Add the rice and heat through. You should have about 2 cups of filling.

Preheat the oven to 350°. Cut the tops from the tomatoes. Hollow them out and sprinkle the inside lightly with salt and pepper. Heat the rice mixture. Stuff the tomatoes and set in a baking pan. Cover with foil and bake 5–10 minutes or until heated through. Serve, if desired, with a dollop of sour cream or Crème Fraîche.

VARIATIONS
Add cooked shellfish or sausage to the filling, stuff 4 large tomatoes instead of 6–8 small ones, and serve as a light entrée.

Dust with Parmesan cheese before baking and garnish with minced parsley.

SAUTÉED GREEN BEANS
WITH HAZELNUT CRUMBS

Serves 6

½ cup ground or finely chopped toasted hazelnuts
½ cup fine fresh bread crumbs or ¼ cup dry bread
    crumbs
1 pound green beans, stemmed
6 tablespoons butter
1 tablespoon minced shallots
¼ teaspoon salt
¼ teaspoon pepper

Combine the nuts and crumbs and set aside. Blanch the green beans in boiling salted water for 2–3 minutes. Refresh under cold running water and drain. Heat the butter in a sauté pan. Add the shallots and sauté until softened. Add the green beans, salt, pepper, and hazelnut crumbs. Sauté several minutes to heat through. Serve at once.

SAUTÉED BROCCOLI
WITH GARLIC BUTTER

Serves 2–3

This recipe demonstrates a technique of vegetable preparation that we favor in our restaurants. At some point earlier in the day, a vegetable (such as broccoli, green beans, cauliflower, or carrots) is blanched to "fix" its bright color and partially cook it. It is given a cold-water bath to halt the cooking, drained well, and refrigerated until just before serving time, when it is quickly reheated in butter for a beautiful crisp-tender result.

½ pound broccoli
¼ cup butter
½ teaspoon very finely minced garlic or 1 tablespoon
    minced shallots
¼ teaspoon salt
⅛ teaspoon pepper

Trim and discard the bottom 2″ of the broccoli, which tend to be very woody. Peel the remaining stems with a vegetable peeler. Cut the stems into ¼″ slices and the flowers into bite-size pieces. Bring to a boil 2 quarts of water. Add the stems and cook 1 minute (start timing as soon as you add the broccoli). Add the flowers and cook 1 minute more, while stirring once or twice. Drain in a colander and run under cold water until the broccoli is cool. Separate the flowers and gently squeeze them in paper toweling to remove excess water (they are like sponges). At this point, the broccoli can be covered and refrigerated for several hours.

Just before serving, heat the butter until it bubbles. Add the garlic and stir 5–10 seconds. Add the broccoli, salt, and pepper and stir over medium-high heat for 1 minute or until very hot. Serve at once.

BRUSSELS SPROUTS WITH BACON, ROASTED PEPPERS, AND BALSAMIC VINEGAR

Serves 4

If so many mothers hadn't tried to feed us overcooked Brussels sprouts when we were young, perhaps this lovely vegetable wouldn't be so maligned. This recipe, developed for The Market, could be just what is needed to convert even the most devout Brussels sprouts hater. Crisp bits of bacon, snippets of sweet roasted peppers, and piquant vinegar successfully complement the sprouts. We've even enjoyed them taken straight from The Market and not reheated at all.

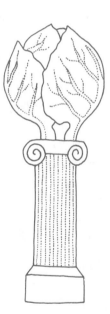

¼ pound bacon, diced
2 teaspoons butter
⅓ cup finely chopped mushrooms
1 teaspoon minced shallots
2 tablespoons olive oil
¼ cup finely chopped red onions
2 tablespoons chopped roasted red peppers
1 tablespoon minced parsley
3 tablespoons balsamic vinegar or red wine vinegar
¼ teaspoon salt
¼ teaspoon pepper
1 (10-ounce) basket Brussels sprouts

Fry the bacon until crisp and drain on paper toweling. Heat the butter in a small skillet. Add the mushrooms and shallots and sauté until all the liquid has evaporated and the mixture is very dark. In a small skillet, heat the olive oil. Add the onions and sauté until soft. Add the mushroom mixture and peppers and sauté briefly to blend. Add the bacon, parsley, vinegar, salt, and pepper. Set aside. Trim the Brussels sprouts and cook until just tender in boiling salted water. (Check after 2 minutes by cutting one in half.) Drain and rinse with cold water. Slice the sprouts in half toward stem. Heat the bacon-onion mixture. Add the sprouts and just heat through. Serve at once.

209

SAUERKRAUT
WITH APPLE CIDER

Serves 4–6

Cider and sauerkraut here meld their respective sweet and sour natures in a felicitous match—another of those spontaneous kitchen experiments that took place one day at old Frog when Steven was rummaging in the walk-in for something to serve with kielbasa for lunch. The piquant sweetness of this dish works particularly well with such rich roast meats as pork, pheasant, and duck.

6 cups filtered apple cider
2 pounds fresh sauerkraut, drained
1 teaspoon caraway seeds

CARAWAY

Reduce the cider over high heat to 1 cup (watch at the end so it doesn't burn). Add the sauerkraut and caraway seeds. Simmer 5 minutes on low heat. Serve hot.

One Christmas season when we wanted to decorate The Commissary's tree with carrots, we held a "carrot ornament" contest. Our customers came forth with sequined carrots, papier mâché, carrots, carrot mobiles... it was a wonderful tree. ☆ Another year, we used "bread dough" to make all kinds of food things for the tree. The recipe is:

ELMER'S GLUE
+ WONDER BREAD
ELVES, CARROTS, PEAS, APPLES, TURKEYS, SHEEP, CHEFS, etc. Tear up 4 dried-up, crustless slices of white bread. Add 4 tablespoons of Elmer's Glue. Mix with your hands for about 10 minutes or until a smooth ball forms. (It will!) Shape bits of dough as you like. Poke a hole or insert a paperclip (for hanging) into the top of each ornament. Air-dry for 24 to 48 hours, turning occasionally. Then paint with acrylic paints and finish with a clear polymer glaze.

DILLED CARROT TIMBALES

Serves 8

1 pound peeled carrots, sliced ⅛" thick
¼ cup minced shallots
¼ cup butter
3 tablespoons minced fresh dill
4 eggs
1¼ teaspoons salt
¼ teaspoon pepper
1 cup heavy cream
Sprigs of dill for garnish

Cook the carrots in boiling water for 12–15 minutes or until very tender. Drain well. In a small sauté pan, sauté the shallots in the butter for 2–3 minutes. Set aside. Purée the carrots in a food processor, scraping down the sides once or twice. Add the shallots, dill, eggs, salt, and pepper and whiz until smooth. Turn into a bowl and stir in the cream. **Preheat the oven to 400°.** Butter eight 6-ounce ramekins or timbale molds well (or any watertight 6-cup mold). Fill with the carrot mixture and set in a large pan of very hot water. Bake for 25 minutes or until the center is as firm as the edges and has puffed up. (Bake a 6-cup mold at 375° for 45 minutes.) Remove from the oven and let rest 10 minutes before molding. To unmold the timbales, knock the bottom of each mold on each of its four "corners" to loosen it. Shake it and firmly invert onto a plate. Gently lift the mold away. Serve the timbales warm, garnished with sprigs of fresh dill.

NOTES AND VARIATIONS

These can be made up to 2 days in advance if stored unmolded and well wrapped in the refrigerator. To reheat the timbales, set the molds on a plate on a rack over simmering water in a covered steamer for about 10 minutes.

Try substituting 1½ tablespoons minced fresh coriander for the dill. Instead of carrots, try turnips, rutabaga, or parsnips. Slivers of Smithfield ham would also be a nice addition.

SPICED PURÉE OF BUTTERNUT SQUASH WITH HONEY

Serves 3–6

This is a splendid melt-in-the-mouth addition to any dinner plate, not to mention the visual lift its vibrant color gives. Thus, this purée is a favorite component of our catering menus during the cooler months.

3 pounds butternut squash
4 tablespoons butter
½ teaspoon cardamom
¼ teaspoon ground cloves
½ teaspoon salt
2 tablespoons honey
¼ teaspoon pepper

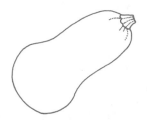

Preheat the oven to 400°. Halve the squash lengthwise, scoop out the seeds, wrap the squash loosely in foil, and bake for 1 hour or until tender. Let the squash cool until easily handled, then scrape out the flesh and purée in a food processor or through a food mill. Mix in the butter and the seasonings. Stirring constantly, reheat the purée over medium heat and serve hot.

4550 pieces are hand-washed in tubs in the basement with water carried from another floor.

KNIVES
CONT. RENTAL

BACKSTAGE at a CATERED PARTY • DRAMA GUILD '81

SCENARIO • Cocktails and dinner for 350 after the January opening of a new play at Annenberg Center. Proceeds to benefit the Drama Guild. Food donated by Steven.

ACT I • Commitment to do the party is made the previous fall. We know Annenberg Center and its limitations (specifically a lack of kitchen facilities) which means rental of all equipment and a menu that requires a minimum of oven/stove use. We brainstorm a menu. "Let's do veal chops like the ones for Pavarotti. We could grill 'em outside like the ribs for the World Series parties. So what if it's cold out." The result:

Raw Bar and Hors d'Oeuvres
Smoked Salmon Mousse with Watercress Purée and Caviar
Grilled Veal Chop with Demi-glace and Pink Peppercorns
Sautéed Fennel and Red Peppers
Spiced Purée of Butternut Squash with Honey *
Poached Pear in Chocolate Robe in Pastry Shell

ACT II • Recipes are developed and tested. The enormous rental order is placed, strategy plotted, food ordered and staff lined up.

ACT III • The catering machine is in full gear by 8 a.m. the day of the party. By 5 p.m., 42 staff are in action setting up the site. (The raw bar alone takes 6 man hours.) All 350 chops make it to the grill (in 5° weather and in the dark). For a finale, 4550-odd-pieces of tableware are handwashed. By 5 a.m., it's over. Cast disperses, exhausted but satisfied.

* See recipe on this page.

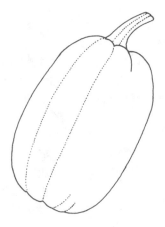

SPAGHETTI SQUASH WITH CARROTS, RED PEPPERS, AND BASIL

Serves 6

One of our newest acquaintances in the vegetable family is spaghetti squash, whose bright yellow flesh is combed out into crunchy, spaghettilike strands after cooking. The squash can be cooked in advance and then served hot or cold later in any number of guises. This particular preparation with its Thai overtones of sugar, rice vinegar, basil, and peanuts, is delicious hot or cold.

1 small spaghetti squash (about 2 pounds)
2 tablespoons corn oil
1 cup julienned red peppers (1½"-long strips)
1 cup julienned carrots (1½"-long strips)
½ teaspoon salt
1 teaspoon sugar
¼ teaspoon pepper
3 tablespoons unseasoned rice vinegar
¼ cup chopped fresh basil
OPT. ¼ cup chopped roasted peanuts

Preheat the oven to 350°. Prick the squash in several places with a long-tined fork, put in a baking pan, and set in the oven for about 1½ hours or until the flesh is tender. Let the squash cool until it can be easily handled, then split it in half and remove and discard the seeds. With a fork, comb out the flesh into spaghettilike strands.

In a large skillet, heat the corn oil. Add the carrots and red peppers and stir-fry for 2 minutes over medium-high heat. Add the salt, sugar, and pepper and blend well. Add the squash and stir-fry until very hot. Sprinkle on the vinegar and blend well. Because basil discolors quickly, add it only just before serving. Sprinkle, if desired, with peanuts.

VARIATIONS
Substitute broccoli (blanched) for the carrots.

Spaghetti squash can literally be treated like pasta. For instance, after baking the squash, you can sauté the flesh in butter and toss with Parmesan cheese or top it with nearly any pasta sauce. Try it also with Tomato Basil Butter.

Breads and Muffins

TODAY'S MUFFINS
Apple Coconut
Cinnamon Butter

Oh great! Here he comes with the muffins now... and they're probably still warm. I'll have to have one of each kind. I'll play an extra hour of squash to make up for the indulgence. Those

FOUR-GRAIN BREAD   *Makes one 9" × 5" × 3" loaf*

With this bread our goal was to produce a lighter, moister whole grain bread in contrast to the heavier varieties commonly found. Starting with an original recipe from Anne's mother, we developed what is today perhaps our top-selling bread at The Market. What this bread will do for a sandwich! And, to take a tip from The Market, try serving it instead of crackers with a selection of soft cheeses.

An important note with this bread is not to let the second proofing go more than twenty minutes. If it overproofs, the loaf will be like a brick. The grains somehow react with the yeast and sugar to make the dough grow very quickly. Also be sure to have the oven preheated before the twenty minutes are up.

⅓ cup bulgur wheat
¾ cup old-fashioned oats
¼ cup brown sugar
2 tablespoons shortening
2 teaspoons salt
1 cup boiling water
¾ cup milk
2 packages yeast (¼ ounce each)
¼ cup toasted sesame seeds
2 tablespoons poppy seeds
¾ cup whole wheat flour
2½ cups high-gluten flour or regular flour
1 egg white
1 teaspoon poppy seeds
1 teaspoon sesame seeds

Combine the bulgur, oats, brown sugar, shortening, and salt in a mixing bowl. Pour the boiling water over them, stir once or twice, and let cool to room temperature. Heat the milk until lukewarm (105°–115°). Pour into a bowl and sprinkle the yeast over it. Let yeast soften several minutes, then stir to dissolve. Add to the grain mixture. Add the sesame and poppy seeds, whole wheat flour, and bread flour. Knead by hand for 10 minutes or beat in an electric mixer fitted with a dough hook for 3 minutes. The dough will be soft. Put in a greased bowl, cover with plastic wrap, and let rise 30–40 minutes in a warm spot (about 70°) or until doubled in bulk. Punch down. Roll the dough to an 8" × 10" rectangle, press out any air bubbles, and roll up the dough, starting from one of the shorter sides. Put it in a greased 9" × 5" × 3" loaf pan. **Preheat oven to 350°.**

Cover the dough and let rise 20 minutes. Brush the dough with the egg white and sprinkle on the poppy and sesame seeds. Bake for 55 minutes. Immediately remove from pan and cool on a rack.

WALNUT ONION MUSHROOM BREAD   *Makes two 8″ × 4″ × 3″ loaves*

Team this bread with a hearty soup and cheese at supper or use it as the basis for a hefty meat and cheese sandwich as we do in The Commissary's Piano Bar. At Anne's house, this bread has become as traditional at Thanksgiving dinner as the turkey.

5 cups high-gluten flour or regular flour
1 tablespoon salt
2 tablespoons sugar
2 packages dry yeast (¼ ounce each)
2 cups warm milk
½ cup plus 1 tablespoon olive oil
½ cup coarsely chopped walnuts
½ pound mushrooms, sliced
¾ cup minced onions
1 egg, beaten

In the bowl of an electric mixer fitted with a paddle attachment (or in a regular mixing bowl), combine the flour, salt, and sugar. Dissolve the yeast in the warm milk. Add the yeast mixture to the flour along with ½ cup of the olive oil. Mix to combine and beat or knead 2 to 3 minutes. Add the walnuts. Cover the dough and let rise in a warm spot for 1½ hours or until doubled. Meanwhile, sauté the mushrooms in the remaining 1 tablespoon of olive oil until all the liquid is gone.

After the first rising, punch down the dough and knead in the mushrooms and onions. Divide the dough in half, roll each piece to a 7″ × 11″ rectangle, press out any air bubbles, and roll up from the short end like a jelly roll. Set in two greased 8″ × 4″ × 3″ bread pans. Cover the pans and again let the dough rise in a warm spot until doubled, about 30–45 minutes.

Preheat the oven to 350°. Lightly brush the tops of the loaves with the beaten egg. Bake for 45 minutes or until done. Remove the loaves from their tins and cool on racks.

GLAZES for BAKING
We've devised a little chart to help guide you.
EGG YOLK + CREAM = very dark
EGG YOLK = dark
EGG = medium
EGG + WATER = light
EGG WHITE = clear shine

Flour marketed specifically as "bread flour" has been milled from a hard wheat with a higher gluten content than regular flour. It is the gluten that allows the dough to absorb more water and expand to a greater degree because it forms little "balloons" of sorts that trap the gas formed by the interacting yeast and wheat. This is how the bread rises.

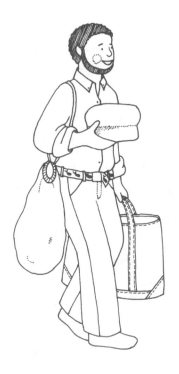

BASIL PARMESAN BREAD *Makes two 8" × 4" loaves*

After a restorative vacation on Nantucket one summer, Steven returned laden with marvelously shaped loaves of a wonderful savory herb cheese bread that he had found being baked on the island and served in one of his favorite restaurants there. Anne was presented with one of the loaves, along with the suggestion that we should produce something similar. Basil Parmesan Bread resulted and was quickly a hit in the Piano Bar, The Market, and the second-floor restaurant at The Commissary. This bread makes up quite easily, and should there be some left a day or two later, it makes terrific toast.

2 packages (¼ ounce each) dry yeast (5 teaspoons)
2½ cups warm water
6–6½ cups high gluten flour or regular flour
1 tablespoon salt
2 tablespoons sugar
1 teaspoon Tabasco
¼ cup olive oil
⅔ cup grated Parmesan cheese
1½ cups shredded Gruyère or Jarlsberg cheese
¼ cup minced fresh basil or 1 tablespoon dried
1 egg, lightly beaten
OPT. Sesame seeds or grated Parmesan cheese for
sprinkling on top

Sprinkle the yeast over the warm water in a bowl and let sit several minutes to soften. Stir a bit to dissolve.

Combine 6 cups of the flour with the salt and sugar. Add the dissolved yeast mixture, Tabasco, and olive oil. When well combined, knead the dough by hand on a well-floured surface for 10 minutes or in an electric mixer fitted with a dough hook for 3 minutes. (Add the additional ½ cup of flour if needed.) Turn the dough into a large greased bowl, cover the bowl, and leave in a warm spot (70°–80°) for 1½ hours or until doubled in bulk. Punch down the dough and work in the cheese and basil. Let rest 10 minutes, then cut the dough in half. Lightly roll out each piece until approximately 7" × 11". Press out any air bubbles, and then roll up beginning at the short end. Set in two well-buttered 8" × 4" loaf pans. Cover the loaves and leave again in a warm spot to double, about 45 minutes.

Preheat the oven to 375°. Brush the loaves with the egg and, if desired, sprinkle with the sesame seeds or Parmesan cheese. Bake for 30–40 minutes. Immediately turn the loaves out of their pans onto a rack to cool.

BRIOCHES

Makes 12 individual brioches

What would breakfast at The Commissary be without those big, airy, buttery, silken, melt-in-your-mouth brioches? We can hardly talk about them without gushing. They are not difficult to make at home either. You only need leave enough time for the three leisured risings that help develop that wondrous brioche texture.

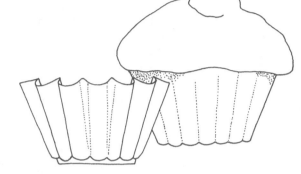

¼ cup milk
½ pound butter, in bits
½ cup sugar
½ teaspoon salt
1 package dry yeast (¼ ounce each)
¼ cup warm water
6 eggs
5½ cups flour (1½ pounds)
1 egg yolk

Gently heat the butter with the milk until the butter melts. Put the sugar and salt in the bowl of an electric mixer and pour on the warm milk-butter mixture. Stir to dissolve the salt and sugar. Cool to lukewarm.

Meanwhile, sprinkle the yeast over the warm water in a small bowl. Let sit 1–2 minutes, then stir to dissolve. Add to the milk mixture. Add the eggs and mix until smooth. Add 3½ cups of the flour and again mix until smooth. If your mixer has a paddle or dough hook, switch to that; otherwise stir in the remaining flour by hand with a wooden spoon. The dough will be too sticky to knead but should begin to pull away from the sides of the bowl; this may take 5–10 minutes of mixing.

Cover the bowl tightly with plastic wrap and let the dough rise in a warm spot until doubled, about 1–1½ hours. Punch down the dough and lightly knead in the bowl for 1–2 minutes. Cover again and let rise once more in a warm spot until doubled (about 1 hour). Punch down and knead for 1–2 minutes. With floured hands, divide the dough into 14 pieces (3½ ounces each). Shape 12 of the pieces into balls and set one in each of 12 greased individual 3–4 ounce brioche tins. Divide the remaining 2 pieces into 6 pieces each and roll them into little balls. Poke a hole with your finger in the top of each brioche and put one of the small balls in each indentation for a "topknot." Set the brioches in a warm spot to rise until very light and doubled in bulk; this could take ½–2½ hours depending on whether dough has been refrigerated.

Preheat the oven to 375°. Beat the egg yolk and brush it lightly over the brioches as a glaze (be careful not to let it drip down the sides, because it could seal the brioche to

BRIOCHE FRENCH TOAST with STRAWBERRIES

Do you eat the topknot first... or save it until last?

the tin). Bake for 15 minutes. Let cool several minutes before removing from the tins. Serve warm.

NOTES

Lots of sweet butter and jam are the natural companions to freshly baked brioches. Try them with our Strawberry Butter.

If you don't have the fluted brioche molds, use twelve 3" muffin-pan cups.

Leftover brioches are pretty special, too. They make wonderful french toast to serve with powdered sugar and strawberries. Smoked salmon and caviar know no better footing than toast made from thinly sliced brioche. Hollowed-out and toasted whole brioches make elegant and tasty cases for such savory contents as truffled scrambled eggs, creamed dried beef in Cheddar sauce, or whatever combination inspires you. See also our recipe for Sausage and Eggs in Brioche.

If you want to have just baked brioches for breakfast (as we do at The Commissary) without having to get up at some ungodly hour, prepare the dough the night before and give it its first rising. For the second rising, set the bowl in the refrigerator. Check on it periodically over the next 2 hours and punch it down when necessary, because until the dough reaches the temperature of the refrigerator, it will rise too quickly. Get a good night's sleep. In the morning, pull the dough from the refrigerator and proceed with the shaping and final rising. Bake and enjoy.

If you do bake the brioches the night before, cool them completely and then wrap well. Don't refrigerate them. In the morning, rewrap them loosely in foil and reheat at 350° for 5–7 minutes before serving.

The dough can also be frozen after the second rising, but we suggest that you first refrigerate it for several hours, punching down occasionally, until it has cooled enough to inhibit the rising. Then, wrap well and freeze. To use, cut the frozen dough into golf-ball-size pieces (so it will defrost uniformly), defrost at room temperature, or in the refrigerator and then proceed with the shaping and final rising.

CHOCOLATE MARZIPAN BRIOCHE
COFFEECAKE   *Makes 2 coffeecakes serving 10 each*

This is a festive variation on our Brioche recipe and just
the thing for a special brunch or holiday breakfast. We
served this to George Lang when he was in town to speak
at The Victorian Society's Ninth Symposium and came to
The Commissary for the opening of an exhibit in our
Gallery room of his collection of Victorian menus.

FILLING
¾ pound almond paste
1 egg white
4 tablespoons unsalted butter, softened
¼ teaspoon salt
½ teaspoon cinnamon
¼ teaspoon almond extract
4 ounces semisweet chocolate, melted

ASSEMBLY
1 recipe Brioche dough (see p. 217), taken through the
  second rising and ready to be shaped

GLAZE
6 tablespoons unsalted butter
1½ cups powdered sugar
¼ cup hot water
½ teaspoon vanilla extract
½ cup toasted sliced almonds

FILLING
In a food processor or by hand, combine the almond paste,
egg white, butter, salt, cinnamon, and almond extract. Stir
in the melted chocolate.

ASSEMBLY
Divide the dough in half. Roll each piece into a rectangle
about 10″ × 14″ thick and smear all over with half the
filling. For each coffeecake, mentally score the dough into
thirds vertically. With a sharp knife, make diagonal cuts
down the side thirds (see diagram) and alternately fold
the side pieces over so that they overlap across the middle
third. Seal the ends by pinching together and tucking
under. Set the coffeecakes on foil-lined and greased baking
sheets and leave in a warm spot to double in size (about
1 hour). Meanwhile, **preheat the oven to 350°**. Bake coffeecakes about 25 minutes. Remove to cooling racks and
let cool to room temperature.

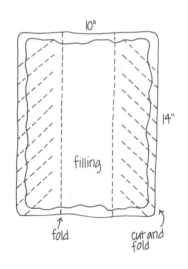

GLAZE
Melt the butter in a small pan and cook until it turns a

golden brown. Blend in the sugar, remove from the heat, and add the water, 1 tablespoon at a time, until mixture is of spreading consistency. Add the vanilla and drizzle the glaze over the cooled coffeecakes. Sprinkle on the almonds and let the glaze set.

NOTES
The filling is also good for sandwiching cookies or to spread in a tart shell to be topped with pastry cream and glazed fruit.

Another quick method for shaping the coffeecakes would be to simply roll up each of the rectangles as you would a jelly roll and set seam side down in two greased 10″ tube pans or (as we did for Mr. Lang) in a large brioche mold, reserving a piece of dough for the topknot.

COFFEE WALNUT CHOCOLATE CHIP MUFFINS
Makes twelve 3″ muffins

Quite honestly, these should really be called cupcakes and put in the dessert section, but we've always made them for breakfast at The Commissary. Our customers just love them, as decadent as these muffins are when consumed before noon.

½ cup unsalted butter
½ cup brown sugar
½ cup white sugar
3 tablespoons instant coffee
2 teaspoons vanilla extract
2 eggs
⅔ cup milk
1¾ cups flour
½ teaspoon salt
1 tablespoon baking powder
¾ cup semisweet chocolate chips
1½ cups coarsely chopped walnuts

Preheat the oven to 350°. Grease and flour twelve 3″ muffin-pan cups. Cream the butter with the sugars, coffee, and vanilla. Beat together the eggs and milk. Combine the flour, salt, and baking powder. Alternately add the wet and dry ingredients to the butter mixture. Stir just to combine. Add the chips and walnuts. Fill the tins full. Bake for 20–25 minutes. Cool 5 minutes, then remove from the tins and cool on racks.

LEMON POPPY SEED MUFFINS

Makes twelve 3" muffins

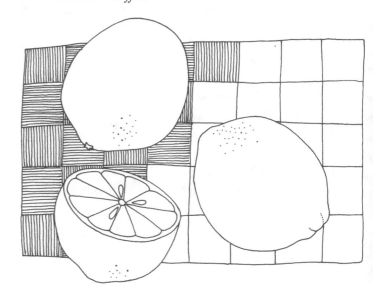

MUFFINS
6 tablespoons butter
6 tablespoons shortening
1 cup sugar
1 tablespoon baking powder
1 teaspoon salt
2 eggs
3 cups flour
⅔ cup milk
3 tablespoons poppy seeds
grated zest of one lemon

GLAZE
¼ cup lemon juice
2 cups powdered sugar
1 teaspoon vanilla

MUFFINS
Preheat the oven to 350°. Grease twelve 3" muffin-pan cups. Cream together the butter, shortening, sugar, baking powder, and salt. Beat in the eggs. Alternately add the flour and milk to the batter, mixing just to combine. Stir in the poppy seeds and lemon zest. Divide the batter among the 12 muffin cups. Bake for 25 minutes.

GLAZE
While the muffins are baking, combine the lemon juice, sugar, and vanilla in a small bowl. When the muffins are done, let them sit a minute and then turn them out onto cooling racks. When they have cooled about 10 minutes, dip the tops one by one into the warm glaze and set them back on a rack over wax paper.

VARIATION
Substitute ½ cup finely chopped walnuts for the poppy seeds.

And then there were the 1400 box lunches... A crew of 8 pulled an "all-nighter" since the production took over most of The Commissary and the boxes had to be en route by 9 a.m. There were mushroom caps filled with Herb-Garlic Cheese, honey-ginger glazed chicken breasts, Oriental vegetable salads, rolls, cheese, fruit, and ... Coffee Walnut Chocolate Chip Muffins. One fellow spent the night first assembling each of the 1400 boxes and then stacking the boxes in floor-to-ceiling pyramids that nearly filled the back dining room on The Commissary's 1st floor.

APPLE COCONUT MUFFINS *Makes twelve 3" muffins*

½ cup unsalted butter
1 cup sugar
½ teaspoon vanilla extract
2 eggs
½ cup milk
2½ cups flour
2½ teaspoons baking powder
½ teaspoon salt
¼ teaspoon nutmeg
3 ounces shredded sweetened coconut (1 cup plus 2 tablespoons)
1½ cups finely chopped peeled apple

Preheat the oven to 350°. Grease twelve 3" muffin-pan cups. Cream together the butter, sugar, and vanilla. Beat the eggs and milk together. Combine well the flour, baking powder, salt, and nutmeg. Alternately add the wet and dry ingredients to the creamed mixture. Blend until just combined. Stir in the coconut and the apples. Fill the cups full. Bake for 25–30 minutes. Cool 5 minutes and then remove from the tins to cool further.

THE COMMISSARY

CINNAMON BUTTER MUFFINS

Makes twelve 3" muffins

Warm, tender, butter-and-cinnamon-dipped muffins for breakfast . . . they almost melt in your mouth. Add to that aroma of freshly ground and brewed coffee, the sweet eye-opening tang of just squeezed orange juice and perhaps some crisp, smoky bacon. Who could resist such a breakfast?

This is perhaps the most universally loved muffin we've encountered. Do try it! These are best eaten while still warm from the oven, although they also freeze very well and can be wrapped in foil and reheated.

MUFFINS
6 tablespoons unsalted butter
6 tablespoons shortening
1 cup sugar
2 eggs
1 teaspoon salt
½ teaspoon nutmeg
1 tablespoon baking powder
¾ cup milk
3 cups flour

CINNAMON TOPPING
1 cup unsalted butter, melted
1 cup sugar
1 tablespoon cinnamon

MUFFINS
Preheat the oven to 350°. Grease twelve 3" muffin-pan cups. Cream the butter, shortening, and sugar together. Beat in the eggs, salt, nutmeg, and baking powder. Stir in the flour alternately with the milk until the mixture is just combined. Fill the muffin cups full. Bake for 20–25 minutes.

TOPPING
Have ready the melted butter and combine the cinnamon and sugar in a bowl. When the muffins are done, let them cool for a minute and then turn out onto cooling racks. Immerse each muffin briefly in the melted butter and let the excess drip off. Roll each in the cinnamon sugar.

Desserts

I just love a good little dessert buffet. It really makes the party. I'll just have a little smidgen of each, please, with just a tad extra of the Chocolate Mousse Cake. I starved mys...

1710 SANSOM STREET

In 1977, The Commissary opened with a distinctive, hand-drawn logo that symbolized, we felt, our unique new restaurant with its good, simple food as well as the hand-crafted quality of what we were doing. As the years went by, we came to feel the need to update and simplify our image. Because customers were always asking about the significance of the neon carrots hanging on the first floor of The Commissary (no significance... just an opening day gift) and because our Carrot Cake had developed a city-wide reputation, we opted for a simple bunch of carrots as our new logo. After a year of floating by themselves, the carrots came to rest against a simple box of a background from which they still herald customers to come inside for Carrot Cake... or a Heart Tart, Chocolate Mousse Cake, Chocolate Chip Fudge Cake, etc.

COMMISSARY CARROT CAKE   *Serves 16–20*

THE BEST CARROT CAKE

Carrot Cake—The Commissary's legendary dessert. Though years ago it was deemed too mundane to serve at old Frog and dropped from the menu, the recipe was resurrected and refined when The Commissary opened. Customers immediately latched on to this special version, which boasts one of the richest fillings imaginable. It sandwiches layers of moist, spicy cake laden with raisins and pecans, which are then covered with a tangy cream cheese frosting and finished with the gilded crunch of toasted coconut. Commissary Carrot Cake, in fact, has become so synonymous with the restaurant that when we went to change our logo a few years back, a sprightly bunch of carrots seemed a natural motif. A mixed greens salad (which leaves plenty of room) and Carrot Cake are an often seen Commissary luncheon choice, and the bakery long ago lost count of all the "Carrot" wedding cakes it has sent out. (And then there was the Carrot Cake Ice Cream!) Many of us, too, will never forget the trays and trays and trays of giant Carrot Cake sheet cakes produced for the various Philadelphia outdoor restaurant festivals, and how, at one festival, after selling out of 2,500 pieces, we were begged by the crowd still mobbing our booth to sell them the crumbs.

This cake is most easily made if you start it at least a day ahead, since the filling, for one thing, is best left to chill overnight. In fact, the different components can all be made even several days in advance and stored separately until you are ready to assemble the cake.

PECAN CREAM FILLING
1½ cups sugar
¼ cup flour
¾ teaspoon salt
1½ cups heavy cream
6 ounces (¾ cup) unsalted butter
1¼ cups chopped pecans
2 teaspoons vanilla extract

CARROT CAKE
1¼ cups corn oil
2 cups sugar
2 cups flour
2 teaspoons cinnamon
2 teaspoons baking powder
1 teaspoon baking soda
1 teaspoon salt
4 eggs
4 cups grated carrots (about a 1-pound bag)

Can cut recipe ∩ ½

1 cup chopped pecans
1 cup raisins

CREAM CHEESE FROSTING
8 ounces soft unsalted butter
8 ounces soft cream cheese
1 1-pound box of powdered sugar
1 teaspoon vanilla extract

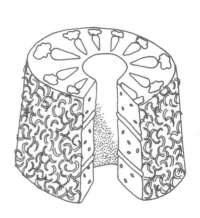

ASSEMBLY
4 ounces shredded, sweetened coconut (1½ cups)

PECAN CREAM FILLING
In a heavy saucepan, blend well the sugar, flour, and salt. Gradually stir in the cream. Add the butter. Cook and stir the mixture over low heat until the butter has melted, then let simmer 20–30 minutes until golden brown in color, stirring occasionally. Cool to lukewarm. Stir in the nuts and vanilla. Let cool completely and then refrigerate, preferably overnight. If too thick to spread, bring to room temperature before using.

CARROT CAKE
Preheat the oven to 350°. Have ready a greased and floured 10" tube cake pan. In a large bowl, whisk together the corn oil and sugar. Sift together the flour, cinnamon, baking powder, baking soda and salt. Sift half the dry ingredients into the sugar-oil mixture and blend. Alternately sift in the rest of the dry ingredients while adding the eggs, one by one. Combine well. Add the carrots, raisins, and pecans. Pour into the prepared tube pan and bake for 70 minutes. Cool upright in the pan on a cooling rack. If you are not using the cake that day, it can be removed from the pan, wrapped well in plastic wrap and stored at room temperature.

CREAM CHEESE FROSTING
Cream the butter well. Add the cream cheese and beat until blended. Sift in the sugar and add the vanilla. If too soft to spread, chill a bit. Refrigerate if not using immediately, but bring to a spreadable temperature before using.

ASSEMBLY
Preheat the oven to 300°. Spread the coconut on a baking sheet and bake for 10–15 minutes until it colors lightly. Toss the coconut occasionally while it is baking so that it browns evenly. Cool completely. Have the filling and frosting at a spreadable consistency.

Loosen the cake in its pan and invert onto a serving plate. With a long serrated knife, carefully split the cake into 3 horizontal layers. Spread the filling between the

layers. Spread the frosting over the top and sides. Pat the toasted coconut onto the sides of the cake. If desired, reserve ½ cup of the frosting and color half with green food coloring and half with orange. Then decorate the top of the cake with green and orange icing piped through a ¹⁄₁₆″ wide, plain pastry tube to resemble little carrots. Serve the cake at room temperature.

NOTES AND VARIATIONS
The assembled cake can be refrigerated for up to 48 hours. It also freezes very well.

Substitute 4 cups unpeeled, grated apples or zucchini for the carrots.

Batter can also be baked as cupcakes, loaves, sheet cake, or petits fours.

Any leftover filling makes a wonderful ice cream topping if you warm it slightly first.

SACHERTORTE   *Serves 12*

We know a number of people who believe that this is *the* best chocolate dessert on earth. It truly is quite wonderful, and those of us who have had the original Sachertorte will tell you that this version is even better. Glorious chocolate is richly textured with finely ground nuts, touched with a tart sweetness from the barest layer of apricot jam and perfectly finished with a smooth-as-glass chocolate icing that is ridiculously easy to make. And, as if that weren't enough, the cake can be made in advance and freezes beautifully—even iced. (Freeze unwrapped first to set icing, then wrap well.)

CAKE
8 ounces semisweet chocolate
8 ounces unsalted butter, softened
1 cup sugar
¾ teaspoon salt
2 teaspoons vanilla extract
⅓ cup flour
8 ounces walnuts, very finely ground
8 egg yolks
8 egg whites
⅔ cup apricot jam

ICING
½ cup heavy cream
2 teaspoons instant coffee
6 ounces semisweet chocolate, chopped (Do not use chocolate chips.)

228

CAKE

Butter and flour a 9″ by 2½″ cake pan with a removable bottom or a springform pan. **Preheat the oven to 350°.** Melt the chocolate and cool until lukewarm. Cream the butter with the salt, vanilla, and sugar. Toss together the flour and walnuts. Add the egg yolks one by one to the butter-sugar mixture. Stir in the chocolate and nuts. Beat the egg whites to soft peaks and stir ¼ of them into the chocolate mixture to lighten the batter. Fold in the remaining whites. Pour the batter into the prepared pan and bake 1 hour. Let cool in the pan for 20 minutes and push down the puffed-up sides so that they are flush with the middle. Remove the sides of the pan and invert the cake onto a cooling rack set over wax paper. (The bottom has now become the top of the cake.) Cool completely. Heat the apricot jam, push it through a sieve, and brush over the top and sides of the cooled cake. Let glaze set for about half an hour before icing the cake.

ICING

In a metal mixing bowl or sauce pan, scald the cream. Whisk in the coffee and add the chocolate. Stir 1 minute over the heat, then remove and continue to stir until the chocolate has completely melted. Cool from hot to warm and pour over the cake. Rotate the cake while spreading the icing evenly with a spatula. Chill the cake on its rack until the icing is completely set. Transfer (2 quiche bottoms are helpful) to a serving plate and refrigerate. Bring to room temperature before serving.

VARIATIONS AND SERVING SUGGESTIONS

Whatever you do for a garnish, keep it simple. A few candied violets around the perimeter seem appropriate, and at Christmas time, sprigs of fresh holly are lovely. Oh! and don't forget the requisite whipped cream to serve alongside.

Cranberry Sachertorte (especially nice at Thanksgiving and Christmas) Add 1½ cups coarsely chopped fresh cranberries and 1 tablespoon grated orange rind to the batter when you add the chocolate and nuts. If you like, decorate the top with whole cranberries.

Try almonds instead of walnuts, add a small amount of finely chopped candied orange peel to the batter and/or glaze with sieved orange marmalade instead of apricot jam.

CHOCOLATE MOUSSE CAKE WITH GRAND MARNIER CUSTARD SAUCE

Serves 20

This is surely one of the grandest of desserts . . . oh so elegant and not overly sweet . . . a silken, semisweet, Grand Marnier-scented chocolate mousse encased in a genoise shell enrobed in more Grand Marnier-infused chocolate and served in a pool of ever-so-light custard sauce, also betraying that exquisite Grand Marnier perfume. It was the special dessert one Mother's Day at Frog and has been on the dessert list at both Frog and The Commissary ever since. In our opinion, it has few rivals.

Production of this masterpiece at home is not difficult . . . it just involves a number of steps. The cake can be assembled and left unfrosted 1–2 days in advance, and the sauce and frosting can also be done several days ahead. Relax, enjoy yourself, and be prepared for an avalanche of compliments when you serve this spectacular cake.

GENOISE
4 ounces unsalted butter
7 eggs
1 cup sugar
1 teaspoon vanilla extract
1¼ cups flour
¼ teaspoon salt

CHOCOLATE MOUSSE
30 ounces semisweet chocolate, chopped
½ cup strong coffee
½ cup Grand Marnier
3 egg yolks
2 cups heavy cream
8 egg whites (1 cup)
¼ cup sugar

FROSTING
6 ounces semisweet chocolate, chopped
6 tablespoons Grand Marnier
½ pound soft unsalted butter

GRAND MARNIER CUSTARD SAUCE
2 cups half-and-half
7 egg yolks
⅓ cup sugar
⅛ teaspoon salt
2 teaspoons vanilla extract
3 tablespoons Grand Marnier

GENOISE

Line a 10″ × 15″ jelly roll pan with wax paper and butter the paper. Melt the butter and set aside. Put the eggs in a large bowl of hot water for 10–15 minutes to warm them. Change the water when necessary to keep it hot. Meanwhile, measure out and set aside the flour and salt. Have ready the sugar and vanilla.

Preheat the oven to 350°. Pour the water off the eggs and break them into the bowl of an electric mixer. With the mixer on medium speed, add the sugar and vanilla all at once. Beat for 5–10 minutes until about quadruple in volume. Sift the flour and salt over this mixture in 6–8 parts, folding in gently, but thoroughly, with a spatula. Work quickly. Put about ⅕ of this batter into a separate mixing bowl. Add the lukewarm butter and whisk it thoroughly into the small amount of batter. Pour this butter mixture over the rest of the batter and very gently and quickly fold the two together. Pour the batter into the prepared pan, filling the corners. Put at once into the preheated oven and bake 20–25 minutes. Set the pan on a rack to cool. If not using within the day, wrap the cooled cake well, otherwise invert onto wax paper and remove the pan and liner.

Using the bottom of the 9″ round pan as a template, cut a 9″ circle from the cake and cut the remaining cake into 2 rectangles as shown in the diagram. With a long thin serrated knife, carefully halve each piece of cake horizontally so that you have 2 circles and 4 rectangles. Cut a 9″ circle of wax paper and fit into the bottom of a 9″ × 3½ ″ falsebottom cake pan. (Do not use a springform pan.) Trimming them to fit, use 3 of the 4 strips of cake to line the sides of the pan. Fit one of the circles of cake (cut side down) into the bottom of the pan. Reserve the second circle to put on top of the mousse filling.

CHOCOLATE MOUSSE

Have ready the cake-lined pan.

Bring 2 inches of water to a simmer in a 3-quart saucepan. Combine, off the heat, in a large metal mixing bowl the chopped chocolate, coffee, and Grand Marnier. Place the bowl over the simmering water. Do not stir the mixture while it is melting and keep the heat as low as possible. Off the heat, stir to blend and cool to room temperature. Whisk in the yolks. Whip the cream to soft peaks and set aside. Whip together the whites, salt, and sugar until soft peaks form and fold into the chocolate mixture. Carefully fold in the whipped cream. Be sure the mixture is homogeneous. Pour the mousse into the cake-lined pan and top with the second circle of cake. Wrap the pan tightly with plastic wrap and chill at least 6 hours or up to 3 days. (The cake can be frozen at this point.)

CHOCOLATE TERMINOLOGY
- Unsweetened chocolate has no added sugar and the most intense flavor.
- Bittersweet, semisweet and sweet chocolates all have added sugar and cocoa butter in varying degrees.
- Milk chocolate is sweet chocolate made milder by the addition of milk.
- White chocolate is cocoa butter with sugar and milk but no chocolate liqueur.

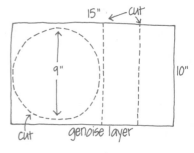

genoise layer

CAKE SCRAP USES

- Cut the scraps into small bits, fold into softened ice cream and refreeze. We have made Carrot Cake and Brownie ice creams this way.
- "Junk Balls"- a commissary favorite. Scraps, a good dose of rum, and leftover frosting are combined, rolled into balls, dusted with cocoa or chopped nuts and set in miniature cupcake papers.
- Staff breakfast, lunch, or dinner. Who can resist? Sachertorte and Carrot Cake scraps are tied for most popular.
- Make trifle by sprinkling scraps with a liqueur of choice and layering them in tall glasses with fruits, custard or mousse, crushed praline, and whipped cream.

Grand Marnier
Custard Sauce

GRAND MARNIER CUSTARD SAUCE

Have ready a large bowl of ice water (heavy on the cubes) and a separate metal mixing bowl. Scald but don't boil the half-and-half. Whisk together the yolks, sugar, and salt. Pour the scalded half-and-half all at once over the yolks while whisking well. Pour back into the saucepan and cook over medium heat without boiling, stirring constantly, until just thickened and mixture coats a spoon. Immediately pour the custard into a metal bowl set over the bowl of ice water and whisk constantly until it has cooled down somewhat. Strain the custard to be sure it is smooth. Whisk in the Grand Marnier and vanilla. Cover and chill until ready to serve.

FROSTING

Invert the cake in its pan onto a serving plate. Pressing down on the removable bottom, carefully lift up the sides. Remove the bottom and the wax paper.

Have ready a large bowl of ice water (heavy on the cubes). In a double boiler over simmering water, melt together the chocolate and Grand Marnier. Remove from the heat and stir in the butter. Set the pan in the bowl of ice water and whisk the frosting until it is of a mayonnaise-like consistency. Remove from the ice and use the frosting immediately. (If the frosting becomes too hard, whisk over simmering water to soften it and then return to the ice water and beat to the proper consistency.) Keep the cake chilled until ready to serve.

To serve, cut the cake in thin elegant slices, wiping off the knife after each cut to keep the slices neat. (The first slice is almost always difficult to coax out cleanly and may have to be sacrificed to the cook.) Serve each piece in a pool of the custard sauce.

NOTES

For those who like to plan and cook ahead, the unfrosted cake freezes quite well if wrapped tightly in its pan.

This recipe, we admit, calls for a goodly bit of Grand Marnier. That makes it a rather expensive cake, and so we've tried the cake substituting strong coffee for the liqueur in the mousse and frosting and have had fine results.

The custard sauce is really wonderful with its potent undercurrent of Grand Marnier. Make it sometime on its own to serve with fresh or poached fruit, pound or angel cake, steamed puddings, etc.

CHOCOLATE CHIP FUDGE CAKE
(KILLER CAKE)

Serves 16

In the race for the most "chocolaty" dessert, this cake is a very strong contender. Underneath a creamy fudgelike frosting is a dense cake made even more intense by the addition of chocolate chips—hence its nickname "Killer Cake." Chocolate freaks are advised not to miss it!

CAKE
6 ounces unsalted butter
6 ounces unsweetened chocolate, chopped
6 eggs
3 cups sugar
½ teaspoon salt
1 tablespoon vanilla extract
1½ cups flour
1½ cups chocolate chips

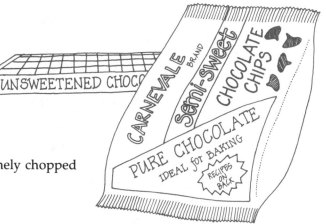

FROSTING
1¼ cups sugar
2 tablespoons instant coffee
1 cup heavy cream
5 ounces unsweetened chocolate, finely chopped
4 ounces unsalted butter
1½ teaspoons vanilla extract

CAKE
This cake is best mixed by hand. A mixer may overbeat the batter and incorporate too much air into it so that when the cake bakes, an unwanted crispy layer will form on top. (The same thing can happen to brownies.)

Preheat the oven to 350°. Grease two 9" × 1½" cake tins and line bottoms with wax or parchment paper.

Melt the butter and chocolate together over simmering water. Cool to lukewarm. In a large bowl whisk together for 1 minute the eggs, sugar, salt, and vanilla. Whisk in the butter-chocolate mixture. Stir in the flour and chocolate chips. Pour the batter into the prepared pans and bake for 30–35 minutes. (Do not overbake. Cake tester should *not* come out clean.) Cool on racks and remove from pans as soon as cooled. Wrap the layers well if not using the same day.

FROSTING
Combine the sugar, coffee, and cream in a deep, heavy saucepan. Stirring, bring to a boil. Reduce the heat and simmer 6 minutes without stirring. Remove from the heat. Add the chopped chocolate and stir until it is melted and blended. Add the butter and vanilla. Whisk well. Chill until the mixture begins to thicken. (If made the day before,

bring back to room temperature and beat until of spreading consistency before using.)

ASSEMBLY

Put one cake layer bottom-side-up on a cake plate. Spread with ⅓ of the frosting. Top with the second layer, also bottom-side-up. Trim the circumference of the cake of excess crusty protrusions so it is smooth and can be frosted evenly. Pour all but ½ cup of the frosting on top of the cake, spreading it over the top and then the sides. Put the reserved icing into a pastry bag fitted with a small star tip and pipe 16 rosettes around the top of the cake. Refrigerate if not serving immediately, but bring to room temperature before serving. Serve with lightly sweetened whipped cream.

MOCHA FUDGE CAKE   *Serves 12–16*

Don't be alarmed that there isn't any flour in this cake. Its name is "Mocha Fudge" and like fudge it is. Terribly rich, divinely moist, and counterbalanced by a "light-as-air" whipped-cream frosting, even a very small piece of this cake should satisfy and greatly please the most avid chocoholic. If you wish, the cake (minus its frosting) can be made up to a week in advance and kept, tightly wrapped in its pan, in the refrigerator. But do plan to bake it at least one day before serving it, since it needs a good amount of time to set up.

CAKE
1 cup strong coffee
1 pound semisweet chocolate, chopped
2 cups sugar
2 cups unsalted butter
8 eggs, lightly beaten

FROSTING
1½ cups heavy cream
¼ cup powdered sugar
½ teaspoon vanilla extract

CAKE
Preheat the oven to 250°. Butter a round 9″ × 3″ cake pan with a removable bottom and line with 1 piece of foil, pushing the foil onto the bottom, up the sides and over the rim smoothly and without tearing. (Foil which is 12″ wide can be used, but you will then need two pieces. Overlap them and fold them together as smoothly as

234

possible. You do not want the batter to leak through.) Lightly but thoroughly butter the foil.

In a large saucepan, combine the coffee, chocolate, sugar, and butter. Stirring all the while, cook the mixture over medium heat until it is about the temperature of hot bath water (130°). Remove from the heat and gradually whisk in the beaten eggs. Pour the batter into the prepared pan and bake 1½ hours (the center will seem uncooked, but will firm up on its own as its cools). Let cool, then cover, and chill overnight (or up to 1 week).

FROSTING

Shortly before serving, trim away any cake not level with the center. Invert the cake onto a serving plate and remove the foil. Whip together the heavy cream, sugar, and vanilla until stiff enough to spread. Frost the top and sides of the cake, leaving some of the cream to put into a pastry bag fitted with a star tip. Pipe rosettes of the reserved cream around the rim of the cake and top each rosette with a strawberry, a nut, or some shaved chocolate.

BASIC SOUR CREAM CHEESECAKE
WITH VARIATIONS   *Serves 12–16*

Back in the days of The Commissary cooking classes, Anne Clark volunteered to do some cheesecake classes and found herself faced with the task of organizing and presenting the fifteen or so different cheesecake recipes that The Commissary alternately offers on its menu. After a great deal of frustration and testing, she chose to handle the problem by creating a basic recipe that could then be flavored and altered to suit the whims of the maker.

This basic cheesecake by itself is lovely—light, creamy, not too sweet, and an ideal foil for fresh fruit. The real fun begins, though, when you start playing with the variations. There are first the wonderful traditional Commissary combinations, such as Munich, with its lemon base and streusel topping; Banana, with a chocolate crust and topping; Chocolate Mint Chip; Amaretto, with nut crust and whipped cream topping; Kahlúa; and so on. Beyond that, it's up to you. The possibilities seem almost limitless.

Plan to make this dessert the day before you intend to serve it, as it requires a good bit of time to first bake and then chill. We bake it at a very low temperature because it seems to crack less that way and the resulting product is as creamy around the edges as it is in the center. Also, if you are dying for cheesecake but don't really want to

Anne surveys her list of cheesecakes to be organized for her class.

make a recipe to serve 12, simply halve the ingredients and use a 6″ × 3″ or 9″ × 1½″ cake pan with a removable bottom. (Use full amount of crust and topping, though, for the 9″ × 1½″ pan.) Bake the 6″ × 3″ size for 1 hour at 325° or for 35 minutes if using the 9″ × 1½″ size.

CRUST
⅔ cup flour
3 tablespoons sugar
4 tablespoons cold butter, in bits

FILLING
2 pounds cream cheese, at room temperature
1 cup sugar
4 eggs
1 cup sour cream
4 teaspoons vanilla extract
¼ teaspoon salt
OPT. 6 tablespoons lemon juice

SOUR CREAM TOPPING
1½ cups sour cream
2 tablespoons sugar
1 teaspoon vanilla extract

CRUST
Preheat the oven to 350°. In a food processor or with a pastry blender, blend the ingredients until very fine crumbs are formed. Press onto the bottom of a 9″ × 3½″ cake pan with a removable bottom. Bake for 15–20 minutes or until done. Cool completely.

FILLING
With an electric mixer, beat the cream cheese until smooth. Add the sugar and beat until well blended, occasionally stopping to scrape the sides and bottom of the bowl. Add the eggs, one at a time. When smooth, add the sour cream, vanilla, salt, and lemon juice. Mix just to combine.

   Preheat the oven to 275°. Pour the filling into the prepared pan and bake for 2 hours and 15 minutes. Remove from the oven (center may seem undercooked but will firm up on its own as it chills). Run a knife around the edges to a depth of ½″ to loosen the cheesecake and help prevent cracking. Cool on a cooling rack. When the cake is at room temperature, cover with plastic wrap flush against the cheesecake and refrigerate in the pan overnight, or for at least 6 hours.

TOPPING
Preheat the oven to 450°. Whisk together ingredients.

236

Spread evenly over the chilled cheesecake while still in the pan. Bake for 7 minutes, watching carefully so that the sour cream does not brown at all (tiny bubbles will appear all over the surface). Cool 2 hours or more before serving. If it is to be kept longer, cover tightly but not flush with plastic wrap, to prevent edges from turning gray, and refrigerate.

NOTES

The cheesecake is best if allowed to come to room temperature before serving. For tidier-looking pieces, wipe off the knife between cuts.

A cheesecake *without* a topping can be made and refrigerated up to 48 hours in advance. It also freezes quite nicely.

VARIATIONS

CRUSTS

Nut: Add ⅔ cup coarsely ground nuts and 1 teaspoon cinnamon.

Chocolate: Substitute ¼ cup unsweetened cocoa for ¼ cup of flour.

Lemon or orange: Add 2 teaspoons grated rind.

Coconut: Add ⅓ cup sweetened coconut and decrease sugar by 2 tablespoons.

Spice: Add 1 teaspoon cinnamon or other spice.

FILLINGS (*omit* the 6 tablespoons of lemon juice in the basic recipe)

Chocolate: Add 1 pound semisweet chocolate, melted and still hot, and OPT. ¼ cup liqueur of choice.

Banana: Add 3 medium ripe bananas mashed with ¼ cup lemon and decrease sour cream by ½.

Amaretto: Add ¼ cup each Amaretto and Cognac or brandy with 1½ teaspoons almond extract.

Mocha: Add 8 ounces melted and still hot semisweet chocolate and 2 tablespoons instant coffee dissolved in ½ cup hot water.

Kahlúa: Follow instructions for Mocha Cheesecake but omit the chocolate, dissolve instant coffee in Kahlúa instead of hot water and add (OPT.) ½ teaspoon cinnamon.

Lemon: Add ½ cup lemon juice and 1–2 teaspoons grated lemon rind.

Chocolate chip mint: Add ¼ cup crème de menthe and ¼ teaspoon peppermint extract to the batter. Sprinkle 1 cup mini chocolate chips over the top and stir them in with your finger so that they are just covered with batter.

Pumpkin: Add 1½ cups pumpkin purée, 1 teaspoon cinnamon, ½ teaspoon each ginger and nutmeg and ¼ teaspoon cloves.

Carrot: Add 1 cup carrot purée.

Nut: Add 1½ cups finely chopped nuts (lightly toasted if almond or hazelnut).

TOPPING

Chocolate sour cream—add 2 tablespoons unsweetened cocoa and an additional 2 tablespoons sugar to Sour Cream Topping

MUNICH CHEESECAKE TOPPING

(for Munich Cheesecake: lemon cheesecake and basic crust base)

1½ cups raisins (regular, golden, or mixture)
Grated peel of 1 lemon
¾ cup sugar
3 ounces half-and-half
1–2 tablespoons lemon juice
6 tablespoons brown sugar
6 tablespoons flour
¼ cup cold butter

Combine the raisins, peel, sugar, and half-and-half in a small saucepan. Cook and stir over low heat about 20 minutes. Chill. If necessary thin with the lemon juice until the consistency of jam. Combine the brown sugar and flour. Cut in the butter. Spread the raisin mixture over a completely cooled and chilled cheesecake still in the pan. Sprinkle on the streusel mixture. Watching carefully broil 4″ from broiler for 2–3 minutes or until the butter bubbles and the streusel is lightly browned. Cool before serving.

CHOCOLATE GLAZE

4 ounces semisweet chocolate, chopped
½ cup heavy cream

In a small heavy pan, melt the chocolate in the cream over low heat. Stir to blend. Pour over a cooled cheesecake in the pan and tilt the pan to spread evenly. Chill 30 minutes or more to set glaze.

VARIATIONS

Mocha: Add 1 teaspoon instant coffee.

Liqueur-flavored: Add 1 tablespoon liqueur of choice.

DACQUOISE

This is truly the queen of desserts at both Frog and The Commissary. It is a bliss-inducing assemblage of crisp, nutted meringue layers sumptuously sandwiched with a vanilla butter cream whispering essence of rum and elegantly finished in chocolate butter cream and toasted almonds.

The meringue layers can conveniently be made several days in advance and stored at room temperature loosely covered with plastic wrap. The butter creams should be made and the whole assembled the day you intend to serve it, since butter cream does not keep its texture well (nor does it refrigerate well) and the meringue will begin to lose its crispness if frosted two or three days ahead.

MERINGUE LAYERS
¼ pound toasted blanched almonds
¼ pound toasted hazelnuts
4½ teaspoons cornstarch
1¼ cups sugar
1 cup egg whites
½ teaspoon cream of tartar
¼ teaspoon salt
½ teaspoon almond extract
½ teaspoon vanilla extract

BUTTER CREAM
6 egg yolks
1 cup sugar
¾ cup half-and-half
2 ounces unsweetened chocolate
1 pound unsalted butter, at room temperature
2 tablespoons dark rum
1 teaspoon vanilla extract

ASSEMBLY
1 cup sliced blanched almonds, toasted

Toast nuts by spreading them in a single layer on a rimmed baking sheet and putting them in a preheated 350° oven for 5 to 10 minutes until they just begin to turn a pale golden brown.

MERINGUE LAYERS
Grease and flour the bottoms of three 9" cake pans with removable bottoms (returning them to their pans) or enough baking sheets to trace three 9" circles on. **Preheat the oven to 400°**. Grind the nuts very finely and combine with the cornstarch and 1 cup of the sugar in a large bowl.

With an electric mixer, whip the egg whites until frothy. Add the cream of tartar and salt. With the mixer on, add half of the remaining ¼ cup sugar. Add the extracts and then the rest of the sugar. Continue beating until stiff but not dry peaks are formed. In 3 additions, gently and quickly fold the egg whites into the nuts. Spread the mixture in the 3 cake pans or over traced circles. Put in the oven and *immediately* reduce the heat to 275°. Bake for 65–70 minutes or until dry to the touch. Cool 15 minutes, then carefully loosen from the pans with a broad spatula and transfer to racks to cool further. The layers baked on the traced circles will need trimming. Trim them using a 9″ circle as a guide.

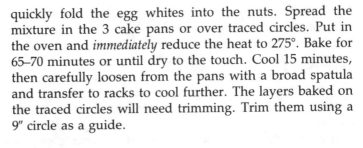

BUTTER CREAM
Make the butter cream only shortly before assembling the cake.

Have ready a large mixing bowl of ice water (heavy on the cubes.) Whisk together the egg yolks and sugar until light-colored. Scald the half-and-half. Whisking well, pour the half-and-half all at once over the yolk-sugar mixture and beat to combine. Return to the saucepan and heat while stirring over low heat until very thick. Do *not* boil. Pour into a mixing bowl, preferably metal, set over the bowl of ice water to help the mixture cool as quickly as possible to just slightly above room temperature.

Melt the chocolate in a small saucepan over simmering water. Put the custard, now at room temperature, into the bowl of an electric mixer and begin beating in the butter, bit by bit, waiting until each bit is absorbed before adding the next. Add the rum and vanilla. Measure off half (1½ cups) of the butter cream and whisk the melted chocolate into it.

ASSEMBLY
Do not attempt to assemble the dacquoise in a room hotter than 85° or the frosting will melt all over. Put 1 trimmed meringue layer on a serving plate. Spread with a little less than half the rum butter cream. Top with a second layer and spread with the same amount (there should be about ½ cup rum butter cream left for the sides). Add the third meringue layer and spread the remaining rum butter cream around the sides. Spread ¾ cup of the chocolate butter cream over the top. Put the rest into a pastry bag fitted with a small star tip. Press the sliced almonds around the sides of the cake. "Tie" the sides of the cake to the top with a border of chocolate butter cream stars or repeated shells. Store in the refrigerator, but *serve* at room temperature (about 70°).

NOTES AND VARIATIONS
If, when you are adding the butter to the custard mixture for the butter cream, the mixture begins to look curdled, whisk for a few seconds over direct heat. If it is too runny after all the butter has been added, whisk over ice a bit until it is of spreading consistency.

Dacquoise freezes well. First freeze it unwrapped to set the frosting, then wrap well in plastic wrap and replace in freezer. To defrost, unwrap the frozen cake and defrost in the refrigerator.

Play with different butter cream flavors—mocha, praline, raspberry, coffee, and so on.

Try baking the meringue layers in different shapes. We often do heart-shaped dacquoises for weddings.

ZUCCOTTO

Serves 12

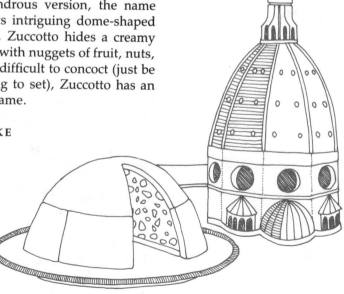

What's in a name? "Zuccotto" barely gives the faintest clue other than its resemblance to the Italian words for pumpkin (zucca) and sugar (zucchero) which could refer to its shape and sweetness. To those, though, who have partaken of this special dessert in its native Florence or have reveled in our own wondrous version, the name means true delight. Beneath its intriguing dome-shaped shell of chocolate chiffon cake, Zuccotto hides a creamy sweet filling brilliantly studded with nuggets of fruit, nuts, and chocolate. Really not at all difficult to concoct (just be sure to allow time for the filling to set), Zuccotto has an elegance that belies its funny name.

CHOCOLATE CHIFFON CAKE
¼ cup unsweetened cocoa
½ cup boiling water
¾ cup flour
1 cup sugar
¾ teaspoon baking soda
½ teaspoon salt
4 egg yolks
1 teaspoon vanilla extract
¼ cup corn oil
4 egg whites
¼ teaspoon cream of tartar
OPT. 6 tablespoons Grand Marnier

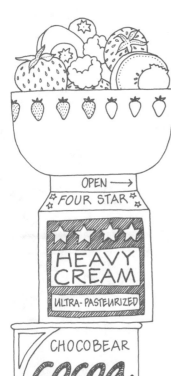

FILLING

4 ounces fine-quality semisweet chocolate, chopped to pieces half the size of a pea (or use mini chocolate chips)

¾ cup coarsely chopped toasted hazelnuts or almonds

4 cups diced fresh fruit (strawberries, bananas, blueberries, kiwis, peaches, raspberries, or others, except for fresh pineapple)

¼ cup Grand Marnier or orange juice

1 small package gelatin (2½ teaspoons)

½ cup sugar

⅓ cup flour

¼ teaspoon salt

3 egg yolks

1 cup milk

2 teaspoons vanilla extract

3 cups heavy cream

CHOCOLATE CHIFFON CAKE

Preheat the oven to 350°. Line a 10″ × 15″ jelly-roll pan with wax paper and butter the paper.

Combine the cocoa and boiling water in a small bowl. Into the bowl of an electric mixer, sift the flour, sugar, baking soda, and salt. Make a well in the dry ingredients and add the cocoa mixture, egg yolks, vanilla, and corn oil. Beat for 3 minutes at medium speed. In a separate bowl, beat the egg whites and cream of tartar until stiff. Gently but thoroughly fold in the whites. Turn the batter into the prepared pan, filling the corners. Bake for 20–25 minutes. Remove from the oven, sprinkle with 3 table-spoons of the Grand Marnier, if desired, and let cool. Turn the cake out of the pan and remove the wax paper. Sprinkle with the remaining Grand Marnier, if desired. If not using in the next hour, wrap well.

Have ready a 3-quart bowl, 9″ in diameter. Using the bowl as a template, cut a 9″ circle of cake. Cut the remaining cake into 2 equal strips (see diagram). With a long serrated knife, carefully halve each piece horizontally. Line the bowl with plastic wrap, leaving several inches hanging over the edge. Center one of the circles of cake, cut side down, into the bottom of the bowl. Reserve the second circle and line the sides of the bowl with the strips of cake, trimming where necessary so that the cake is flush with the rim of the bowl.

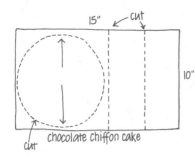

FILLING

Have ready the chocolate, nuts, fruit, and cake-lined bowl. If using chopped chocolate, spread it on a plate and refrigerate so that it doesn't become so soft that it will later bleed into the filling.

Sprinkle the gelatin over the Grand Marnier in a small cup and let sit several minutes to soften. Meanwhile, combine the sugar, flour, and salt in a small saucepan. Whisk in the egg yolks and milk. Set over medium heat and cook, while stirring continuously, until the mixture is thick and boiling. Remove from the heat and immediately whisk in the gelatin mixture. Stir until the gelatin dissolves. Cool to room temperature. Whisk in the vanilla. Whip the cream until stiff and stir 1 cup of it into the custard. Carefully fold in the remaining cream along with the nuts, chocolate, and fruit. Pour the filling into the cake-lined bowl, being careful not to leave air pockets. If the filling for some reason doesn't quite fill the bowl, trim the cake so that it is flush with the filling. Top with the reserved circle of cake. Cover tightly with plastic wrap and chill at least 6 hours. To serve, unmold onto a serving plate, remove the plastic wrap, and, if desired, dust the top with powdered sugar in a decorative pattern.

NOTES AND VARIATIONS

Uncut, the zuccotto will keep up to 3 days in the refrigerator. It also freezes very well.

Substitute Amaretto or Frangelico for the Grand Marnier.

Try varying the fruits and nuts in the filling. You could also substitute one of our recipes for Pumpkin, Lemon, or Orange Walnut Mousse as the filling.

Substitute regular Genoise for the chocolate chiffon cake and frost the unmolded zuccotto shortly before serving with Sachertorte Frosting.

LINZERTORTE

Serves 10

Strictly speaking, we should probably rename this recipe "Raspberry Butter Tart," for it omits the cinnamon, cloves, and ground nuts that traditionally flavor Austria's famous Linzertorte. But the recipe, contributed by a Commissary baker years ago, came to us with this name and we have simply never changed it. The shape, though, is quite traditional. A very buttery, lemon-scented dough is pressed into a long rectangular mold, jam is spread over the dough, and the remaining dough is arranged in a lattice pattern on top. Serve with a little whipped cream on the side, if you dare.

243

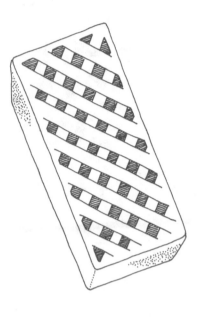

CRUST

½ pound unsalted butter
½ cup sugar
2 egg yolks
1 tablespoon lemon juice
1 teaspoon grated lemon rind
2¼ cups flour
1½ teaspoons baking powder

ASSEMBLY

1 (12-ounce) jar seedless raspberry jam (1 cup plus 2
  tablespoons)
1 tablespoon lemon juice
OPT. Powdered sugar

CRUST

Preheat the oven to 350°. Cream together the butter and sugar. Add the egg yolks, lemon juice, and rind. Beat smooth. Add the flour and baking powder and combine well. Set a 4½" × 14" rectangular tart mold on a buttered baking sheet or substitute a round 9" tart pan with removable bottom or springform pan for the rectangular mold. With your fingers, press ⅔ of the dough (15 ounces) into the mold, covering the bottom and building up a ½" rim.

ASSEMBLY

Combine the jam and lemon juice and spread over the crust. On a floured surface, roll out the remaining dough until ³⁄₁₆" thick. Cut strips of dough ⅝" wide and arrange them diagonally ½" apart in a lattice pattern over the tart (see diagram). Be sure no dough overhangs the rim. Bake for 40 minutes. Cool thoroughly on a rack and remove the mold by lifting straight up and away.

If desired, dust with powdered sugar. First cover any jam spots with small bits of wax paper, sift the powdered sugar over and carefully remove the wax paper. Transfer the torte (2 quiche pan bottoms make this easy) to an oblong tray or serving board. Cut into 1½"-wide slices to serve. Do not refrigerate.

VARIATIONS

Play with different flavors of jams.

Add ½ cup finely ground almonds, hazelnuts, or walnuts to the dough.

Make **Linzer Bites** (as we do for The Market) by rolling balls of the dough and placing them into miniature cupcake papers. Make a depression in the center of each and fill with jam. Bake about 30 minutes. Makes about 28 pieces.

STRAWBERRY HEART TARTS

Makes 6 individual heart-shaped tarts

One day just prior to the opening of The Commissary, Anne found herself pondering the questions of what new desserts to open the restaurant with and what to do with all the heart-shaped gelatin molds lying about Frog after one Valentine's Day bout with coeur à la crème. On a whim, she draped pastry dough over the backs of the molds and baked them. The Heart Tart was born! The muses then went to work on the filling; chocolate, pastry cream, and strawberries converged. The Commissary opened serving 12 a day; then came a catering order for 70, and the Heart Tarts were off and running. The process soon had to be streamlined to meet the demand—pastry cream became cream cheese filling, and a machine was purchased to mix huge batches of dough. Now, the daily average of tarts sold is 150, with a high of more than 400 on Valentine's Day!

A dessert truly original to The Commissary, the Heart Tart has claimed a legion of followers who adore its combination of crisp crust, toothsome chocolate lining, rich cream filling, and crowning of glazed jumbo berries. Anne's husband, Chris, is one of those fans, and in her wedding vows, Anne promised him "unlimited Heart Tarts."

The tart's elegant appearance belies its ease of preparation, especially once you have the heart-shaped gelatin molds in hand. The pastry takes just seconds in a food processor, and when baked, the shells can be kept on hand in the freezer (don't remove from the mold when freezing them), ever ready to dazzle unexpected guests or brighten a midweek dinner. The filling will easily keep a week in the refrigerator, and the chocolate and berries are very simple last-minute additions.

VALENTINE'S DAY DINNER
Skip the mob scenes in the restaurants and share this elegant little dinner at home instead. (Oh! And leave the dishes for the morning!)
Pasta with Bay Scallops and
    Champagne Cream Sauce *
Roast Fillet of Beef with Green
    Peppercorn Butter
Sautéed Cherry Tomatoes
Bibb and Watercress Salad with
    Champagne Vinegar Dressing
Strawberry Heart Tarts *(freeze
    the other 4 tart shells)

*see Index for recipe page number

TART SHELLS
1½ cups flour
2 tablespoons sugar
6 tablespoons butter
2 tablespoons vegetable shortening
3 tablespoons cold water

CREAM CHEESE FILLING
8 ounces softened cream cheese
3 tablespoons sugar
1 tablespoon Grand Marnier
½ teaspoon vanilla extract

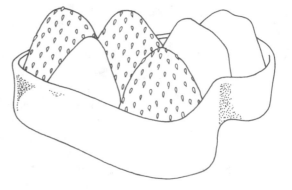

245

HEART TARTS
CUISINE MINCEUR

In 1977 when Michel Guérard's Cuisine Minceur had just exploded on our gastronomic horizon, we were asked to cater a fund-raising gala with "Disco à la Régine" as its very contemporary theme. Dinner was to be à la Cuisine Minceur since Guérard was the consultant to the kitchens of Régine's international discos. To M. Guérard's book we went running. Banishing cream and butter from our thoughts, we interpreted and improvised on the master's tenets. What we proposed included sushi, marinated squid with lemon and ginger, salmon in aspic with green peppercorns, boned chicken legs stuffed with marjoram and sweetbreads, and almond jelly with kiwi. Almond jelly? Who wanted to be that noble? The least we could do, we decided, was serve a dessert people would like. So, Heart Tarts, as antithetical as they were, came to crown our Cuisine Minceur menu. (As it turned out, some guests reputedly sent out for corned beef sandwiches, but no one quibbled about dessert.)

ASSEMBLY
3 ounces semisweet chocolate, chopped
2 pints of strawberries
⅓ cup sieved or seedless raspberry jam

TART SHELLS
In the bowl of a food processor, combine the flour, sugar, butter, and shortening. Whiz for several seconds until crumbly. Add the water and whiz until the dough forms a ball. Wrap the dough in plastic wrap and let rest at room temperature for ½ hour. (It can also be held in the refrigerator for up to 4 days but bring it to room temperature before using.)

To roll and bake the shells, **preheat the oven to 350°.** Bring the dough to a workable temperature and divide into 6 equal portions. On a floured surface, roll each portion of dough into a circle large enough to drape over the back of one of the gelatin molds. Trim off any excess and prick the molded dough several times with a fork. Set the 6 molds dough-side-up on a baking sheet and bake for 15–20 minutes or until pale gold and crisp. Cool the shells completely while still on the molds.

CREAM CHEESE FILLING
In a mixer or food processor, combine all the ingredients until smooth. Refrigerate if not using immediately.

ASSEMBLY
Fill the tarts as close to serving time as possible. If you are not serving them immediately, do at least keep them well chilled.

Remove the shells from their molds and set upright. Melt the chocolate in a small pan over simmering water, then divide it among the 6 shells and spread evenly over the bottom of each. Let the chocolate cool 10 minutes before filling. Divide the cream cheese filling among the 6 shells. Stem the strawberries and toss gently with the jam to coat. Top each tart with 5–8 berries (depending on their size) stem-end-down.

SERVING SUGGESTIONS AND VARIATIONS
Serve each tart with a healthy dollop of whipped cream—some swear it helps the tart slide down.

For an especially attractive presentation, set several flat green galax leaves (available from a florist) or a fresh grape leaf under each tart as you would a doily.

Other fruits can be substituted for the strawberries. Try raspberries, blueberries, peaches, bananas, or a mixture of fruits. Use different jam flavors, too.

To make the pastry with an electric mixer, first bring the butter to room temperature. Then, combine the butter, shortening, flour, and sugar in the mixer (fitted with a paddle or dough hook) until crumbly. Add the water and continue to beat until the dough forms a ball.

Instead of using heart-shaped gelatin molds, substitute 4" quiche or tart pans instead. We have even made smaller "one-strawberry-size" tarts to pass as petits fours after dinner.

MOCHA BUTTERCRUNCH PIE *Serves 8–10*

An amazingly sensuous pie with an addictive candy-bar crust and a silken, decadently rich filling that melts in the mouth and lies in wait under an elegantly sculptured cloud of coffee-flavored whipped cream. Frog's patrons have been ecstatic after indulging.

For something so divine, the preparation seems ridiculously simple. Make the pie in advance, if you like, and add the topping just before serving. It is best if not served icy cold, but do be careful on very warm days that it doesn't begin to melt.

CRUST
1 cup flour
¼ teaspoon salt
⅓ cup brown sugar
⅓ cup cold butter
3 tablespoons finely chopped chocolate, sweet or
    semisweet
¾ cup finely chopped walnuts
1 teaspoon vanilla extract
2 teaspoons water

FILLING
½ pound soft unsalted butter
1 cup brown sugar
4 teaspoons instant coffee
2 teaspoons vanilla extract
3 ounces unsweetened chocolate, melted
4 eggs

TOPPING
2 cups very cold heavy cream
2 tablespoons plus 1 teaspoon instant coffee
½ cup powdered sugar
2 tablespoons unsweetened cocoa
1 teaspoon vanilla extract
OPT. Grated chocolate or chocolate curls

247

CRUST

Preheat oven to 350°. Combine the flour, salt, and brown sugar. With a pastry blender or 2 knives, cut in the butter. Stir in the chocolate and nuts. Mix the vanilla and water and add to the crumbs. Work the mixture with your hands to combine. With floured fingers, push the mixture into a 9" pie shell, covering the bottom, sides, and rim. Bake for 20 minutes. Cool completely.

FILLING

In an electric mixer, cream the butter until fluffy and smooth. Add the sugar, coffee, and vanilla and beat until smooth. Add the melted chocolate. Again beat smooth. Add the eggs one by one, beating for several minutes after each addition. Spread the mixture into the pie shell. Chill several hours. (At this point, the pie can be wrapped and frozen. Defrost in the refrigerator for 6–8 hours.)

TOPPING

Just before serving, whip together the cream, coffee, powdered sugar, cocoa, and vanilla until stiff enough to hold a shape. Spoon into a pastry bag fitted with a large star tip and cover the top of the pie with large rosettes. Garnish with grated chocolate or chocolate curls. Refrigerate until ready to serve.

FLAKY PASTRY FOR PIE CRUSTS

For single-crust 9" pie

This is the best, most trouble-free pie crust we know. The recipe is high on fat and low on water so that it is especially flaky. We've also found that the method of rolling out the dough between wax paper (as described below) works best for this crust.

1½ cups flour
½ teaspoon salt
½ cup plus 1 tablespoon cold vegetable shortening or use half butter and half shortening
2–3 tablespoons cold water

In a large bowl combine the flour and salt. Using a pastry blender or 2 knives, cut in the shortening until the mixture is coarse and crumbly. Sprinkle on the water, 1 tablespoon at a time, while tossing the mixture with a fork. Gently gather up the dough with your hands and pat firmly into a ball. This is best used immediately.

To roll the dough, set the ball of dough on a sheet of

wax paper and press it into a 6″ circle. Top with a second sheet of wax paper and roll the dough from the center out into a 12″ circle; it will extend 1″ out from the sides of the paper. Loosen the top sheet of wax paper and put it back on the dough. Flip the dough over on the counter and discard what is now the top sheet of wax paper. Center the pie pan upside down over the dough. Slide one hand under the bottom sheet of wax paper, put your other hand on the pie pan, and flip the dough and pan right side up. Center the dough in the pan and remove the wax paper. Lift the edges to gently fit the dough into the pan. Trim the edges for a ½″ overhang (if necessary, piece the dough together to achieve an even overhang). Roll this overhang under to sit on the rim of the pan and crimp decoratively or attach small pastry cut-outs of leaves made from any scraps of dough. Chill until ready to use.

PECAN PIE   *Serves 8*

Some people, like ourselves, never tire of pecan pie. We're especially fond of this version, which is more buttery than most, and the pie is absolutely irresistible when served slightly warm with whipped cream or vanilla ice cream.

1 recipe Flaky Pastry for Pie Crusts (see p. 248)
1 cup brown sugar
4 teaspoons flour
¼ teaspoon salt
4 eggs
1¼ teaspoons vanilla extract
1⅓ cups light Karo corn syrup
5 ounces butter, melted
OPT. ¼ cup bourbon plus 1 additional tablespoon flour
2 cups pecan halves

Line a 9″ pie pan with the pastry. Chill until you are ready to fil it. **Preheat the oven to 400°.** By hand, combine the brown sugar, flour, and salt in a large bowl. Whisk in the eggs, vanilla, corn syrup, and butter. If desired, add the bourbon and the additional tablespoon of flour. Either mix in the nuts and pour into the pie shell or pour the filling into the chilled pie shell and arrange the pecan halves in concentric circles on top, pushing them down slightly into the "goo" without spoiling the arrangement. Put the pie on the bottom rack and bake 10 minutes, then reduce the heat to 350° and bake 45–55 minutes more or until the edges of the filling are puffed and begin to crack. The pie will seem loose but will firm up on cooling.

APPLE CRANBERRY CURRANT PIE   *Serves 8*

Make this pie a new tradition for your Thanksgiving table. It is a large, impressive, old-fashioned-looking pie, and we can never make up our minds whether to serve it *à la mode*, with hot brandy sauce, or simply graced with a small wedge of good Vermont Cheddar.

⅓ cup brandy
2 teaspoons grated orange rind
1 cup currants
½ cup flour
1¾ cups sugar
2 teaspoons cinnamon
1 teaspoon nutmeg
¼ teaspoon salt
¼ teaspoon ginger
3 pounds tart apples, peeled, cored, and thinly sliced
½ cup orange juice
2 cups whole cranberries
¼ cup cold butter, in bits
Double recipe of Flaky Pastry for Pie Crusts (see p. 248)
1 egg yolk, beaten

Bring the brandy to a boil with the orange rind and currants in a small saucepan. Lower the heat, cover, and simmer 5 minutes. Take off the heat, uncover, and set aside. Meanwhile, combine the flour, sugar, cinnamon, nutmeg, salt, and ginger and toss with the apples. Add the orange juice and brandy mixture. Toss thoroughly. Add the cranberries and butter. Set aside.

Divide the Flaky Pastry dough into 2 balls, one about 25% bigger than the other. Roll the smaller ball between 2 sheets of wax paper (see p. 248) to fit a 9" pie pan and then gently fit the dough into the pan. Trim the edges to leave a ½" overhang.

Preheat the oven to 450°. Fill the pie shell heaping full and pack down the filling. Roll out the reserved dough between wax paper until it is 14" in diameter. Transfer to the pie. Pinch the top and bottom crusts together and roll them under so that the roll rests on the rim of the pie pan. Crimp the edges well with your fingers. Cut several air vents in the top. If desired, decorate the top with any extra dough cut into shapes. Then brush with the egg yolk. Set the pie on a rimmed baking sheet lined with aluminum foil to catch any juices which may overflow.

Bake on the lowest rack for 15 minutes. Then, lower the heat to 350° and bake 55 minutes more or until golden and bubbly. Let cool completely before cutting (or it will run all over the place). Store at room temperature.

APPLE SOUR CREAM STREUSEL PIE   *Serves 8*

A is for Apple Pie, of course, and in our alphabet that means Apple Sour Cream Streusel Pie, one of The Commissary's all-time most popular desserts. Tart apple slices are coated with a creamy, lightly spiced filling and baked in a tender, flaky crust under a crunchy crowning of walnut streusel. Ummmmmmm . . . it is worth making this pie for the baking odors alone.

STREUSEL TOPPING
⅓ cup white sugar
¼ cup brown sugar
½ cup plus 2 tablespoons flour
2 teaspoons cinnamon
3 ounces cold butter
½ cup coarsely chopped walnuts

FILLING AND ASSEMBLY
1 recipe Flaky Pastry for Pie Crusts (see p. 248)
¾ cup sugar
2 tablespoons flour
3 eggs
1½ cups sour cream
1 teaspoon cinnamon
1½ teaspoons vanilla extract
¼ teaspoon grated lemon rind
¼ teaspoon nutmeg
¼ teaspoon salt
4 cups peeled, thinly sliced tart apples (about 5 apples)
   (Granny Smiths or McIntoshes are good)

STREUSEL
Combine the white sugar, brown sugar, flour, and cinnamon. Cut in the butter until crumbly. Toss with the walnuts. Refrigerate to keep butter from melting into dough.

FILLING
Line a 9" pie pan with the pastry. **Preheat the oven to 350°.** Blend together the sugar, flour, and eggs. Whisk in the sour cream, cinnamon, vanilla, lemon rind, nutmeg, and salt. Fold in the apple slices. Turn into the pie shell. Bake the pie on the bottom shelf of the oven for 20 minutes. Remove the pie from the oven and distribute the Streusel over the top. Return to the oven and bake 25–30 minutes more or until the topping is crisp and browned. Let cool completely before cutting and serving.

Instead of apples, try pears, cranberries, blueberries, raspberries, peaches or other fruit. For the berries, use 3 cups rather than 4 cups of fruit (the blueberry version needs 1 pint of berries).

OATMEAL CHOCOLATE CHIP
WALNUT COOKIES
Makes about 4 dozen

We sell this cookie the way McDonald's sells burgers: They fly out the door. Since day one at The Commissary, a jar of these cookies has sat up front by the cashier as one last temptation for the customer. They really are irresistible—just ask any of the cashiers, since they're the ones who get to snack on any broken cookies. One always encounters people munching (or furtively nibbling) these cookies on the streets around the restaurant.

Like the Carrot Cake, the cookies have a very strong following, and when we had to raise the price five cents per cookie several years ago, we felt compelled to put out an explanatory little letter to our customers. There's also a running controversy about whether these cookies are better soft or hard and crunchy. Personally, we love them best when they're soft and chewy and still warm from the oven.

To give those cookies you baked yesterday (or even 5 days ago) that just-out-of-the-oven appeal again, put them on a baking sheet tray, turn on the oven to 350°, and heat the cookies for 3 to 5 minutes.

1 cup unsalted butter, softened
1 cup brown sugar
1 cup white sugar
2 teaspoons vanilla extract
2 eggs
2 cups flour
1 teaspoon salt
1 teaspoon baking soda
1 teaspoon baking powder
2½ cups old-fashioned oats (not instant)
12 ounces semisweet chocolate chips (2 cups)
1½ cups chopped walnuts

Preheat the oven to 350°. Cream the butter with the sugars in a mixture or by hand. Add the vanilla and the eggs. Add the flour, salt, baking soda, and baking powder to the creamed mixture and beat to combine. By hand, stir in the oats, chips, and nuts. Drop 1½" apart on greased cookie sheets. Bake for 10–12 minutes. Let sit 1 minute, then remove to cooling racks.

For fatter cookies, chill dough overnight, then roll into 1"
balls, set on the cookie sheets, and bake.

Substitute raisins for the chocolate chips or pecans for
the walnuts.

Double the chocolate chips.

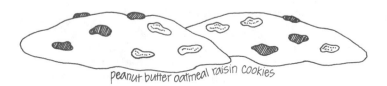

peanut butter oatmeal raisin cookies

PEANUT BUTTER OATMEAL
RAISIN COOKIES

Makes 4 dozen

¾ cup unsalted butter, softened
¾ cup peanut butter
1 cup white sugar
1 cup brown sugar
2 eggs
2 tablespoons milk
1 teaspoon vanilla extract
2 cups flour
1 teaspoon baking soda
1 teaspoon salt
¼ teaspoon cinnamon
2 cups old-fashioned oatmeal (not instant)
2 cups raisins

Preheat the oven to 350°. Cream together the butter, peanut
butter, and sugars. Beat in the eggs one by one. Add the
milk, flour, salt, baking soda, and cinnamon. Beat until
well blended. Stir in the oatmeal and raisins. Drop rounded
teaspoonfuls of batter 1½" apart on lightly greased baking
sheets. Bake for 10–12 minutes until lightly browned and
still chewy.

VARIATIONS
Substitute chocolate chips for the raisins.

Add 1 cup chopped peanuts.

For fatter cookies, chill the dough, roll it into 1" balls,
and set them on the baking sheets.

COLD ORANGE WALNUT SOUFFLÉS

Serves 5
Makes about 1¼ quarts

1 packet unflavored gelatin (2½ teaspoons)
¼ cup lemon juice
2 egg yolks
6 tablespoons plus ¼ cup sugar
1 cup orange juice
1½ tablespoons grated orange rind
⅛ teaspoon salt
1 teaspoon vanilla extract
2 egg whites
1 cup heavy cream
¼ cup finely chopped walnuts

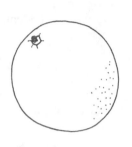

COLLARING that SOUFFLÉ

Tear off a 6"-wide piece of waxed paper, fold it in half so that it is a 3"-wide band, and wrap it around the outside of a ramekin so that it extends 1½" above the rim. Secure the collar with a rubber band or masking tape. (for cold soufflés)

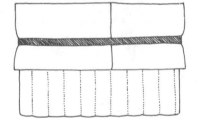

Prepare five 6-ounce soufflé ramekins with collars or have ready a 1-quart soufflé dish fitted with a collar, a 1½-quart serving bowl, or five individual dessert dishes/glasses.

Sprinkle the gelatin over the lemon juice in a small dish to soften. Beat together the egg yolks and 6 tablespoons of the sugar. Whisk the orange juice, rind, salt, and vanilla into the yolk mixture and pour it into a saucepan.

Cook, stirring, until mixture is slightly thickened. Do not boil. Remove from the heat and whisk in the softened gelatin until it is dissolved. Pour into a bowl and chill until the mixture just begins to set and mounds slightly when dropped from a spoon. Whip the cream until soft peaks form. Beat the egg whites until stiff with the remaining ¼ cup of sugar. Gently fold in the whites and then the cream until the mixture is just blended. Add the walnuts. Spoon the soufflé into the prepared ramekins or serving dish. Chill until set, at least 4 hours.

VARIATIONS

Garnish with rosettes of sweetened whipped cream and chopped walnuts, chocolate curls, orange twists, or knotted strips of candied orange peel.

The nuts can be omitted if you prefer a smooth texture, or you can use them as garnish.

PUMPKIN MOUSSE

Makes eight 6-ounce servings

Jumping jack-o'-lanterns! A pumpkin has probably never known such an ethereal demise as when transformed into this heavenly mousse, an autumn-winter dessert regular in our restaurants.

1 packet unflavored gelatin (2½ teaspoons)
¼ cup dark rum
1 (1-pound) can unsweetened pumpkin purée
1 cup sugar
2 egg yolks
¼ teaspoon nutmeg
⅛ teaspoon allspice
1 teaspoon cinnamon
½ teaspoon ginger
1½ teaspoons vanilla extract
½ teaspoon salt
2 cups heavy cream

Sprinkle the gelatin over the rum in a small heatproof cup. Let soften several minutes while you combine the pumpkin purée, sugar, egg yolks, nutmeg, allspice, cinnamon, ginger, vanilla, and salt in a large bowl. Set the cup of gelatin in a pan of gently simmering water and stir the gelatin until it has dissolved. While the gelatin is still hot, whisk it into the pumpkin mixture. Whip the cream to soft peaks and carefully but thoroughly fold it in. Fill eight 6-ounce ramekins or a large glass serving bowl. Refrigerate at least 4 hours or overnight.

SERVING SUGGESTIONS

Decorate with rosettes of sweetened whipped cream and sprinkle with minced candied ginger, crushed praline, or chopped walnuts.

Chill the mousse until it begins to mound. Put it into a prebaked 9″ pie shell (gingersnap crust would be a good choice) and chill 4–6 hours. Garnish with whipped cream.

COLD LEMON SOUFFLÉ
WITH BLUEBERRY
OR LEMON CURD FILLING

Serves 6–8

Makes about 1 quart

A lemon dessert is always a refreshing ending to any meal, and our choice along those lines would be for this very light, creamy, and definitely "lemony" cold soufflé. It is lovely served simply with a flourish of whipped cream and a few fresh berries, but sometimes we also like to gussy it up with the visually dramatic addition of one of the two lush fillings we suggest here.

While the fillings can be prepared ahead of time, plan to make and assemble the soufflé mixture without a break—at least 4 hours before serving, as it needs time to set up.

OPT. Filling (see following recipes)
1 packet of unflavored gelatin (2½ teaspoons)
¼ cup cold lemon juice
3 egg yolks
¾ cup sugar
OPT. ½ teaspoon grated lemon rind
⅓ cup lemon juice
3 egg whites, beaten stiff
1 cup heavy cream, beaten stiff

LEMON SOUFFLÉ
If you have decided to add a filling, prepare that first, then proceed with the soufflé.

Sprinkle the gelatin over the ¼ cup of lemon juice in a Pyrex or stainless steel measuring cup. Let sit 5 minutes to soften. Then set the cup in a pan of simmering water and stir until the gelatin dissolves. Have ready a large mixing bowl of ice water (heavy on the ice). Whisk together the egg yolks and sugar. Whisk in the lemon rind and additional ⅓ cup lemon juice. Add the dissolved and still warm gelatin and whisk in well. Whip the cream to soft peaks. Set the bowl of gelatin mixture in the bowl of ice water and stir the mixture gently and continuously with a spatula to help it cool and prevent it from setting up on the bottom. When the mixture is syrupy, remove it from the ice to prevent it from setting up. Immediately beat the egg whites to soft peaks and fold them into the gelatin mixture over the ice again. Then fold in the whipped cream. Spoon the soufflé into individual glasses (clear glasses are best if you are adding a filling), ramekins, or an attractive serving bowl. (If using glasses, fill each only three-quarters full to allow for the addition of a filling.)

OPTIONAL: If you are adding filling, spoon the filling into a pastry bag fitted with a ¼"-wide tip. Immerse the tip into the soufflé around the edge so that the tip is touching the side of the container. Squeeze out some of

USING A PASTRY BAG
Put the pastry bag, tip down, in a tall glass and fill about two-thirds full with whatever it is you are going to pipe. Twist the top of the bag closed just above the filling and hold the bag with one hand lightly at the bottom to guide the tip and the other hand up top by the twist to gently squeeze. Practice first, if you wish, on waxed paper. If you are decorating a cake, trace or mark your design with a toothpick before piping on the icing.

the filling so that it "streaks" against the sides. Pull the pastry bag out and repeat the process at various points around the sides of the container(s).

Chill the soufflé, filled or unfilled, for at least 4 hours before serving.

BLUEBERRY FILLING

1 pint fresh or frozen blueberries
½ cup sugar
1½ teaspoons lemon juice
¼ teaspoon cinnamon

Pick over and wash the blueberries and put them in a saucepan. Crush them with a spoon to extract some of the juice. Stir in the sugar. Over medium heat, stir and cook the blueberries until the sugar has dissolved. Then, let boil, uncovered, for 10–15 minutes until the mixture is of jamlike consistency. Cool the mixture. Stir in the lemon juice and cinnamon.

LEMON CURD FILLING

6 egg yolks
½ cup plus 1 tablespoon sugar
½ cup lemon juice
1½ teaspoons grated lemon rind
¼ cup unsalted butter, cut in bits.

Combine all the ingredients in a small nonaluminum saucepan over medium heat and stir until the butter is melted and the mixture is hot. Lower the heat and whisk constantly until the mixture has thickened and is just about to boil, but *don't* let it boil. Mixture should be thicker than custard. Strain into a bowl and cover with plastic wrap. Refrigerate until completely cool (or speed up process by putting over ice).

SERVING SUGGESTIONS AND VARIATIONS

Decorate the soufflé shortly before serving with rosettes of whipped cream piped through a pastry tube and garnish with candied violets, lemon twists, blueberries, or the like.

Soufflé mixture will also fill a 9″ prebaked pie shell. In this case, let it begin to set up a bit so you can pile it high. You might first line the bottom of the pie crust with one of the fillings, top with the soufflé, chill until set, and then decorate with whipped cream. Or use the soufflé to fill individual tart shells that have first been lined with chocolate, *à la* Strawberry Heart Tarts. Garnish each with a strawberry.

The Blueberry Filling, by itself, makes a delicious jam.

The Lemon Curd is worth making for itself alone. Try it on toast with afternoon tea; as a filling for coconut cake,

BLUEBERRIES

With a bushel of blueberries you could make pancakes, muffins, shortcakes, grunt, pie, turnovers, buckle, and coffee-cake. You could lavishly strew them on cereal, fruit salads, lemon mousse, and mixed fruit tarts. Then, you could freeze some, stew some, and pop the rest as is into your mouth. Blueberry heaven! You can identify the addicts by their blue teeth and tongues. They'll tell you, too, that the tiny low-bush berries are best and then reminisce about some secret patch they know of in New England. ☆ For a quick blueberry pie, make and prebake a graham cracker crust. Fill it with blueberries. Melt a jar of currant jelly and pour evenly over the berries. Chill until set. Before serving, cover the top of the pie with sour cream or whipped cream.

This menu is derived from a dinner shared by friends who gathered at Steven's one summer's evening to bid "Bon Voyage" to 2 of the group who were about to embark on a European jaunt. Casual, redolent of the season and set against a backdrop of spacious lawn, trees, and champagne bubbles, the menu took its cues from the nearby herb and vegetable garden.

- Crudités (zucchini, kohlrabi, and sugar snaps) with sea salt
- Greek and Niçoise Olives
- Salmon Cru (thinly sliced raw salmon brushed with sesame oil, dusted with chives, and served with soy sauce and wasabi)
- Whole Wheat Pasta with Goat Cheese and Fresh Herbs*
- Tomatoes and Garden Greens with Olive Oil Vinaigrette
- Grilled Marinated Boneless Leg of Lamb
- White Chocolate Ice Cream* with Raspberries

*See Index for recipe page number.

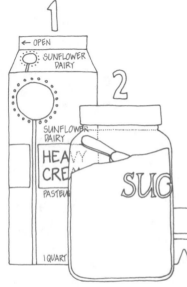

cake roll, or cookies; or as a tart filling to be topped with meringue.

WHITE CHOCOLATE ICE CREAM
Makes 1½ quarts

White chocolate makes the smoothest and probably the richest ice cream we've ever tasted. At Frog, where it is one of the few dessert menu constants, we serve it by itself and unadorned, since its delicate flavor is easily overwhelmed by other additions. We have, however, upon occasion experimented with fanciful presentations for very special catered affairs. At one big benefit dinner with a circus theme, White Chocolate Ice Cream sat alongside a scoop of Mocha Rum Ice Cream under an ethereal cloud of cotton candy touched by an earthly leaf of chocolate. Even more elaborate was the version concocted for a wedding rehearsal dinner given by a very prominent political family where individual heart-shaped cakes were filled with the ice cream, frosted with whipped cream, decorated with the names of the betrothed piped in pink icing, and set afloat in a pool of raspberry purée.

1 quart half-and-half
¾ cup sugar
12 egg yolks
1 pound white chocolate, finely chopped

Scald the half-and-half. Whisk together the sugar and egg yolks in a large bowl. Whisking constantly, pour the scalded half-and-half over the yolk-sugar mixture. Pour the mixture back into the saucepan and over moderate heat cook and stir the mixture until it thickens slightly and coats a spoon. Do not allow it to boil. Have ready a large bowl of ice. Off the heat, add the chocolate to the custard mixture and stir until melted. If there are any lumps, strain the mixture. Turn into a mixing bowl, preferably metal, and set over the bowl of ice. Stir to help it cool quickly. Proceed according to the directions for your ice cream machine.

PISTACHIO ICE CREAM   *Makes about 3 quarts*

The real thing . . . and no green food coloring! This ice cream is marvelously creamy and delicately nutty. It is a standard on the menu at 16th Street Bar & Grill, where some of us *always* order it for dessert, and at Frog, where they serve it topped with hot fudge sauce!

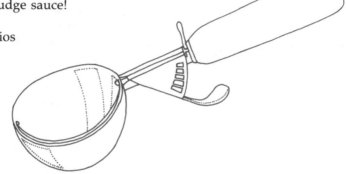

2 cups shelled unsalted pistachios
1⅔ cups sugar
⅛ teaspoon salt
8 egg yolks
2 cups milk
6 cups heavy cream
1 tablespoon vanilla extract
½ teaspoon almond extract
1 tablespoon dark rum

Preheat the oven to 300°. Toast the pistachios for 10 minutes. Let cool, then coarsely chop.

In a large bowl, whisk together the sugar, salt, and egg yolks. Scald the milk with 2 cups of the cream. Whisking all the while, pour the hot milk-cream over the yolk mixture. Return to the saucepan and whisk over medium heat until the mixture thickens. *Do not allow it to boil.* Pour into a large bowl. Add the flavorings. Chill thoroughly and add the remaining 4 cups of cream. Freeze according to the directions for your ice cream machine. When the ice cream is half frozen, stir in the nuts. Finish freezing.

VARIATIONS

Vanilla: Omit almond extract and nuts. Add 4 split vanilla beans to the milk-cream mixture. Heat to scalding. Let steep 30 minutes. Remove beans and scrape seeds back into milk-cream, or add ¼ cup (yes) of real vanilla extract. Proceed as directed with rest of recipe.
Hazelnut: Substitute hazelnuts for pistachios.
Cinnamon Walnut: Omit almond extract, substitute walnuts for the pistachios, and add ¾ teaspoon cinnamon.

MOCHA RUM ICE CREAM

Makes 5½ cups

6 egg yolks
1 cup sugar
¼ cup dark rum
3½ cups heavy cream
¾ cup strong coffee
4 ounces unsweetened chocolate, chopped
6 ounces semisweet chocolate, chopped
1½ tablespoons vanilla extract

Whisk together the egg yolks and ½ cup of the sugar. Bring the rum and 1½ cups of the heavy cream just to a boil and pour over the yolk mixture while whisking constantly. Return the mixture to the saucepan and whisk over medium heat until slightly thickened. *Do not allow to boil* or it will curdle. Pour into a large bowl and set aside. Heat together the coffee and the remaining ½ cup of sugar. Stir until the sugar has dissolved. Remove from the heat and add the 2 kinds of chocolate. Return to a very low heat and whisk well until the chocolate has just melted. While still warm, scrape the chocolate mixture into the bowl of a food processor and whiz 20 seconds. This step will prevent the ice cream from having a chalky feel and non-homogeneous look. Add this chocolate mixture with the vanilla to the custard. Cover with plastic wrap and chill thoroughly. Stir in the remaining 2 cups of heavy cream and freeze according to your ice cream machine's instructions. Serve topped with additional dark rum, if you like.

MINTED LEMONADE

Make a simple syrup by heating equal amounts of water and sugar until the sugar has dissolved. Add plenty of chopped fresh mint to the syrup and let steep until the syrup is cool. Strain the syrup and add an equal amount of lemon juice. Add cold water or club soda to taste, serve over ice, and garnish with mint sprigs.

MINTED LIME SORBET

Makes 2 quarts

By the time we had finished our third run-through on this recipe in the test kitchen, we had achieved the effect we were looking for—an incredibly refreshing, mouth-tingling sorbet that clearly reads of both lime and fresh garden mint. We also made sure that there was room for the leftovers in our freezer there, because we quickly became addicted to this sorbet to relieve our palates after heavy-duty tasting sessions.

SYRUP
3 cups water
2½ cups sugar
1 cup loosely packed fresh mint leaves

SORBET

2 cups strained fresh lime juice (about 14–20 limes)
3 cups cold water
3 tablespoons finely chopped fresh mint leaves

SYRUP

Heat together the water and sugar, stirring until the sugar dissolves. Add the mint leaves and bring the mixture to a boil. Reduce the heat and simmer 5 minutes. Remove from the heat. Strain the syrup, squeezing as much liquid from the mint as possible. Discard the mint. Chill the syrup thoroughly.

SORBET

Combine the chilled syrup with the cold water, lime juice, and chopped mint leaves. Put into your ice cream machine and proceed according to the manufacturer's instructions.

NOTES

Serve as a dessert or an intermezzo and garnish with fresh mint leaves and/or a twist of lime.

Would also be very good served with melon or topped with a splash of rum, gin, or dry vermouth . . . which leads us to the following suggestion: For a quick icy summer drink, put several scoops of the sorbet in a blender with a healthy dose of your choice of liquor, whiz briefly, pour into a glass, and then sit back and put your feet up.

"COME SEE OUR DAFFODILS" DINNER

When spring officially arrives, and the daffodils trumpet the news, have your friends come early, before dusk, to drink in some of the flowers' soul-warming brightness. Then, herald the season at your dinner table with the following spring-touched menu.

Szechuan Shrimp* on Shredded Greens
Baked Glazed Country Ham
Assorted Mustards & Chutneys
Potato Gratin with Chives
Asparagus with Hazelnut Crumbs (see recipe for Green Beans with same on page 208)
Coconut Lemon Sorbet*
Strawberries

*See Index for recipe page number.

LEMON COCONUT SORBET   *Makes 3 quarts*

We've known some normally very proper people who have devoured three bowls of this sublime dessert at one sitting, even after a generous dinner. Very smooth, addictively sweet, yet refreshingly tart, it seems more like an ice cream in texture than a sorbet because of the nature of the coconut cream.

3 (15-ounce) cans sweetened coconut cream at room
    temperature
3 cups water
3 cups lemon juice
1 tablespoon grated lemon rind

In a large bowl whisk the coconut cream until very smooth. Add the remaining ingredients. Put immediately into your ice cream machine and proceed according to the manufacturer's instructions. Do not chill before freezing because

A BASIC SORBET FORMULA

Make a simple syrup of equal parts sugar and water by boiling until the sugar has dissolved. Let cool. Juice or purée and strain the fruit(s) of your choice and add simple syrup until it tastes good to you. Add a little lemon juice to counteract the sweetness of the simple syrup. Citrus sorbet bases may need to have water added to them. If a sorbet separates after being frozen, that could mean too much sugar. If it is rock-hard, it probably has too little sugar. ☆ Proportions for Raspberry Sorbet, for example, are as follows: 3 quarts raspberries puréed and sieved for 5 cups of purée, 3 cups cold simple syrup, and ½ cup lemon juice. Freeze according to the manufacturer's instructions for your ice cream machine.

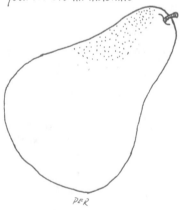

PER

the fat in the coconut cream hardens and forms little globules.

SERVING SUGGESTIONS

Garnish each serving with a lemon twist and a sprig of mint, or top with a splash of rum.

Turn it into a decadent summer drink by whizzing several scoops in a blender with a liberal dose of rum.

PEAR-RIESLING SORBET   *Makes about 1½ quarts*

This is a heavenly dessert, redolent of pears at their peak of ripeness. It is best made and served the same day, because the alcoholic liquid, which has a lower freezing point than the rest of the ingredients, tends to separate out with time. For the Riesling, we use a medium-dry Alsatian brand, but you can do just as well with a California or German Riesling as long as you are aware that you may have to adjust the amount of sugar since some Rieslings are much sweeter than others. Pears, too, vary in sweetness, so it is a good idea in general with this recipe to be careful to taste it as you go and adjust when necessary.

2½ pounds perfectly ripe pears, preferably of a less
   grainy variety
1 bottle (a fifth) Alsatian Riesling wine
¾ cup sugar
3 tablespoons lemon juice or to taste

Peel, core, and slice the pears. Put them in a saucepan with the wine and sugar and poach until very tender. Allow to cool fully. Purée in a food processor or blender until smooth. Add the lemon juice and freeze in an electric ice cream machine according to the directions.

SERVING SUGGESTIONS

Top with a splash of Pear Williams, Lillet, or Framboise, sauce with raspberry purée, or decorate with lightly sweetened raspberries.

Index.....................

Page numbers in italics refer to information in boxes and recipes in margins adjacent to the text.

Recipes that may be untitled and are to be found in the section of a recipe called Variations are followed in the index by *var.*, and the page number.

Full titles have occasionally been shortened because of space limitations.

268

Apple Sour Cream Streusel, 251–52
Blueberry Sour Cream Streusel, *var.*, 252
Cranberry Sour Cream Streusel, *var.*, 252
Mocha Buttercrunch, 247–48
Peach Sour Cream Streusel, *var.*, 252
Pear Sour Cream Streusel, *var.*, 252
Pecan, 249
Raspberry Sour Cream Streusel, *var.*, 252
Pimento Mayonnaise, 18
Pistachio
  Chicken, with Herb-Garlic Cheese Filling, 123–24
  in Country Pâté, 42–43
  Ice Cream, 259
Pizza
  Clam, with Fresh Herbs, 177–78
  Crust, 174–75
  Deep-Dish, 16th Street's, 174–75
  Goat Cheese, 176–77
  Mussel, 178–79
  Sauce, 174–75
Poppy Seed Muffins, Lemon, 221
Pork
  and Chicken "Lasagna," 134–36
  Chops, with Bacon, Cheese, and Corn, 152
  with Garlic and Nam Pla, 153
  in Spring Rolls, 28–29
Poultry. *See* specific types
Potato(es)
  Gratin, *var.*, 202
  Oven-Roasted, 204
  with Peperonata, 203
  -Rutabaga Gratin, 202
  in Taramasalata, 13
Prosciutto
  in Italian Scrambled Eggs, 186
  in Loin of Veal, 147–48
Pumpkin
  Cheesecake, *var.*, 237
  Mousse, 255
  Waffles, 194–95

Q

Quick Ideas for Appetizers and Hors d'Oeuvres, 22–23

R

Rack of Lamb with Mustard, 154
Raita Salad Dressing, 70–71
Ramen with Broccoli and Peanuts, 26–28
Raspberry
  jam, in Linzertorte, 243–44
  Sour Cream Pie, *var.*, 252
  Vinegar Sauce for Duck, 138–41
Raw bar, how to set up, 17
Red Lentil Salad, Curried, 63
Rice
  Fragrant, with Eggs, 187–88
  Salad with Shrimp, 84
  and Spinach in Tomatoes, 207

Ricotta and Spinach Filling for Pasta Roll, 160–61
Riesling and Pear Sorbet, 262
Roquefort
  Filling for Chicken, 120
  -Herb Salad Dressing, 95
Rosemary-Rum Salad Dressing, 93
Rum
  Ice Cream, Mocha, 260
  -Rosemary Salad Dressing, 93
Rutabaga(s)
  -Potato Gratin, 202
  Timbales, *var.*, 211

S

Sachertorte, 228–29
Saffron
  Mayonnaise, 78–80
  on Pizza, with Mussels, 178–79
Sage Cream Sauce for Pork, 152
Salad Dressing, 90–101
  Almond-Yogurt, *var.*, 99
  Anchovy
    -Feta, 98
    -Herb, 77–78
  Apricot-Yogurt, *var.*, 99
  Basic Clear Vinaigrette, 90
  Basic Creamy Vinaigrette, 94
  Basil, Lime, and Peanut, 92
  Chili-Cumin, 97
  chilling, importance of, *91*
  Cider Vinaigrette, 93
  Curried,
    Creamy, 70–71
    Vinaigrette, 74–75
  Dijon, Creamy, 94
  Fig-Yogurt, *var.*, 99
  Frog's Mustard, 62
  Garlic Vinaigrette, 84
  Hazelnut Vinaigrette, *var.*, 91
  Herb Vinaigrette, 94
  Horseradish Vinaigrette, 97–98
  Lime, 81–82
  Mayonnaise. *See* Mayonnaise
  Olive Oil–Anise Seed, 96
  Onion, Sweet, Vinaigrette, 76–77
  Orange-Tarragon, 73
  Oriental, 69–70
  Parmesan, Creamy, 85–86
  Parsley-Shallot Vinaigrette, 95
  Peanut, Spicy, 75–76
  Raita, 71–72
  Roquefort-Herb, 95
  Rum-Rosemary, 93
  Sesame
    Fragrant, 65–66
    -Ginger Vinaigrette, 82–83
    Herbed, Warm, 66–67
  Soy-Mustard Vinaigrette, 92
  Strawberry-Yogurt, 99
  Sweet Onion Vinaigrette, 76–77
  Tahini-Yogurt, 45
  Tomato Vinaigrette, 90–91
  Vinaigrette
    Basic Clear, 90
    Basic Creamy, 94
  Walnut
    Vinaigrette, 91

- -Yogurt, 99
Yogurt
  Almond, *var.*, 99
  Apricot, *var.*, 99
  Fig, *var.*, 99
  Raita, 71–72
  Strawberry, 99
  Tahini, 45
  Walnut, 99
Salad(s), 62–88
  Avocado with Tahini Yogurt, 45
  Beef, Thai, with Spicy Peanut Dressing, 75–76
  Bouillabaisse with Saffron Mayonnaise, 78–80
  Caponata, 206
  Chicken
    Classic, with Horseradish Juniper Berry Mayonnaise, 67–68
    -Corn with Dill Mayonnaise, *var.*, 81
    Curried, 70–71
    Indian, with Raita, 71–72
    -Melon with Orange-Tarragon Dressing, 73
    Oriental, 69–70
    Pepperoni, Italian, with Rice and Garlic Vinaigrette, *var.*, 84
  Combination ideas, 87–88
  Cucumber, Sweet and Sour, *130*
  Duck with Curried Vinaigrette, 74–75
  Frog's, Mixed, with Mustard Dressing, 62
  greens, about, *94*
  Lamb, Warm, with Pine Nuts, Raisins, and Sweet Onion Vinaigrette, 76–77
  Lentil, Red, Curried, 63
  Minestrone with Basil Garlic Mayonnaise, 64–65
  Niçoise with Anchovy Herb Dressing, 77–78
  Pasta
    Buckwheat with Shellfish and Vegetables, Sesame-Ginger Vinaigrette, 82–83
    Niçoise, 77–78
    Orzo, with Fragrant Sesame Dressing, 65–66
    Orzo, with Shrimp or Chicken, Italian, *var.*, 84
    Parmesan with Broccoli and Salami, *var.*, 86
    Smoked Mozzarella with Roasted Peppers, Spinach, and Parmesan, 85–86
  Peperonata with Potatoes, 203
  Rice and Shrimp with Garlic Vinaigrette, 84
  Scallop
    Bay, and Corn with Dill Mayonnaise, 80–81
    Oriental, *var.*, 69–70
    South American with Lime Dressing, 81–82
  Shrimp, Oriental, *var.*, 70
  Slaw, Mixed Vegetable, 64

Pine Nuts, and, 207
Spring Rolls with Sweet and Sour
   Sauce, 28–29
Squash
   Butternut, Spiced Purée, 211
   See also Spaghetti Squash
Star Anise
   about, *146*
   Braised Beef, 146–47
   in Szechuan Stir-Fry, 133–34
Stew
   Seafood, with Aïoli, 109–10
   See also Curry(ied); Soups
Stir-Fry
   Broccoli, Garlic Butter,
      208–9
   Chicken
      Basic Oriental Sauce, 131–32
      Garlic Sesame Sauce, 132
      Szechuan Sauce, 133
   Duck, Chinese Sausage, 136–37
Strawberry
   Butter, 196–97
   Heart Tarts, 245–47
   Soup, *var.*, 99
   -Yogurt Dressing, 99
Streusel Topping for Pies, 251–52
Strudels
   Crab and Brie, *var.*, 3
   Honeyed Lamb, *var.*, 5
   Mushroom Gruyère, *var.*, 6
   Spinach, Feta, Pine-Nut, 4
Stuffings, Bread
   Apricot, Almond, and Apple,
      for Chicken, 200
   Bacon, Corn, and Cheese, for
      Pork Chops, 152
   Corn Bread and Wild Mush-
      room, 200–1
Sunchokes
   about, *107*
   Lobster Curry with Asparagus
      and, 107
Sun-Dried Tomatoes
   about, *176*
   Pizza, with Mussels, Saffron,
      and Three Cheeses, 178–79
   Poached Eggs, Sausage, and
      Brioche with, 189–90
Sweetbreads
   Lemon-Hazelnut Butter, 149–50
   Roasted Chestnuts and Sherry
      Vinegar Butter, *var.*, 150
Sweet Onion Vinaigrette, 76–77
Sweet Potato Fritters with Apples
   and Raisins, 205
Swiss Chard–Stuffed Chicken
   with Lemon Pecan Sauce,
   125–26
Swordfish
   Grilled Marinated, 115
   Smoked, Oriental, with Vegeta-
      ble Salad, 39–40
Szechuan
   Shrimp, 37
   Stir-Fry Sauce, 133–34
Syrup, Hot Cider, 194–95
Szechuan Peppercorns, about, *35*

T

Tahini-Yogurt Dressing, 45
Tapenade Mayonnaise, 17
Taramasalata, 13
Tart(s)
   Cream Cheese Filling for, 245–
      47
   Crust, Savory, 180
   Crust, Sweet, 245–47
   Eggplant and Pepperoni, 180
   Strawberry Heart, 245–47
Thai
   Basil, Lime, Peanut Dressing,
      92
   Beef Curry, 144–45
   Chicken Curry, 129–30
   Chicken in Romaine Leaves,
      34–36
   cooking, *155*
   Curry Glaze for Duck, 137–38
   Curry Paste, about, *129*
   Lamb Curry, 155–56
   Popcorn, 144
   Pork with Garlic, 153
   Salad, with Beef, 75–76
   Soup, with Shrimp, 55
   Spring Rolls, 28–29
   Three-Noodle Appetizer, 26–28
Timbales
   Carrot, Dilled, 210–11
   Parsnip, *var.*, 211
   Rutabaga, *var.*, 211
   Turnip, *var.*, 211
Three-Noodle Appetizer, 26–28
Tofu, Scrambled, Western, 188–89
Tomato(es)
   Butter
      Basil, 114
      Parsley, *var.*, 114
      Tarragon, *var.*, 114
   Chutney, 32–34
   Coulis, 102
      for Soufflé Roll, 192–94
      for Pasta Roll, 160–61
   peeling, how to, *102*
   Sauce
      Minted, 187–88
      Pizza, 174–75
      Provençale, 116–17
      Tarragon Cream, 164–65
   Soup, Sausage, and Eggplant,
      59
   Stuffed with Spinach, Rice, and
      Pine Nuts, 207
   Vinaigrette, 90–91
   See also Sun-Dried Tomatoes
Tortellini
   Blue Cheese Filling, 162–63
   Goat Cheese Filling, *var.*, 163
Tostados, in "Lasagna," 134–36
Tuna
   Caper Mayonnaise, 18
   in Niçoise Salad, 77–78
Turkey Scallops with Lemon-Ca-
   per Butter, 142
Turnip Timbales, *var.*, 211

VWXYZ

Vanilla
   Ice Cream, *var.*, 259
   Walnuts, 14
Veal
   Loin Stuffed with Spinach, Pro-
      sciutto, and Funghi Por-
      cini, 147–48
   Scallops with Lillet Cream
      Sauce and Violets, 148–49
Vegetables. *See* Salads; names of
   vegetables
Vegetarian
   Chili, 51
   Eden Burger, 181
Vichyssoise, Carrot, 52–53
Vinaigrettes. *See* Salad Dressings
Vinegar
   balsamic, about, *203*
   Raspberry, *139*

Waffles
   Buckwheat, with Strawberry
      Butter, 196–97
   Cornmeal, with Westphalian
      Ham, 196
   Oatmeal Sunflower Seed, with
      Honey Butter, *var.*, 198
   Pumpkin, with Hot Cider
      Syrup, 194–95
Walnut(s)
   Bread, Onion Mushroom, 215
   Butter for Pasta, 166–67
   Chocolate Chip Oatmeal Cook-
      ies, 252
   Coffee Chocolate Chip Muffins,
      220
   Curried, 14–15
   Ice Cream, Cinnamon, *var.*, 259
   Muffins, Lemon, *var.*, 221
   Soufflé, Cold Orange, 254
   Vanilla, 14
   Vinaigrette, 91
   Yogurt Dressing, 99
Whipped Cream
   Horseradish, 101
   Mocha, for Buttercrunch Pie,
      247–48
   for Mocha Fudge Cake, 234–35
White Chocolate Ice Cream, 258
Whole Wheat Pasta, Goat Cheese,
   and Fresh Herbs, 159
Wontons, Crab-Brie, *var.*, 4

Yogurt
   Fragrant Sauce, 122–23
   Soup, Strawberry, *var.*, 99
   See also Salad Dressings

Zuccotto, 241–43